THE STATE AND ECONOMIC LIFE

EDITORS: Mel Watkins, University of Toronto; Leo Panitch, York University

19 MURRAY E.G. SMITH

Invisible Leviathan: The Marxist Critique of Market Despotism beyond Postmodernism

As we experience yet another deep economic recession, people throughout the world are feeling the symptoms of capitalist crisis, from unemployment to bankruptcy to deficits to cutbacks and so on. With this timely book, Murray E.G. Smith invites readers to a reconsideration of the themes pertinent to an understanding of capitalist economic crises and to discussion of the ways to overcome them.

The text is broad-ranging, integrating eleven studies that consider the theory of labour-value from historical, philosophical, and economic perspectives. Smith incorporates a thorough review of the controversy that has raged around Marx's theory of labour-value, reporting the key arguments of orthodox Marxists, neo-Ricardians, neo-orthodox Marxists, and fundamentalist Marxists. He concludes that the Marxian theory of labour-value remains a logically coherent and theoretically sound basis for understanding capitalism's historical-structural crises. Also included is a reconsideration of Marx's law of the falling tendency of the rate of profit along with a statistical analysis of long-term trends in the Canadian economy that lend support to Marx's views.

This original and important contribution to Marxist debates will appeal to an international community of political economists and Marx scholars. Its comprehensive reporting and analysis will also attract a broader audience of historians and philosophers.

MURRAY E.G. SMITH is a member of the Department of Sociology, Brock University.

D0162248

Invisible Leviathan:
The Marxist Critique of
Market Despotism beyond
Postmodernism

MURRAY E.G. SMITH

University of Toronto Press
Toronto Buffalo London

© University of Toronto Press Incorporated 1994
Toronto Buffalo London
Printed in Canada

ISBN 0-8020-0589-6 (cloth)
ISBN 0-8020-7190-2 (paper)

⊖

Printed on acid-free paper

Canadian Cataloguing in Publication Data

Smith, Murray E.G. (Murray Edward George), 1950–
  Invisible Leviathan : the Marxist critique of
  market despotism beyond postmodernism

  (The State and economic life ; 19)
  Includes bibliographical references and index.
  ISBN 0-8020-0589-6 (bound)   ISBN 0-8020-7190-2 (pbk.)

  1. Labor theory of value.   2. Marxian economics.
  I. Title.   II. Series.

  HB206.S55 1994   335.4'12   C94-931472-2

University of Toronto Press acknowledges the financial assistance to its
publishing program of the Canada Council and the Ontario Arts Council.

This book has been published with the help of a grant from the Social Science
Federation of Canada, using funds provided by the Social Sciences and
Humanities Reseach Council of Canada.

*Dedicated to my wife Rún, my daughter
Elizabeth, my son Evan, my mother Elsie, and
the memory of my father Edward*

Contents

Preface

This book is unified by a concern to reassert the pivotal importance of Marx's theory of labour-value – 'the labour theory of value,' as it is more commonly known – to an understanding of our social world and its historical development. The broad picture that I draw challenges the idea, more hegemonic in the early 1990s than at any time since the First World War, that 'free-market economics' (a euphemism for the set of socio-economic relations that form the basis of capitalism) are better suited to meeting human needs than any conceivable alternative. It does this by building a case for the proposition that the capitalist market economy has substantially exhausted its potential to further human progress, notwithstanding the collapse of 'socialism' in the former Soviet bloc and in spite of the triumphalist declarations of Francis Fukuyama and his ilk that liberal-democratic capitalism now stands at the 'end of history.'

In brief, the principal thesis proposed here is that, while 'value relations' have played a role of paramount importance in the development of human society, the point has been reached where these relations need to be superseded by a new set of social arrangements that must, at a minimum, provide for a qualitative increase in the degree to which human social and economic affairs are governed by *conscious* decision-making at the level of the human collectivity as a whole. The individualistic rationality of Adam Smith's fabled 'invisible hand,' linked to the idea that the clash of economic interests individually pursued will produce the greatest amount of wealth and well-being for the largest number of people, must be definitively supplanted by a form of rationality that takes the social whole as its starting-point and the 'all-round development' of each and every human being as its goal.

A secondary theme of the book, intimately linked with the latter point, is the book's defence of Marx's *dialectical reason* against both the 'subjective reason' invoked by the currently fashionable school of so-called Analytical Marxism and the 'cynical reason' promoted by poststructuralism and conservative postmodernism. Today more than ever, a reassertion of the claims of Marx's dialectical reason is indispensable to sustaining belief in humanity's continuing potential for social progress and therefore to a world-view informed by 'historical optimism,' an outlook that has been in rather pronounced decline in recent years.

In making these arguments I realize that I am swimming against some very powerful currents. The recent dismantling of the Stalinist administrative-command systems in Eastern Europe has strengthened the claims of neoliberals and neoconservatives that 'planned economies' are neither workable nor desirable. Yet the case against planned economies – while ideologically vital to legitimating policies that give freer reign to capital and that erode social gains previously won by working people in the West (in the 'shadow' of 'actually existing socialism') – is insubstantial and based to a considerable extent on impressionistic analysis, myopic ideology, and selective memory-loss. Impressionistic analysis because it attributes the failure of the administrative-command system to the 'planning principle' rather than to the real and intensifying contradictions of an order that was constitutively incapable of stimulating and harnessing the consciousness, creativity and inter-subjectivity necessary for a *rationally planned* economy. Myopic ideology because it assumes that the 'free-market economies' of the West are not themselves characterized by significant elements of economic planning: for example, the 'military Keynesianism' of the Reagan White House and the large-scale planning of those few hundred corporate giants that accounted recently for some 70 per cent of the industrial output of the global capitalist economy. And selective memory-loss because it 'forgets' that Soviet planning, for all its contradictions and irrationalities, permitted a rate of economic growth over a period of several decades that was well above that of the capitalist West.

The debate between proponents of socialist planning and corporate capitalism (tendentiously peddled as 'free-market economics') is far from over, despite the defeat that has been inflicted on a decrepit travesty of socialism beaten black and blue by a world capitalist order commanding many times its resources. Indeed, the endemic inability of world capitalism to satisfy even the basic needs of the great majority of the world's population ensures that this debate will not only be re-engaged in scholarly discourse but will eventually be joined to a struggle of living social forces on a scale never before seen.

The plan of the book is as follows. Chapter 1 addresses the issue of the contemporary relevance of Marx's theory of labour-value by connecting it to several recent events and trends within the world economy. In chapter 2, I discuss the place of value relations (and 'the law of value') in the broad sweep of human history, focusing especially on the significance of the 'value' (or commodity) abstraction to precapitalist historical development as well as its relation to the basic principles of Marx's materialist conception of history. Chapter 3 provides a capsule description of the career and vicissitudes of 'the labour theory of value,' establishing in particular its intimate historic connection to practical politico-ideological as well as scientific concerns. Chapters 4 through 6 provide an in-depth conspectus and evaluation of Marx's theory of value and the controversy surrounding it, while chapters 7, 8, and 9 address the implications of Marxian value theory for the theory of capitalist crisis and the uneven development of the world capitalist economy. In chapter 10, I explore the issues of class structure, class consciousness, and class struggle, as well as some of the political-programmatic implications of value theory, arguing that it provides little support for a *reformist* working-class politics or for the 'market socialism' idea that has come into vogue as a by-product of the decay and collapse of Stalinist 'real socialism.' Finally, in chapter 11, I address the implications of value theory and the value controversy for issues currently being debated by social theorists and philosophers under the rubrics of 'modernity' and 'postmodernism,' arguing that the dialectical reason informing Marx's critique of value relations provides both a durable and indispensable foundation for intellectual as well as socio-economic progress.

The greater part of this book represents a substantially revised version of certain sections of my doctoral dissertation 'The Value Controversy and Social Theory: An Inquiry into Marx's Labour Theory of Value' (Department of Sociology, University of British Columbia, 1989). The dissertation was written under the guidance of an advisory committee composed of David Schweitzer (supervisor), Bob Ratner, and Blanca Muratorio, all of whose criticism, good counsel, and insistence upon clarity helped me to hone arguments on a theoretical terrain somewhat remote from their own areas of specialization. I can only now fully appreciate how rare a privilege it was to have been allowed the intellectual latitude and freedom afforded to me by this committee. They, and I, had the good fortune to rely on the specialized knowledge of Bob Chernomas of the Department of Economics at the University of Manitoba. Professor Chernomas's conscientious critical review of several chapters pertaining to value theory, capitalist crisis, and the history of political economy – performed, it should be said, on an entirely unofficial and voluntary basis – contributed greatly both to a theoretical strengthening of the dissertation and to the peace of mind of the members of my advisory committee. I thank all four of these colleagues for their advice and friendship. Thanks are also due to Graham Johnson and Derek Sayer for their roles in the final examination of the dissertation. Professor Sayer, in particular, made several valuable suggestions that have been duly incorporated into the present work.

My dissertation and this work grew out of an intensive study of Marx's critique of political economy that began in 1980. Since then I have been fortunate to receive fellowship support from the University of Manitoba, the University of British Columbia, and the Social Sciences and Humanities Research Council of Canada; to each I express my gratitude. I owe my thanks as well to the many teachers, colleagues, and friends who have assisted me in my research, influenced my thinking, and critically reviewed my literary production since 1980. In addition to those already cited, I would like to mention Wayne Taylor, Mikhail Vitkin, Ken Campbell, John McAmmond, Ken Waldhauser, Don Forgay, Roy Turner, David Mole, Michael Lebowitz, David Laibman, Grant Amyot, Gregory Albo, Leo Panitch, and two anonymous readers of the manuscript originally submitted to the University of Toronto Press. While few of the above are likely to be fully comfortable with all of the arguments developed in this book, I gratefully acknowledge that each has contributed something of importance to its general lineaments. I should also like to extend special thanks to Virgil Duff, the executive editor of the University of Toronto Press, for his advice and encouragement over the past two years; and to my family, for suffering with good humour the frequent petulance of a distracted academic author who has been juggling too many workloads for rather too long a time.

Finally, I wish to acknowledge the permissions I have received to reproduce or quote certain materials in this book. Four journal articles that I have published in recent years have found inclusion, in somewhat modified form, as chapters or parts of chapters. 'Understanding Marx's Theory of Value: An Assessment of a Controversy,' which first appeared in volume 28:3 (August 1991) of *The Canadian Review of Sociology and Anthropology*, has found a new incarnation as sections of chapters 4, 5, and 6. 'Respecifying Marx's Value Categories: A Theoretical and Empirical Reconsideration of the Law of the Falling Rate of Profit,' originally published in *Studies in Political Economy* 35 (Summer 1991), is the basis of chapter 8. 'The Value Abstraction and the Dialectic of Social Development,' originally published in *Science & Society* 56:3 (Fall 1992), has been reprinted with only minor changes as chapter 2. Finally, several passages from 'Alienation, Exploitation and Abstract Labor: A Humanist Defense of Marx's Theory of Value,' which appeared in the *Review of Radical Political Economics* 26:1 (1994), have been incorporated into chapters 6 and 11.

The following publishers have kindly consented to reproduction or extensive quotation of copyrighted materials: Penguin Books, Ltd., for passages from *Grundrisse* by Karl Marx (1973, trans. Martin Nicolaus); Blackwell Publishers, for three graphs that appeared in *The Imperiled Economy*, vol. 1 (URPE 1987); *Scientific American*, for a graph that originally appeared on page 190 of its September 1982 issue (Leontieff 1982); Humanities Press, for passages from *Marx's Theory of Scientific Knowledge* by Patrick Murray (1988); Verso, for figures that originally appeared on page 49 of *Marx After Sraffa* by Ian Steedman (1981) and on page 280 of *The Value Controversy* by Ian Steedman et al. (1979); and Verso, for passages from Anwar Shaikh's 'The Poverty of Algebra,' which appeared in *The Value Controversy* by Steedman et al. (1979).

Murray E.G. Smith
St Catharines, Ontario
January 1994

Invisible Leviathan: The Marxist Critique of Market
Despotism beyond Postmodernism

1 Value, Wealth, and Human Development: Reflections on the Invisible Leviathan and Some Recent Events

I authorize and give up my right of governing myself, to this man, or to this assembly of men, on this condition, that thou give up thy right to him, and authorize all his actions in like manner. This done, the multitude so united in one person is called a COMMONWEALTH, in Latin CIVITAS. This is the generation of that great LEVIATHAN, or rather, to speak more reverently, of that mortal god, to which we owe under the immortal God, our peace and defence.
Thomas Hobbes, *Leviathan* (1651)

[Every individual generally] neither intends to promote the public interest, nor knows how much he is promoting it. ... [H]e is in this case, as in many cases, led by an invisible hand to promote an end which was no part of his intention.
Adam Smith, *The Wealth of Nations* (1776)

Labour is not the source of all wealth. Nature is just as much the source of use-values (and it is surely of such that material wealth consists!) as labour, which itself is only the manifestation of a force of nature, human labour power ... [A] socialist programme cannot allow such bourgeois phrases to pass over in silence the conditions that alone give them meaning.
Karl Marx, *Critique of the Gotha Programme* (1875)

Early in 1992 the United Nations Development Programme 'honoured' Canada by ranking it first among the member states of the United Nations according to its 'Human Development Index.' The HDI is a quantitative measure of human well-being, based on life expectancy, literacy, and purchasing power, for purposes of international comparisons of socio-economic development. The Conservative government of Prime Minister Brian Mulroney quickly seized upon the distinction and launched a stirring 'Take Pride in Canada' public-relations campaign designed to reverse its flagging fortunes in public-opinion polls. On 25 June 1992, the Economic Council of Canada dampened this cynically contrived 'celebration' by releasing a report stating that one in three Canadians would be poor at some point in their working lives and that poverty rates would likely worsen owing to increasing social and economic stresses associated with 'family breakdown' and 'labour market instability.' The Council report added to the bleak picture that had already been drawn by Statistics Canada reports showing that over the course of 1979–91 the median (before-tax) family income in Canada had actually declined slightly in real (constant-dollar) terms. In light of the fact that the average Canadian family was contributing more labour time to the economy in 1991 than in 1979 (owing to a large increase in the number of two-income families) and that the tax burden on this average family had increased over this period (owing to a considerable expansion of regressive sales, excise, and 'sin' taxes), the conclusion was quite unmistakable: Canada, the country ranked first on the UN Human Development Index, had suffered a significant decline in average living standards since at least the late 1970s.

In late 1991, Giovanni Arrighi published an article in *New Left Review* entitled 'World Income Inequalities and the Future of Socialism.' Marshalling empirical evidence for a 'world-system' twist on the theme that 'the rich get richer and the poor get poorer,' Arrighi argued compellingly that the global spread of 'free market' relations in this century had contributed to a dramatic increase in the per-capita GNP gap between the rich and poor countries of the capitalist world economy. 'The wealth of the West,' declared Arrighi, 'cannot be generalized because it is based on relational processes of exploitation and relational processes of exclusion that presuppose the continually reproduced relative deprivation of the majority of the world population ... Processes of exploitation provide wealthy states and their agents with the means to initiate and sustain processes of exclusion. And processes of exclusion generate the poverty necessary to induce the rulers and subjects of comparatively poor states to continually seek re-entry into the world division of labour on conditions favourable to wealthy states' (1991: 58–9). Despite this historical verdict, the post-Communist states of the former Soviet bloc, with widespread though hardly unanimous support from their populations, had just opted for the most massive and unprecedented 're-entries' in the history of capitalism – their rulers promising 'eventual' prosperity after a painful but endurable transition to a 'free-market economy.'

Far from welcoming these moves with a new Marshall Plan of significant assistance to these converts to free-market economics, the developed capitalist countries adopted a posture of relative indifference, as if to confirm that the original Marshall Plan had been motivated pre-eminently by Washington's geo-political determination to 'save' Western Europe after the Second World War from the very real prospect of continental socialist revolution. In the present context, it would appear that Washington and the capitalist West in general now consider such a massive economic assistance package as either well beyond their present economic means or unnecessary to prevent a sharp left turn and socialist outcome to the still-fluid and highly volatile events now unfolding in the post-Communist states.

Tying much of this together nicely is a piece produced by François Moreau for the inaugural issue of *Socialist Alternatives* in the Fall of 1991. Reprising some of Arrighi's world-system themes as well as Immanuel Wallerstein's (1983) thesis that the 'absolute immiseration of the working class' (as anticipated by the young Marx) may apply on a *world* scale if not to the condition of the working classes of advanced capitalism, Moreau took the UN Human Development Index data and showed that the claims currently being made for capitalism's capacity to generate human well-being (that is, 'development') are entirely vacuous. While 'core' capitalist countries like Canada rank highest on the HDI, 'peripheral' capitalist countries like India and Bangladesh rank lowest. Moreover, the 'transitional' (Communist) countries – as of 1987, when they were still nominally 'socialist' – ranked well above the average HDI for the capitalist world. The average HDI for the capitalist world (inclusive of capitalist core and periphery) was 629, while the average HDI for Eastern European and Third World transitional societies was 764. Interestingly, the Eastern European transitional countries by themselves had an average HDI score of 916, only slightly below the 970 average boasted by the capitalist core. Summing up, Moreau commented: 'What the UNDP analysis shows, no doubt without consciously intending to do so, is that transitional societies have actually achieved a higher level of "human development" for a given level of economic development than capitalist countries ... [M]uch of the third world could indeed achieve a significantly higher level of "human development" with a different socio-economic system' (1991: 141–2).

Moreau predicted that the return of capitalism to the Eastern European countries would likely produce results precisely opposite to those anticipated by the 'free market' fideists. The change in socio-economic system and full re-entry into the world capitalist system, if accomplished, would in most cases lead to a falling HDI – an outcome anticipated by Arrighi's thesis concerning the oligarchic and concentrated character of 'wealth' in the capitalist world system. 'To see what the condition of the working class is like under capitalism, and what awaits Eastern European countries if they turn capitalist,' averred Moreau, 'one should indeed turn, not to Sweden or Austria, but rather to "newly industrialized" countries such as Mexico. With an estimated GDP per capita of 4,624$, adjusted for purchasing power, this country actually stands very close to the world average for capitalism as a whole, as computed by the UNDP' (ibid.: 142). This 'average' capitalist country, which has in recent years been in the vanguard of Third World trends toward trade liberalization and privatization, has seen a cumulative decline in real wages of 60 per cent since 1976, compared to the 15 per cent decline experienced by the relatively affluent Canadian workforce. At this writing, Mexico and Canada are about to tie their economic fates closer together by joining with the United States in a North American Free Trade Agreement – one of the goals of which is evidently to further erode wages and living standards and increase levels of exploitation in all three countries in order to restore profitability and make North American capital competitively supreme in an increasingly predatory world market.

What, then, does all of this have to do with Marx's theory of labour-value? The short answer is, *everything*. Despite the ideological hoopla attending the 'death of Communism' in the early 1990s (a celebration cut short by the onset of a severe and long-lasting global depression), Marxist theory remains the only serious framework for grasping the contradictory, irrational, and increasingly dangerous trajectory of the capitalist mode of production – an ensemble of social relations and human capacities, of technology and societal organization, that, more than ever, demands to be understood in a *world-wide* context and that, no less than in the past, remains in the grip of a law that its own social relations and forms of social organization imperiously necessitate: the capitalist law of labour-value.

The terms of our discourse to this point – development, growth, purchasing power, labour time, wages, wealth, profitability, concentration, inequality, exploitation, competition – are all part of the vocabulary of Marxian value theory: they are the concepts that capture both the objective presuppositions of the capitalist law of value and its real effects. Most of them play some role in non-Marxian accounts of capitalist economy as well, though 'inequality' and 'exploitation' are infrequent players in the discourse of neoclassical economic theory. How much weight these latter concepts are given depends ultimately on how much importance one attributes to them as elements of objective social reality. Apologists for capitalism typically view them as aberrations from some ideal capitalist 'norm.' But this idealized capitalist 'norm' of the true believers in liberal democracy and 'free enterprise' has now had several *hundred* years to assert itself, and, all the while, actually-existing-capitalism has been characterized by soaring exploitation and burgeoning disparities of wealth.

Believers in capitalist 'free market' economies have also long contended that, in principle, the crisis tendencies bred by these economies can be significantly mitigated and eventually fully contained, once the right 'mix' of state economic policies is formulated. But again, the history of actually-existing-capitalism suggests otherwise. Despite the confidence expressed by mainstream economists during the 1950s and 1960s that world capitalism would never again experience a severe depression, the period from 1974 to 1992 saw three of the most severe global recessions/depressions of this century, and the world economy remains today in the grip of a malaise that shows little sign of lifting.

A principal theme of this book is that Marx's theory of labour-value remains the indispensable foundation for explaining economic phenomena that non-Marxist economic thought (whether in its Keynesian, post-Keynesian, monetarist, or institutionalist variants) has manifestly failed to explain or even to anticipate. Why has capitalism been unable to 'outgrow' its tendencies toward severe economic crisis? Why is capitalism so capable on the one hand of stimulating progress in science, technology, and productivity and so incapable on the other of translating this progress into enduring gains in living standards for the great majority of the working population? Why are positive rates of growth in industrial productivity on a world scale accompanied by declining average rates of profit for most capitalist countries?[1] And why has capitalism as a world system ceased to contribute to the development of the 'productive forces' of humankind – most obviously by chronically *underutilizing* the talents and energies of billions of people around the world?[2]

For those who grasp the essential theses of Marx's theory of value, surplus-value, and capital, the answers to these questions are in clear focus. The anomalies and irrationalities of capitalist reality are to be explained fundamentally by the fact that this reality encompasses four tendentially contradictory principles of social organization, four interpenetrated yet distinguishable relations of production and reproduction: the *equalitarian* relation existing between economic subjects (producers, labour, commodities) within the capitalist market; the *exploitative* relation existing between those who monopolize the ownership of the means of production and those who must sell their labour-power for wages or salaries in order to secure a livelihood; the *competitive* relation existing between all economic subjects in the market but most importantly between the owners of capital; and the *cooperative* relation existing between producers in a global division of labour that has become ever more detailed, elaborate, and interdependent. On the face of it, the coexistence and interpenetration of these social relations would appear to be quite problematic. Historically, in fact, their interaction within the totality that is the capitalist socio-economic system has been a source of great dynamism. Yet, while recognizing this fully, Marx insisted that this dynamism was likely to become ever more one-sided and that, at a certain stage in its development, capitalism would exhaust its progressive role in promoting human development. Accordingly, Marx rested his indictment against capitalism not simply on the fact that the system was 'unjust,' but centrally on the system's increasing tendency to generate waste, to block the development of human capacities, and to divert human energies (both physical and mental) into non-productive and even destructive pursuits.

Marx's theory of labour-value is at the core of his indictment against capitalism. At bottom it is an account of what might be described (with apologies to neither Thomas Hobbes nor Adam Smith) as an Invisible Leviathan – a structure of socio-economic relations that has usurped from conscious humanity real control over the socio-economic life process and imposed a set of laws that are both very powerful and deeply hidden from view. Its crowning law, the capitalist law of value, compels humanity to apply a single yardstick to the measurement of 'wealth': the yard-stick of 'value,' of abstract socially necessary labour time.

Within a society founded upon capitalist social relations of production and reproduction, the measurement of social wealth in these terms is both 'unconscious,' in that it is effected through impersonal market mechanisms, and decisive to the developmental trajectory of the economy and the division of labour as a whole. Thus, certain forms of activity will be recognized as 'wealth-generating' (regardless of how socially destructive they may be – for instance, the production of armaments and supermarket tabloids), while other forms will not enter the economic calculus at all, despite their socially valuable character (for example, voluntary care-giving to children and the elderly). This means that as capitalist production as a whole meets the demand generated by aggregate 'purchasing power' with a range of goods requiring less and less labour input, the material wealth of society in physical terms will expand while its measurement in terms of labour time will suggest, rather perversely, that society is actually becoming 'poorer.' This is because the measurement of material wealth in terms of social labour-time (whose phenomenal economic expression is *money*) means, under conditions of labour-saving and labour-displacing technical innovation, that capitalist society *tends* toward a zero-sum situation in which any gains in income or real wealth must come at the expense of other economic agents, and in which it is quite possible for aggregate purchasing power to *decline* (as it does under conditions of economic contraction). The upshot is that social wealth is measured by criteria informed by the *socially antagonistic* (exploitative and competitive) character of capitalist production and exchange.

Marx's theory of labour-value states that the sole source of 'value' within a capitalist society is living human labour and that the sole source of 'surplus-value' (the social substance of profit) is the surplus labour performed by workers in excess of the necessary labour required to produce the value represented by their wages. To the great majority of the population who rely for their livelihood on the sale of their labour-power (whether for a wage or a salary) these propositions should require little proof. Yet the fact that 'proof' can be demanded by the capitalists and their ideological agents attests to the remarkable ability of capital to represent itself as an 'independent' source of 'value' and to confuse the categories of value, money, and wealth. The point of Marx's theory is precisely to establish that the economic category of 'value' – together with those of wages, profit, interest, and so on – is bound up with the existence of the social relations of production/reproduction characteristic of a 'commodity economy,' in particular that of capitalism. *Value and wealth are therefore by no means synonymous.* Indeed, implicit in Marx's theory of value and capital is the thesis that the measurement of wealth in terms of 'value' (socially equalized labour-time) at first stimulates but eventually impedes the production of wealth. Hence, while Marx would doubtless solidarize with the intent of Arrighi's critique of the inequalities and 'oligarchic wealth' that define capitalism today, he would also wish to make the point that wealth (understood as the useful things and services that constitute people's living standards and their ability to continuously satisfy their needs) *can* be 'generalized' to all the world's people once it ceases to be measured in socially antagonistic ways – 'relationally,' to be sure, but centrally in terms of 'abstract socially necessary labour.'

This is a revolutionary suggestion. Yet it flows quite logically from a theory that has had an excellent track record in charting the course of capitalist development. As such it deserves to be considered with the utmost seriousness, particularly when it is appreciated that the long-term rate of growth of the global economy is falling and that higher rates of growth for all sectors of the world economy are absolutely necessary to avert a global ecological catastrophe.[3] For if Marx is right, if 'value relations' *have* exhausted their potential to contribute to the creation of human wealth and to meet human needs *on a global scale*, then it becomes incumbent upon humanity to seek out a new form of socio-economic organization that can transcend these relations while subsuming under itself the tremendous developmental potential of the science, technology, and world division of labour that capital has fashioned over the past few centuries.

I am well aware that the objection will be made that Marx's own prescription for this new social form has been found wanting 'in practice.' Although the purpose of this book is not to refute this rather hoary argument, a few comments are perhaps in order. In my view, Marx's own vision of the transition to a socialist society presupposes several conditions that have been conspicuously absent from *all* of the 'experiments' in 'socialist construction' in this century: a strong and well-organized working class, a functioning democracy of the 'associated producers' *and* consumers, a high level of development of productivity, the availability of ample 'free time' permitting the full involvement of 'ordinary people' in political, cultural, and civic activities, and a well-articulated international division of labour. Lacking many of these conditions, the 'transitional' Communist societies of the East registered many impressive accomplishments – though at a human cost exceeded only by Western capitalism in its era of industrialization and worldwide expansion. They were not, however, able to reach the critical threshhold of truly socialist relations of production. In my opinion, the responsibility for this failure is one that ultimately falls most heavily on those ostensibly socialist and working-class leaders in the West who retreated from the program of social transformation and who justified this retreat by denying the veracity of Marx's value-theoretical critique of capitalism – almost always without having ever bothered to understand it.

Let us speak plainly. The rhetoric of 'free market economics' is the upbeat ideological mantle of a despotism that has most of humanity in its grip, capitalists and workers alike: the *despotism* of the 'invisible hand,' of market forces operating behind the back of the human collectivity whose destiny they shape. This despotism has decreed that the economic life of human beings, the basis upon which all 'modes of life' depend, will be governed by the law of labour-value, whether or not this is consciously understood by its subjects, and whether or not it serves the collective needs of humanity. To break this despotic power will require a conscious decision to return control of the mechanisms of production and reproduction to the *conscious* decision-making of human beings collectively organized. But such a decision must be predicated upon a hard-won prior recognition: that the law of labour-value is not an 'eternal' law of human society and that *it can indeed be transcended*.

The question remains: Can this historically bounded law be transcended in such a way as to allow humanity to contend with our most pressing socioeconomic, cultural, and ecological problems? The record of 'the transitional societies' – for all their manifest failures – provides us with many indications that it can. Yet something of a 'leap of faith' may still be needed, one requiring a rehabilitation of the good name of Human Nature and a rebirth of 'socialist imagination' – something that has been in terribly short supply since pro-

Moscow Communists and capitalists joined together in proclaiming the insidious identity of Stalinism and socialism/communism. Yet it is precisely this sort of imagination that Marx's theory of labour-value can serve to stimulate by challenging the bogus 'inevitability' of value relations and by reaffirming the capacity of human beings to radically alter their socio-economic relations.

Arguing in a similar vein, Frederic Jameson has written:

The market is ... Leviathan in sheep's clothing: its function is not to encourage and perpetuate freedom (let alone freedom of a political variety), but rather to repress it. ... Market ideology assures us that human beings make a mess of it when they try to control their destinies ('socialism is impossible'), and that we are fortunate in possessing an interpersonal mechanism – the market – which can substitute for human hubris and planning and replace human decisions altogether. We only need to keep it clean and well-oiled; it now – like the monarch so many centuries ago – will see to us and keep us in line. (1990: 106)

The notion that the market – and the Invisible Leviathan of capitalist value relations that forms its real basis – will 'see to us' grows thinner and thinner with the passage of time. But it can 'keep us in line' only so long as we fail to understand and expose its most precious secret: that it has *already* overstayed its historical welcome as a means to furthering the material wealth, the social and cultural development, and the general well-being of humankind.

2 The Value Abstraction and the Dialectic of Social Development

The idea that human history evinces a pattern of development rooted in the propensity of human beings toward technical (labour-saving) forms of rationality is fundamental to Marx's materialist conception of history. Yet the 'dialectic of forces and relations of production' as traditionally conceived in historical-materialist discourse has found only weak expressions in social formations dominated by precapitalist modes of production. In this chapter the hypothesis is advanced that simple commodity production and exchange (and therefore rudimentary *value* relations) may be of decisive importance to the historic emergence of cognitive faculties capable of giving a systematic impulse to the development of science and technology, and therefore to a precapitalist forces-relations dialectic. This viewpoint permits a new way of appreciating Marx's 'ranking' of the Asiatic, ancient, feudal, and capitalist modes of production as 'progressive epochs' in the development of human society, while illuminating the socio-historical provenance (and sources of variability) of the categories of human thought. More generally, the chapter offers a philosophical and historical framework for conceptualizing the historically limited contributions of value relations to human progress.

Contemporary debates surrounding Marx's 'theory of history' centre on three overlapping yet distinguishable topics: the feudalism-to-capitalism transition (Hilton 1976; Brenner 1977; Gottlieb 1984; Laibman 1984); the problem of the *specificity* of Marx's 'precapitalist modes of production' and the status of his concept of the 'Asiatic mode of production' (Anderson 1979; Krader 1975; Vitkin 1981; Amin 1985); and the cluster of issues pertaining to the social ontology, philosophical anthropology, and scientific method informing Marx's own accounts of the materialist conception of history (Cohen 1978; Sohn-Rethel 1978; Geras 1983; Sayer 1987).

In broad strokes, it is possible to survey the terms of current historical-materialist debate by citing a series of familiar and recurring theoretical oppositions: evolutionism versus anti-evolutionism; productive-forces determinism versus production-relations determinism; unilinearity versus multilinearity; objective laws of motion versus class struggle; technological determinism versus cultural (or superstructural) determinism; transhistorical prime movers rooted in invariant elements of human nature versus historically specific causal mechanisms rooted in ever-changing human propensities; 'iron necessity' versus law-breaking contingency; and so forth. The very structure of historical-materialist debate suggested by this catalogue of binomial oppositions would seem to invite radical 'deconstruction' – which is precisely what has been proposed by a growing roster of non-Marxist, ex-Marxist, and 'post-Marxist' celebrants of 'postmodernism' and/or 'post-structuralism' (Derrida, Foucault, Baudrillard, Lyotard, Laclau and Mouffe, and so on). But to deconstruct such a structure of argument is a tricky exercise, and one that, in my view, should not be entrusted to intellectuals who call into question or reject such fundamentals of the Marxist world-view as the idea of 'objective truth' or the possibility of progress, while invoking an unbridled 'subjectivism without a subject' (Anderson 1983: 54) as an antidote to the dogmatism, ethnocentrism and productivism of 'modernity.' For instance, if Derrida (1982: 44) is not prepared to embrace a *monistic* social ontology in place of the ontological dualism implicit in the above binomial oppositions (and it does seems to me that in the choice between monism and dualism one cannot meaningfully choose 'différance'!), it is perhaps better to return to Marx for some clues as to how we can make our way out of the theoretical maze and reorient ourselves in the struggle for a better future.

In this chapter I want to show that a satisfactory way of conceptualizing the 'forces-relations' dialectic of human social development *can* be established, despite the less-than-compelling derision for this notion emanating from the postmodernist camp and despite the thoughtful reservations that have been expressed by Giddens (1981) and Sweezy (1981) concerning the pertinence of the concept to precapitalist social development. My starting-point will be three basic 'premisses' that I take to be central to Marx's materialist conception of history.

The first of these is the *monistic* proposition that the reality confronted by human beings is an *ontologically unified* ensemble or totality, embracing natural, social, and ideal aspects. This premiss is consistent with the traditional philosophical-materialist tenet that matter has ontological primacy as the 'substance' of reality; but it breaks from this tradition in its insistence that material reality is subject not only to 'natural law,' but to the transformative influences of human practice as well (that is, the influences of human social relations and consciousness). In my view this is the fundamental theme of Marx's *Theses on Feuerbach.*

The second premiss is that the 'subject' of history is the 'real living individuals' referred to by Marx and Engels in *The German Ideology*; that is, human individuals whose actions are shaped by both natural and social imperatives and constraints. The historical subject, on this view, is most emphatically *not* a transcendental logos, a reified 'first principle,' or an unchanging 'human nature.' Rather it is human beings seeking practical solutions to the natural, social, and intellectual problems they confront ... precisely through natural, social, and intellectual means. The more complex the problems and the more varied the available means of recourse, the greater the *creative* response of human beings is likely to be.

The third premiss is that human beings are driven to seek 'material security' in the face of hostile natural *and social* forces. This is the basis for a certain *duality* within the elusive notion of 'human rationality.' Forms of 'technical' rationality are distinguishable from forms of 'sociological' rationality, but not because of any ontological schism within reality of the type implied in the dualistic social ontologies of Weber, Habermas, or Giddens. They are distinguishable (and *usefully* distinguished within a dialectical social ontology) just because they can and do enter into complex and potentially contradictory relationships with one another. Yet their *common basis* should still be clear: purposive human activity as founded upon the socially mediated transformation of nature (both human and non-human). It seems to me that the tendency to *privilege* 'technical rationality' in general over 'sociological rationality' in general, or vice versa, may well be the unspoken theme behind recurring attempts to attribute deterministic 'primacy' to either the productive forces or the relations of production in the development of society.

The desire to 'privilege' the productive forces (and, inter alia, a technical-instrumental rationality) may well have been the inspiration of Marx's most 'deterministic' historical-materialist text, the 1859 Preface to *A Contribution to the Critique of Political Economy*. It is just this text that happens to contain what is perhaps the most controversial and enigmatic passage in Marx's entire corpus, the one that reads: 'In broad outline, the Asiatic, ancient, feudal and modern bourgeois modes of production may be designated as epochs marking progress in the economic development of society' (Marx 1970: 21).

It will not be my purpose to summarize or even identify the many debates that have devolved from the interpretation of this single passage. However, it should be noted that even a 'soft' reading of it suggests that Marx is *ranking* these modes of production with respect to their potential to engender 'progress' (even though he may not be positing a 'hard' theory of stages through which 'all societies' must pass). Moreover, it *will* be my purpose to defend the central idea implied in the passage – Marx's pivotal notion of a 'universal human history' marked by a determinate (if not 'inexorable') developmental logic. The key that Marx provides to understanding this universal history is precisely the forces-relations dialectic as this unfolds in both precapitalist and capitalist eras.

A caveat is necessary here. The scepticism of Sweezy and Giddens among others concerning the reality of a precapitalist forces-relations dialectic contains an important grain of truth. The objective laws governing the historical movement of capitalist society are *much stronger* than those influencing the economic development of precapitalist social formations. This is so because only capitalism is under the sway of a fully reified 'law of value,' a law that becomes fully determinant only under conditions of market competition (Amin 1985: 204). Capitalism's 'economic law of motion,' moreover, is defined by the contradictory relationship of elements 'internal' to its social-production relations, relations that are at once equalitarian, exploitative, and competitive (Rubin 1973). This distinguishes capitalism from precapitalist societies quite decisively, for it is precisely the interplay of social-production relations (and perhaps of forms of rationality) belonging to *differentiated* modes of production in precapitalist eras that appears to furnish a developmental dynamic conducive to the growth of the productive forces. This is one aspect of Laibman's (1984: 275) important argument concerning the role of simple commodity production during the feudal era in stimulating the development of the 'intensive' (labour-saving) capabilities of the productive forces and thereby creating an 'intensive surplus which enables commodity production to assume a new role, eventually moving to the center of the [production relations].'

I concur with Laibman in regarding simple commodity production as a critical (and much underestimated) element in the forces-relations dialectic of precapitalist history. Indeed, the argument that I present below should be seen as complementary to his stress on the importance of an individually appropriated 'intensive surplus' to the development of the productive forces of Western European feudal societies. But I go beyond Laibman in suggesting that it is not only the competitive relations (and individual acquisitiveness) embryonic in simple commodity production that propel the growth of labour-saving technology, but the 'equalitarian' relations implicit in them as well. Indeed, it is precisely the equalitarian aspects of commodity value (impressively delineated by I.I. Rubin [1973] in his essay 'Equality of Commodity

Producers and Equality of Commodities') that I regard as fundamental to the specific contribution of the 'value abstraction' to the extension of human productive capacities during precapitalist times.

Where I depart from Laibman (and, arguably, from the Marx of the 1859 Preface) is in my rejection of the assumption that human technical rationality *must* prevail over a 'class-appropriative' rationality (or indeed over other forms of 'sociological' rationality) in determining the course of history. No such presumption is, in my view, warranted on 'purely' theoretical grounds. In the end, what must determine the outcome of the clash of these two forms of rationality is the class struggle, and this can issue just as easily in the 'mutual ruin' of the contending classes as in the inauguration of a more progressive epoch.

Marxism, of course, has no pretensions to being a 'pure theory.' It is defiantly a theoretically informed program and a programmatically informed theory – a *practical* project embracing a specific vision of human history and the struggle for a better future. This is why it can likely be said with confidence that even the 'late Marx' of the 1870s and 1880s – who faced something of an intellectual crisis as he moved away from the Eurocentric standpoint of the Preface; who explored a far richer ethnography than he had previously ever imagined; and who even ruminated on the Russian peasant commune as a potential starting-point for socialist development (Vitkin 1981; Shanin 1983) – never wavered from the idea that human history is possessed of a 'meaning' to the extent that the rational human imperative to extend the productivity of labour can be said to hold sway in human history. The propensity of human beings toward labour-saving technical rationality of this sort was a fundamental premiss of his philosophical anthropology – one that held out the promise of the eventual emergence of a mode of human existence in which, for the first time, human individuals would have the chance to develop their many-sided talents and capabilities unconstrained by either material hardship or social antagonism (Geras 1983). All ethnocentrisms and postmodern relativisms aside, this is surely a vision of human emancipation worthy of *all* humanity – and it is certainly just as much a 'guiding thread' of Marx's thought as any other that might be cited.

The Value Abstraction in Precapitalist History: Cognitive Faculties as Forces of Production

The idea that Marx was committed to a definite concept of human progress linked to the propensity of the human species toward technical rationality has been most prominently associated in recent years with the influential work of G.A. Cohen. In *Karl Marx's Theory of History: A Defence* Cohen under-took to champion what he characterized as an 'old-fashioned historical materialism' according to which 'history is, fundamentally, the growth of human productive power, and forms of society rise and fall according as they enable or impede that growth' (1978: x). Cohen readily admitted to a 'technological interpretation' of human history, but was circumspect with respect to whether his account should be termed 'technological determinist.' No doubt this was because his argument was not so much that technology 'dominates' other aspects of human social life as that human beings tend to *select* those social forms that are most propitious to the extension of their productive powers given a certain level of development of technology and technical-scientific knowledge. Human history possesses a pattern because human beings can be expected, in the long run, to behave (collectively) in a technically rational fashion. Cohen's overall theoretic-methodological framework might there-fore be described as a 'rational-choice functionalism' or a 'functionalist praxiology.'

The issue of Cohen's functionalism is not a central concern of the present discussion, although it is certainly prominent among the features that render his account of historical materialism novel, not to mention contentious. Of greater concern is the 'analytically rigorous' fashion in which Cohen insists upon interpreting the 'material-social' distinction in Marx's thought and in the Preface of 1859 in particular. For Cohen the material aspects of human existence pertain strictly to the 'content' of human society (which is always a 'natural content'), whereas the social aspects pertain just as strictly to the issue of 'form' (defined pre-eminently by social relationships of ownership and control of the means of production). It is on this basis that he develops a somewhat 'non-traditional' understanding of the following famous passage from Marx's Preface: 'In the social production of their life, men enter into definite relations that are indispensable and independent of their will, relations of production which correspond to a definite stage of development of the material productive forces. The sum total of these relations of production constitutes the economic structure of society, the real basis on which rises a legal and political superstructure, and to which correspond definite forms of social consciousness' (Marx 1970; quoted in Cohen 1978: vii).

The real novelty of Cohen's interpretation of this passage has to do with the way he specifies (a) the distinction between the forces and the relations of production, and (b) the distinction between the 'economic structure of society' and the 'legal and political superstructure.' According to Cohen, the forces of production belong to the material side of the material-social dis-tinction while the relations of production belong to the social side. Once this is recognized it becomes possible to specify with analytical precision those elements of reality that belong to the 'material forces of production' and those that belong to the 'social relations of production.' At the same time, on this interpretation, the economic structure of society refers to the totality of social relations of production within a particular socio-economic formation and is not at all a synonym for the 'mode of production' concept. That is to say, unlike Marx's concept of mode of production, the economic structure does not at all refer to the material forces of production. Rather the material forces of production (together with the 'material relations of production' bearing on the physical organization of the labour process) belong to a material substratum existing 'below' the economic structure.

If the material aspects of reality are conceptually excluded from the economic structure by Cohen, the ideal aspects of this same reality are just as resolutely excluded from his conception of the social superstructure. For Cohen this superstructure consists exclusively of legal and political *institutions* that function to stabilize and reinforce the economic structure. Accordingly, the superstructure does not, strictly speaking, encompass ideas or consciousness and therefore does not refer to an 'ideal' sphere or level of reality.

There is much in Cohen's restatement of the basic concepts of the Preface that is highly moot; but to some limited extent at least he has admirably captured a key aspect of Marx's social ontology, one overlooked by many other commentators. For Cohen has painstakingly demonstrated that the point of departure of Marx's historical sociology is not the 'material-ideal' distinction that pervades the greater part of bourgeois social theory, but rather a 'material-social' distinction, and that, related to this, ideas and consciousness for Marx are not part of an *independent* realm but are always embedded in the social and material conditions and practices through which human beings make their own history. Hence, it is not only necessary to insist that there are many cultural products that cannot and need not be included in Marx's 'base-superstructure' metaphor; it is also necessary to underscore that 'productively relevant' ideas and knowledge are themselves essential elements of the material forces of production. For tools, productive machinery, and even 'skilled labour power' (the perishable expressions of the productive forces) cannot be said to exist *independently* of such knowledge.

I wish to extend this latter argument still further by suggesting that the practical technical knowledge embodied in the physical means of production is itself predicated upon the capacity of human beings to think in 'problem-solving' ways. Moreover, the premiss of any *systematic* development of the 'productive powers of human beings' is the emergence of cognitive faculties favouring a technical-scientific form of rationality. Unlike Cohen I do not claim that the human propensity toward technical rationality is explicable simply with reference to the human mammal's 'excellent brain.' The existence of such a brain is certainly a *condition* for the development of technical rationality, but the former's existence, even in the context of the 'inclemencies of nature,' fails to account for the non-emergence of technical rationality over vast stretches of human history. My claim is that social forms have decisively mediated the relation between the 'excellent brain of human beings' and the human encounter with an inhospitable (non-human) nature, and that in fact it is only *certain* social forms that have encouraged the emergence of cognitive faculties capable of giving a systematic impetus to the development of labour productivity. These cognitive faculties may themselves be referred to as 'mental elements' of the productive forces at a certain stage of the latter's development.

The cognitive faculties in question refer to the categories of abstract reason to which Kant attributed a *transcendental* origin. Yet any such idealist (non-) explanation of the provenance of the abstract intellect must encounter the same objection as Cohen's explanation of the origin of human technical rationality in the (unmediated) interaction of 'excellent brains' and the 'inclemencies of nature.' Kant's theory cannot account for the fact that over tens of thousands of years of human prehistory and over thousands of years of early civilization there is little evidence of the existence of an 'abstract intellect' or of the influence of the 'categories of pure reason' on human practice.

All of this suggests that Kant's categories must not only have a *social* provenance, as Durkheim following Marx suggested, but also a definite historical origin. Yet it was only with the publication of Alfred Sohn-Rethel's Marxist 'critique of epistemology' in 1978 that a plausible historical-materialist account of the social and historical origins of the categories of reason was finally made. For Sohn-Rethel the emergence of the cognitive faculties associated with classical Greek philosophy, mathematics, and modern natural science was directly connected with the emergence of the 'real abstraction of exchange' attendant to the appearance of commodity production and money.

The implications of Sohn-Rethel's insight are clearly immense with respect to the possible place of simple commodity production/exchange in defining a precapitalist forces-relations dialectic. Moreover, it is perfectly reasonable to hypothesize that the development of simple 'value relations' (as sponsored by rudimentary forms of commodity production) might well have been the spark that ignited a veritable cognitive revolution without which the development of capitalism would have been impossible. It is this cognitive revolution, I contend, that marks a profound epoch-making transition *within precapitalist history.*

Within the classical Marxist tradition such a notion is most clearly fore-shadowed in a passage from Engels's *Origin of the Family, Private Property and the State*:

The appearance of private property in herds of cattle and articles of luxury [among the ancient Greeks] led to exchange between individuals, to the transformation of products into *commodities.* Here lies the root of the entire revolution that followed. ... The Athenians were soon to learn ... how quickly after individual exchange is established and products are converted into commodities, the product manifests its rule over the producer. With the production of commodities came the tilling of the soil by individual cultivators for their own account, soon followed by individual ownership of the land. Then came money, that universal commodity for which all others could be exchanged. But when men invented money they little suspected that they were creating a *new social power*, the one universal power to which the whole of society must bow. (Marx and Engels 1970, 3: 279)

Most contemporary Marxists would agree that Engels rather overstates his case in this passage, according, as he does, a pre-eminence to this 'new social power' that it was unable to really acquire until the emergence of modern capitalism. For money to appear as the 'one universal power to which the whole of society must bow,' commodity production had not only to exist; it had to be well on its way to being 'generalized' – to becoming the *general* social form of production. This was not the case in either Greek or Roman antiquity, despite the considerable extension of trade and commodity production that occurred during this epoch.

Even so, Engels's argument should not be wholly dismissed, nor indeed should his related thesis that the law of value has its historical origins in the value relations established over thousands of years of simple commodity production (Engels 1895). To be sure, such precapitalist value relations must be seen as *rudimentary* antecedents of the capitalist law of value; yet the existence of commodity production and exchange, even where it is decisively subordinated to other modes of production, still signifies the existence, if only in a rudimentary sense, of a trade-based division of labour and of a type of economic activity that is predicated upon the recognition of 'private property rights.' It need hardly be pointed out that such rights, which Sohn-Rethel quite properly defines in terms of the 'laws of the separation of exchange and use,' can have no meaning except where market-exchange has become a significant social form of the process of production (as distinct, say, from the communal, familial, or manorial forms that are so widespread in precapitalist formations). I wish to argue, however, that the impact of this social form and of the new 'social power' it represents may be greater in its 'sponsorship' of new cognitive faculties than in its direct influence upon economic intercourse per se. Not only might simple commodity production sponsor a 'law of value sui generis' that *directly* enters into the forces-relations dialectic of precapitalist history; it may well sponsor a modality of thought that is conducive to labour-saving technological innovation and the extension of the productive powers of humanity. The crucial historiographic issue must then be: to what extent have *particular* precapitalist societies (a) 'permitted' the proliferation of simple commodity production/exchange, together with related social forms; and (b) 'tolerated' the technical-scientific consciousness arising from a trade-based division of labour.

An argument can easily be made that, of all the precapitalist modes of production identified by Marx, only the feudal mode possessed the specific features and the endogenous dynamic that could give a systematic impulse to both of these developments. And it is for *this* reason that capitalism grew out of (West European) feudalism and could not have grown out of either the ancient or Asiatic modes of production. Feudalism should be ranked higher among the 'epochs marking progress in the economic development of society' not only because it encouraged the growth of a trade-based division of labour, but because it erected fewer obstacles to the technical-scientific progress made possible by the unleashing of the abstract intellect.

To buttress the credibility of this argument we need only draw upon a few well-established (and relatively uncontroversial) theoretical and historiographic points pertaining to the specificity of Western European feudalism in relation to other precapitalist modes. The first is that feudalism is distinguished from 'despotic' or 'slave' societies in its decentralized political structure, its 'dispersal of political power' (Amin 1985: 206; Anderson 1979). The absence or weakness of a centralized political authority opens the door to a wide array of social forms, including those based upon the postulates of 'equalitarian' commodity exchange and individual surplus appropriation.

This leads to the second point. It is just such social forms proliferating in the 'pores' of feudal society that may be most responsible for the intensive development of the productive forces stressed by Laibman. The same point extends to Brenner's (1977) important distinction between 'absolute' and 'relative' surpluses in the transition from feudalism to capitalism. 'Pure' feudal relations are likely only to engender an absolute surplus; but feudal societies have a weak ability to maintain their 'purity' (and their ruling elements also appear to have little *will* to do so). Hence, the stage is set for simple commodity production and long-distance trade to stimulate the intensive (labour-saving) productive forces that make possible the appropriation of a growing relative or 'intensive' surplus.

The final point concerns the fact that 'productively relevant' knowledge tends to be less centralized and is more likely to actually be applied to production under feudal conditions than in other precapitalist, class-antagonistic situations. This is not only because the incentive to use such knowledge is greater in feudal societies; it is also because 'despotic states' promote a radical division of intellectual and manual labour as between state functionaries and the direct producers. Non-feudal 'state-classes' are notorious 'hoarders' of knowledge, which they use primarily to reinforce and perpetuate the conditions of their own rule. Such élites are also apt to erect and sustain formidable ideological obstacles to the spread of technical-scientific forms of rationality.

An adequate specification of a 'precapitalist forces-relations dialectic' requires recognition of both the pivotal role played by simple commodity production in developing the forces of production and the limits imposed on this role by other, more dominant, precapitalist forms. Fragile as it might have been in precapitalist eras, and incapable as it might have been of imposing its own norms and laws upon societies ruled by despots, slave-owners, or feudal lords, simple commodity production was nevertheless successful in sponsoring an extremely 'subversive' form of human consciousness – a mode of thinking and of problem-solving that itself must be ranked with land, labour-power, and productively relevant knowledge as a major force of production. Its development, in tandem with the development of the other forces of production, could only eventuate in a challenge to the feudal relations that had (indirectly) nurtured it, particularly when the feudal mode of production itself entered, for numerous reasons, into protracted crisis.

It should be underscored that the 'cognitive revolution' postulated here had an extremely uneven and historically discontinuous development. It began in antiquity, but could not possibly have triumphed in the ancient societies. It was unleashed to some limited extent wherever a trade-based division of labour took root; but it was repeatedly suppressed by social forms as varied as the despotic state and the European guilds. Its ultimate triumph (in Western Europe) was predicated on the emergence of a particular 'balance' of social forms, as well as favourable geographical and historical circumstances. All of which could very easily suggest that this cognitive revolution and the growth of the forces of production that propelled capitalist development had a somewhat fortuitous character. This I take to be true. Yet this in no way contradicts the thesis, which I believe to be central to Marx's historical vision, that *human history possesses a pattern of development to the extent that it is guided by the human propensity toward technical rationality.* There is no hint of a unilinear theory of human history here, still less of any speculative 'historico-philosophical theory' of the type berated in *The German Ideology.* There is also no evolutionary inevitablism implicit in such a formulation. All that can be said is that history *has* unfolded in such a way as to unleash the productive power of technical rationality; that capitalism *has* emerged as the dominant mode of production on a planetary scale; and that this *has* created the potential for a world-wide development toward the sort of socialist society envisaged by Marx and Engels.

This interpretation of Marx's materialist conception of history is free, I believe, of any *idealist* teleology, of the sort that would claim that human history is unfolding according to some transcendental logic toward a preordained goal (communism), via a series of set 'stages.' But it does insist upon the possibility that human history may *assume* a determinate developmental pattern if the balance of social forms comes to favour the full flowering of technical rationality. The reality that Marx was faced with, and that we continue to be faced with, is that in the course of human history such a development *did* occur. And it is only by virtue of this that we can now entertain ideas about the contemporary results and future prospects of a 'universal human history' that has materialized before the eyes of humanity in just the past few centuries.

While Marx never discussed these issues in precisely these terms I believe that the argument set forth here is fully consistent with the fundamental concepts and premises of his historical materialism, particularly as these have been elucidated in recent years in relation to the basic principles of his social ontology and epistemology.

Cohen, Sayer, and Sohn-Rethel on Historical Materialism

The argument presented above departs from Cohen's more traditional account of historical materialism in its stress upon contingency in the historical interplay of social forms and productive forces. At the same time, it is predicated upon a more radical break from the dualistic ontology from which Cohen partially distances Marx. Central to Cohen's account is the role of human technical rationality in promoting the development of the material forces of production and in selecting the social relations of production historically suited to technological progress. Yet this propensity toward technical rationality is never adequately explicated by Cohen; indeed, it appears to exist *independently* of the material-social relation that Cohen quite rightly has identified as the key concept of Marx's historical materialism. It appears to spring from a socially unmediated relation of human beings to 'nature' that Cohen tends to identify with the 'material' or 'natural' *content* of society and that is *externally related* to the social forms assumed and discarded by concrete societies. Thus, in defending the notion that Marx's theory of history highlights the material-social distinction and not a material-ideal opposition, Cohen has disclosed a necessary but not a sufficient basis for reasserting Marx's dialectical social ontology as against the claims of philosophical dualism. Indeed, in his handling of the form-content relation, Cohen has actually succumbed to the typically Kantian (and dualist) habit of regarding this as an *external* relation, and in so doing has readmitted an ontological opposition between 'consciousness' (human rationality as embedded in 'content') and 'social being' (as rooted in the 'form' of society). It need only be assumed that content has ontological priority over form to conclude that human technical rationality must ultimately prevail over all forms of consciousness that are rooted in 'mere' social relations. Here, indeed, is where Cohen's interpretation of Marx finally sanctions a rather crude, and historically indefensible, technological determinism, one quite incapable of accounting for the historical viability and persistence of class-appropriative forms of rationality that have often proved *inimical* to technical rationality.

Cohen's incomplete break with a dualistic social ontology has theoretical consequences that have been most fully explored by Derek Sayer in *The Violence of Abstraction: The Analytic Foundations of Historical Materialism*, a work that represents a substantial advance over Cohen's in its grasp of Marx's historical sociology. Proceeding from an 'internal relations' perspective of the type elaborated by Ollman (1976), Sayer suggests that for Marx neither the material-social distinction nor the form-content distinction has a hard and fast character. Indeed, Marx's dialectical social ontology enjoins us from drawing the sort of 'analytically precise' boundaries between such concepts as the forces of production and the relations of production that Cohen draws: 'we can no longer assume that terms like forces and relations of production, or base and superstructure, refer unambiguously or consistently to different, and mutually exclusive, bits of empirical reality as they would in an atomistic ontology ... On the view argued here, the empirical referents of Marx's concepts may neither be mutually exclusive, nor consistent across space and time' (Sayer 1987: 22). The upshot is that productive forces should not be treated as a 'set of things,' but as 'attributes of human beings in association, their collective capacities' (ibid.: 27), while the relations of production should be conceptualized as 'any and all social relations which are demonstrably entailed in a given mode of production, or "way in which [people] produce their means of subsistence" (Marx)' (ibid.: 75). Such an approach makes it possible to see not only the *internal* relationship of social form and material content but also the social content of 'things' and the 'material forms' assumed by social relations: an analytical agenda splendidly pursued by Marx in his analyses of commodity and capital fetishism.

Sayer's critique of 'traditional historical materialism' (including Cohen's) has the considerable virtue of emphasizing Marx and Engels's seminal historical-materialist proposition that 'the production of life ... appears as a *double* relationship: on the one hand as a natural, on the other as a social relationship' (1947: 18). Thus, the *same* activities must be seen as having social and material (or natural) dimensions. This means that the forces of production have a social dimension as well as a material one, just as it means that the relations of production have both material and social expressions. It is only on this basis that one can explain Marx's repeated reference to such unmistakably *social* phenomena as the community, money, trade, and state activity as 'productive forces' (ibid.: 29). Equally, it is only on this basis that it becomes possible to give an adequate general definition of the concept of relations of production as one that encompasses, in different times and places, 'material relations of production' and 'superstructural relations,' as well as Cohen's 'relations of ownership' or 'relations of effective power over persons and productive forces' (1978: 34, 63).

This already suggests a second major area of Sayer's critique of Cohen and of traditional historical materialism. For if a hard and fast distinction cannot be made between the material and the social, it is no less true that the distinction between the mode of production and the superstructure is necessarily a fluid one. This is particularly so in precapitalist societies, where the organic unity of the human community admits no distinction between 'economy' and 'polity' as discrete spheres. In a very real sense, the notion of a political and legal superstructure arising on the basis of the economic structure could only be articulated from the standpoint of capitalist society, and the transferability of this metaphor to precapitalist formations is therefore highly problematic. Yet Marx's notion of the superstructure involves something more than this. Despite the wording of the Preface, which Cohen takes all too literally, the superstructure is for Marx not so much an institutional sphere as 'the "ideal" form in which the totality of "material" relations which make up the "base" itself are manifested to consciousness' (Sayer 1987: 84). Marx's abundant references to 'ideal' and 'ideological' superstructures in many of his other works make this clear. According to Sayer, the base-superstructure metaphor of the Preface recapitulates Marx's long-standing philosophical position that 'the ideal is nothing else than the material world reflected by the human mind, and translated into forms of thought' (Marx 1873: 19; quoted in Sayer 1987: 86).

Cohen's failure to grasp this aspect of Marx's philosophical perspective is of crucial importance: for it leads him in the direction of a dualistic epistemology in which ideological forms of consciousness are associated with 'social forms' while technical-scientific forms of consciousness are imbricated in the 'material content' of society (the socially unmediated relation of 'excellent brains' and non-human nature). Sayer insists against this that human consciousness, on Marx's view, must always be a projection of the 'double relationship' in which human beings are inescapably implicated: a material world governed by both natural and social relations. This in no way vitiates the necessary distinction between science and ideology as elements of consciousness. But it should sensitize us to the fuller meaning and contradictory implications of Marx's postulate that 'social being determines consciousness.'

At the same time, Sayer's interpretation of Marx's concepts closes the door to the proposition that the forces of production must enjoy 'primacy' over the relations of production in determining the course of history. Once the form-content relation is treated as an internal one, it is no longer meaningful to ponder the sort of question to which Cohen admits he has 'no good answer': namely, 'how productive forces select economic structures which promote their development' (Cohen 1983: 124). Once forms are regarded as *immanent* in contents this problem of 'selection' quite simply disappears. More problematically, however, Sayer suggests that so too does the problem of 'causality,' at least insofar as we are speaking of the interrelationship of relations and forces. After a compelling critique of Cohen's primacy thesis Sayer proceeds to dismantle the converse proposition that social relations of production dominate the productive forces: 'simply to reverse the line of causality between forces and relations obscures the important extent to which, for Marx, the growth of human productive power does remain the fundamental dynamic of historical progress' (Sayer 1987: 35). Yet the point of Sayer's argument is not that an internal-relations perspective absolves Marx or any theorist of the responsibility to specify the 'causal links' existing between phenomena; indeed, Sayer is quite explicit in associating Marx's method and ontology with a 'realist' position which requires that 'giving a causal explanation *necessarily* involves "elaborating" a theory of causal mechanisms' (ibid.: 125). His point is simply that it is mistaken to establish a 'line of causality' between forces and relations understood as discrete and externally related 'categories.' For Sayer, the causal mechanisms identified by Marx 'lie ultimately in the actions of real individuals,' and consequently 'the causal explanation of social phenomena must ... be historical' rather than functional (ibid.: 125). In a related vein Sayer argues: 'Contrary to Cohen, Marx's concepts of forces and relations of production ... do not then denote "items" which are "more basic than actions" [Cohen 1983: 123] ... These "items" *are* actions – forms of human relationship – and the whole point of Marx's critique is to unmask them as such. Behind the authorless theatre of fetishism lie "real living individuals", for Marx the true and the only subjects of history' (1987: 136).

For Sayer, the problem with 'traditional' historical materialism is that it has fetishized and reified Marx's categories of forces and relations of production in the process of theoretically reducing them to lists of empirical items. The all-too-predictable result has been the positing of 'more or less implausible connections at the level of general theory' for which the indicated antidote is 'a minimum of a *priori* theory, and the use of empirically-open general categories which are analytically capable of letting the real world in' (ibid.: 147).

Sayer's critique of Cohen is compelling and his proposed agenda for historical-materialist inquiry attractive. Yet there is something not altogether satisfying about his plea for a more 'empirical' (if not empiricist) redefinition of the historical-materialist project. A clue to the deficiency is to be found in his repeated insistence that the starting-point of analysis must be 'the real, living individuals' invoked by Marx in the *The German Ideology*. What Sayer gives insufficient weight to is the ability of concrete, historically existing individuals through their activities to create those 'reified structures' and 'economic laws' that come to dominate and constrain their existence. Human activity does indeed construct 'the theatre of fetishism'; but once constructed this theatre has a way of transforming its builders into scripted actors who sustain the theatre's operations. It may be true, then, that the operations of the law of value are 'ultimately' rooted in 'the actions of real individuals'; but an adequate causal explanation of these operations must nevertheless consider the real existence of such 'holistic' structural entities as 'abstract labour' and 'the world of commodities,' entities that arise as *collective* expressions of a multitude of individual actions. Oddly, much of Sayer's argument leads away from this consideration and lends itself to a methodologically individualist interpretation of Marx – one that is irreconcilable with his own insistence upon Marx's opposition to 'atomist' ontologies.

A further problem with Sayer is that there is precious little in his account of historical materialism that would enable us to understand what he *means* when he says that, 'for Marx, the growth of human productive power does remain the fundamental dynamic of historical progress' (1987: 35). If human productive power can refer to social relations as well as 'material objectifications,' what criteria can be 'objectively' deployed to assess whether 'growth' and therefore 'historical progress' is occurring? In this connection, it should be noted that in earlier works Sayer has expressed his solidarity with the ultra-voluntarist Maoist notion that even the poorest of societies (in material/technological terms) can 'build socialism' provided the requisite social forms are in place (see Corrigan, Ramsay, and Sayer, *For Mao*, 1979). This may also explain his interest in 'late' Marx's sympathy for Russian populism and for the proposition that the Russian peasant commune could be a base for socialist construction (Sayer and Corrigan 1983). Yet there is no theoretical warrant to proceed from the recognition that the social phenomenon of 'cooperation' (as embodied in a detailed technical division of labour) ranks as *one* of the forces of production in the development of capitalism to the idea that social forms and mental attitudes are *all* that matter in the construction of socialism. As Sayer acknowledges (implicitly 'against Mao'):

The productive power of social labour may indeed, in the course of human development, increasingly become embodied in things – like machines – and undeniably it is through such embodiment that it is most enhanced. This is what is so revolutionary about modern industry; for Marx it represented a qualitative break, a veritable quantum leap in the unfolding of human productive potential comparable only perhaps with the neolithic revoution. Human beings are, distinctively, creatures who purposefully objectify their collective capacities in the material world they create through transforming nature, and this is fundamental to Marx's sociology. (1987: 27)

Yet human beings are also creatures who may purposefully seek to shelter themselves, as individuals, from the worst inclemencies of nature by turning their excellent brains to the enterprise of subjugating and exploiting their fellow humans. This is perhaps *why* the transformation of nature and the growth of human productive potential has been so painfully slow and discontinuous in the course of human history. Throughout this history technical forms of rationality have had to wage a long battle against sociological forms of rationality ('appropriative' forms) rooted in *antagonistic* social postulates – postulates that find expression in class structures and state forms.

This leads to a third critical observation concerning Sayer. Unlike Cohen, who is openly dismissive of Marx's law of value, Sayer regards Marx's value theory as a critically important component of his historical-materialist analysis of capitalist society. But as has been the fashion in Marxist circles in recent years, Sayer fails to address the extent to which value relations might be said to have impacted on *precapitalist* societies.[1] Not surprisingly, in view of this, he also fails to address the issue of the impact of 'real abstractions' on precapitalist history. This is a crucial omission, for it must result in a failure to appreciate the cognitive revolution sponsored by simple commodity production and exchange.

It is here that a closer examination of Sohn-Rethel's argument becomes mandatory. As discussed earlier, Sohn-Rethel's fundamental thesis is that it is the historical appearance of a *real abstraction* – the commodity or value abstraction – that makes possible the development of those conceptual abstractions associated with classical philosophy, mathematics, and modern natural science. In substantiating this thesis Sohn-Rethel begins by pointing to the 'striking similarity' between the value abstraction and the thought abstractions of science:

The economic concept of value [resulting from the commodity abstraction] is characterized by a complete absence of quality, a differentiation purely by quantity and by applicability to every kind of commodity and service which can occur on the market. These qualities of the economic value abstraction indeed display a striking similarity with fundamental categories of quantifying natural science without, admittedly, the slightest inner relationship between these heterogeneous spheres being as yet recognizable. While the concepts of natural science are thought abstractions, the economic concept of value is a real one. It exists nowhere other than in the human mind but it does not spring from it. Rather it is purely social in character, arising from the spatio-temporal sphere of human interrelations. It is not people who originate these abstractions but their actions. 'They do this without being aware of it' (Marx). (1978: 20)

It is important to be clear on what Sohn-Rethel is saying here. The economic concept of value is a 'real abstraction' rather than a 'thought abstraction' because it derives from a real social process: that of commodity exchange (that is, from activities rather than thoughts). The 'reality' of the commodity abstraction, however, defies the standard philosophical criterion for what is 'real' (as opposed to 'ideal'): an empirically specifiable content. It is precisely the empirical emptiness of this abstraction that renders it 'abstract,' just as its provenance in the socio-temporal sphere of actual human interactions, as founded upon definite social norms, renders it 'real.' The existence of such a real abstraction within the human mind suggests a *social* origin for the non-empirical concepts whose basis traditional philosophical materialism has never adequately explained, and whose undeniable importance has been key to the (only comparative) 'success' of philosophical idealism in accounting for the *duality* of the sources of knowledge ('pure reason' as well as sense perception). Sohn-Rethel elaborates as follows:

The entire exchange abstraction is founded upon social postulate and not upon fact. It is a postulate that the use of commodities must remain suspended until the exchange has taken place; it is a postulate that no physical change should occur in the commodities and this still applies even if the facts belie it; it is a postulate that the commodities in the exchange relation should count as equal despite their factual difference ... None of these form-concepts imply statements of fact. They are all norms which commodity exchange has to obey to be possible and to enable anarchical society to survive by the rules of reification. (1978: 68)

The thrust of Sohn-Rethel's argument is thus to establish that an 'inner relationship' *does* obtain between the value abstraction and the thought abstractions of mathematics, philosophy, and natural science, and that, in fact, 'the real abstraction operating in exchange *engenders* the ideal abstraction basic to Greek philosophy and to modern science' (1978: 28; emphasis added). For if any of the elements of the real abstraction of exchange are correctly identified within the human mind, the result must be the formation of concepts (thought abstractions) that are 'as non-empirical as the exchange abstraction itself' (ibid.: 67). Sohn-Rethel's detailed theoretical analysis of the formal elements of the exchange abstraction, as suggested by Marx's theory of value, serves to demonstrate that not only analogy but 'true identity' exists between the formal elements of this abstraction and the formal cognitive constituents of those forms of thought that issued in the development of modern science. In particular, the concepts of 'abstract quantity,' 'abstract time and space,' 'abstract movement,' and 'strict causality' are all notions that have 'real' counterparts in elements of the act of exchange (Sohn-Rethel, 1978: 47–55). Kant's categories a priori, then, are not transcendental properties of the human intellect, but historically produced concepts originating in specific types of social interaction and founded upon a real abstraction. Yet it remains importantly true that 'once the elements of the real abstraction have assumed conceptual form, their character, rooted in social postulates, evolves into the dialectic of logical argument attached to the concepts' (ibid.: 71). The 'autonomy' of this 'dialectic of logical argument' from social being follows from the fact that the exchange abstraction is an abstraction associated with the *actions* of people and not with their thinking. It is an abstraction of which people are not consciously aware, but which is nevertheless reproduced in human consciousness in the form of the 'abstract intellect.'

It is in this rather special sense that 'value' (and its material expression as money) may come to exert itself as a significant 'social power' long before the advent of capitalism. To be sure, so long as exchange does not play a dominant part in giving social form to production, the forms of thought deriving from the value abstraction must wage an 'uphill' battle against forms of thought rooted in different (and often hostile) social postulates: the more-or-less conscious yet pre-scientific forms of socio-economic regulation that are founded on custom, tradition, and social privilege. But this in no way obviates the thesis that the value abstraction *causally influences* the growth of scientific and technical knowledge, and in this specific way enters into the forces-relations dialectic as this unfolds in precapitalist history.

Value Relations and Social Progress

The view that ideas and the categories of thought are rooted in social relations and the activities of 'real, living individuals' originates with Marx. In *The German Ideology* he wrote that 'ideas, categories' are but 'the abstract ideal expressions of ... social relations' (1989: 189), and in a letter to Engels (25 March 1868) he remarked that 'the logical categories are coming damn well out of "our intercourse" after all' (Marx and Engels 1965: 202). The young Lukács was to further pursue the connection between the 'commodity-struc-ture' and the abstract intellect of *bourgeois* society in his essay on 'Reification and the Consciousness of the Proletariat.' But it was left to Sohn-Rethel to provide 'ontological depth' to the analysis of how commodity exchange engenders the categories of thought associated with *technical rationality* and how these could develop even in commodity-producing societies where the fully reified capitalist law of value did not yet hold sway. According to Sohn-Rethel, the relationship between use and exchange as *contrasting* kinds of activity contains the real key to the abstraction of exchange; moreover, this is a relationship that resides at the very heart of the 'formal structure of exchange.' In defining this structure, Sohn-Rethel refers to the following passage from Marx's *Capital*:

So long as the laws of exchange are observed in every single act of exchange – taken in isolation – the mode of appropriation [of the surplus] can be completely revolu-tionized without in any way affecting the property rights which correspond to com-modity production. The same rights remain in force both at the outset, when the product belongs to its producer, who, exchanging equivalent for equivalent, can enrich himself only by his own labour, and in the period of capitalism, when the social wealth becomes to an ever-increasing degree the property of those who are in a position to appropriate the unpaid labour of others over and over again. (Marx 1977: 733)

This passage is noteworthy because it suggests that for Marx the 'laws of exchange' remain invariant *across* socio-economic epochs distinguished by different modes of exploitation. (Note that the notion of 'laws of exchange' is by no means synonymous with the 'law of value.') Moreover, commodity production is characterized by specific 'property rights' that remain *formally invariant* as between simple and capitalist commodity production. For Sohn-Rethel it is precisely the characteristics of commodity exchange as these are articulated on the basis of these rights that are central to the analysis of the value abstraction:

The point is that use and exchange are not only different and contrasting by description, but are mutually exclusive in time. They must take place separately at different times. This is because exchange serves only a change of ownership, a change, that is, in terms of a purely *social status* of the commodities as owned property. In order to make this change possible on a basis of negotiated agreement the physical condition of the commodities, their *material status*, must remain unchanged. Commodity exchange cannot take place as a recognized social institution unless this separation of exchange from use is stringently observed. (1978: 23–4)

All of this suggests that commodity exchange involves a socially specific type of 'restriction of use.' Where such restrictions are associated with 'exploitation based on unilateral appropriation as opposed to the reciprocity of exchange,' we are dealing with instances of what Marx calls 'direct lordship and bondage.' In such instances, the restriction of use is a result of conscious design and deliberate intent, but not of 'objective necessity.' Things stand altogether differently with the restriction of use associated with commodity exchange; and it is this difference that is key to appreciating both the cognitive revolution associated with the exchange abstraction and the significance of the first tentative stages in the transition from 'personal-dependency relations' to 'objective-dependency relations' as promoted by simple commodity production (Marx 1973: 157–64). It was precisely his belief that the latter relations were absent from Oriental life that prompted the young Marx to regard it as a purely natural and 'barbarian' form of human existence, one outside of history, just as it was his later recognition that *some* objective-dependency relations subsisted under the 'Asiatic mode of production' that led him to include the AMP in his sequence of 'historical epochs' (Vitkin 1981).

This point returns us to the issue of Marx's appreciation of 'progress' in human history. At the beginning of this chapter I suggested that Marx's vision of human progress was ultimately shaped by his belief in the realizability of a form of human society that is free of both material insecurity and of social antagonism. Yet the realization of such a society is dependent upon a definite development of the forces and relations of production made possible only by capitalism. In a world-historical sense capitalism is indeed the *necessary* prelude to socialism, in part because it lays the basis for a *world* economy, but also because its encouragement of technical rationality creates the indispensable material premises of socialism and communism. The historical contribution of the capitalist mode of production has been to 'bring together' technical rationality and appropriative rationality by giving technical rationality an appropriative form. This was mainly accomplished through the commodification of labour-power and the subordination of natural science to the demands of surplus-value production and realization (that is, through the 'formal' and then the 'real' subsumption of labour under capital, the latter serving to extend the division of intellectual and manual labour into the very heart of the production process). The corollary to this, however, is that technical rationality has served the development of the productive forces under capitalism *only* to the degree that it has served the appropriation of surplus labour. It is precisely the object of Marx's *Capital* to disclose the limits of the convergence under capitalism of these historically antagonistic principles: labour-saving technological progress, on the one hand, and surplus-labour appropriation, on the other. Indeed, the contradiction between these principles within capitalism is at the very heart of Marx's 'law of the falling tendency of the rate of profit' – a law that Marx considered to be 'in every respect the most important law of modern political economy, and the most essential for understanding the most difficult relations' (Marx 1973: 748; Smith 1991a; chapter 7 below).

But if all this is so, how are we to explain Marx's 'revised' estimation of the Asiatic mode of production and his fascination with the Russian peasant commune as a possible basis for socialist development in the last years of his life? A definitive answer is, I think, beyond our reach. But it would seem that Marx in the 1870s and the 1880s moved toward a position which recognized that capitalism had created a 'world history' to which the 'primary social formations' of the East (including the Russian commune) could now contribute. Marx never embraced the notion that socialism could be achieved 'within Russia' thanks to the collectivist social relations inherited from the peasant commune. But he was prepared to entertain the notion that the task of building *world* socialism might be jointly shouldered by formerly capitalist and Asiatic (or semi-Asiatic) societies alike. Thus, while a socialist revolution might well begin in semi-Asiatic Russia, the construction of socialism would still depend upon the enormous technological resources and productive capacities bequeathed by advanced capitalism: 'The *contemporaneity* of Western [capitalist] production, which dominates the world market, enables Russia to build into the commune all the positive achievements of the capitalist system, without having to pass under its harsh tribute' (Marx 1881: 110). This, along with many of Marx's other formulations in the various drafts of his letter to Vera Zasulich, suggests a position far closer to Trotsky's 'law of uneven and combined development' and his theory of permanent revolution than to either Stalin's or Mao's versions of socialist economic autarchy (that is, the doctrine of 'socialism in one country').

Finally, a few words should be said in defence of technical rationality and the social progress that it has made possible. When all is said and done, Marx's concept of 'human productive powers' (the forces of production) can only refer to the capacities of human beings to transform the world that we inhabit in such a way as to reduce the burden of toil, increase the margin of material security, and attenuate the degree of social antagonism that we collectively confront. Technical rationality has contributed mightily to the development of these powers, and therefore to the potential for human well-being. To free it from its subordination to the logic of appropriation inherent in capitalist social relations, however, requires the promotion of a *socialist rationality* grounded in a vigorous commitment to *human progress* – to the realization of a society in which 'human individuality' can develop unhampered by material hardship or social antagonism. Such a concept of human progress still stands as the loftiest of goals to which human beings can aspire. Yet its realizability and even its desirability must be persistently denied by forms of consciousness no less deeply rooted in the 'exchange abstraction' than is technical rationality. Ironically, the division of exchange and use as contrasting types of activity, together with the division of intellectual and manual labour that has been profoundly ramified by the generalization of commodity relations, must promote an abstract intellect prone to a profoundly *dualistic* world-view, one that habitually views the relations between fact and value, 'is' and 'ought,' freedom and necessity, theory and practice, and so on as 'external' and eternally problematic. For many who share such a world-view the epistemological and cultural relativism that is promoted by postmodernist thought may well appear to be the most humane as well as comfortable of intellectual options. But for those who reject this world-view, together with its social basis, it must appear as the last line of intellectual defence of a social order that has exhausted its progressive historical mission.

A Final Unresolved Issue

A possible implication of my argument is that cognitive faculties based upon the commodity abstraction have not only *stimulated* technical rationality but have in large part been *constitutive* of this form of thought. Yet such a conclusion must be qualified by the observation that, prior to the cognitive revolution associated with the historical appearance of the commodity abstraction, labour-saving technological innovation was not at all unknown (the invention of the wheel and the plough are among the more obvious examples). This suggests that technical rationality may not be *identical* with the 'abstract intellect' referred to by Sohn-Rethel, who, incidentally, regards the non-empirical concepts drawn from the real abstraction as constituting the 'paradigm of mechanistic thinking' (1978: 72). At the same time, it suggests that technical rationality, as promoted by the *particular* cognitive faculties associated with the commodity abstraction, may well be subject to further historical transformations sponsored by the development of new social forms. In other words, Kant's 'categories of pure reason' are by no means the last word in defining the formal constituents of the abstract intellect. As Marx averred, 'the categories are no more eternal than the relations they express. They are historical and transitory products' (1989: 189). Indeed, even the scientific *critique* of these relations, as Marx's own work testifies, may well generate new theoretical categories and perspectives of relevance to the social and the natural sciences alike (for instance, the categories of 'totality' and 'real contradiction'). In light of these considerations it may well be fruitful to explore the question of the socio-historical provenance of quantum theory, scientific realism, and the 'chaos' paradigm as substantial recent examples of an on-going dialectical process of cognitive revolution.

The following chapter examines the vicissitudes of the *theory* of value resulting from its changing relationship to the scientific and ideological requirements of the principal social classes of modern capitalist society.

3 Science, Ideology, and 'Economic Value'

The concept of 'value' has been both a perennial and an elusive one in the history of economic thought. Despite the fact that value and price are usually thought of as coextensive if not synonymous terms, and despite the fact that, in practice, most economists conflate the two notions, there is clearly a sense in which value is considered the *basis* of price, and therefore as something conceptually distinct from it. Consumers, reflecting on the quality and the price of a particular commodity, make a determination as to what is a 'good value' and what is an 'unreasonable price.' Notwithstanding that at this level the value of a good or service is a subjective judgment, it is one that also has a real basis in human experience, especially in the common-sense yet well-grounded notion that price and value do not always coincide (that is, that the *same* commodity can be variously priced).

The inner connection between value and price obscures the fact that the significance of 'value' extends beyond the processes of price formation. Certainly, this was Marx's view. Yet neoclassical economists have maintained an almost dogmatic insistence that any theory of value that cannot be of direct use in the explanation of individual commodity prices is unworthy of consideration. Indeed, it is just this prejudice that sanctions the dismissal by most conventional economists of all notions of 'labour-value' in favour of the marginal-utility theory of value pioneered by Jevons, Walras, and Menger.

To be sure, a growing contingent of non-Marxist economists now dismiss marginalism in the same terms that the marginalists rejected the notion of labour-value: by labelling it 'metaphysical.' Neo-Ricardian, post-Sraffian, and Cambridge School economists, for example, claim to eschew all notions of value as ideological mystification. But the even-handedness displayed by a Joan Robinson in rejecting the scientific claims of both marginal-utility theory and Marx's labour theory of value may only serve to mask a new twist on a familiar ideological bias. Hence, Robinson (1968: 39) could easily have been speaking for the economics profession as a whole when she dismissed the labour theory of value as a convenient, if 'unscientific,' basis for Marx's thesis that capitalists do not *steal* from workers but rather *exploit* them, and averred that such a theory is 'ideologically ... much stronger poison than a direct attack on injustice' since it leads to the conclusion that 'reform is impossible' (Ibid.: 39). In spite of the clumsiness of her critique of Marx, Robinson was on to something here: for the 'operational significance' of Marx's theory of value is precisely that it serves to underpin his rather provocative proposition that 'the true barrier to capitalist production is capital itself' (1981b: 358), thereby establishing the historical necessity to not merely reform capitalism but to replace it with a higher order of socio-economic organization.

The labour theory of value did not always have such 'subversive' implications, at least not in the anticapitalist sense. Indeed, the career of the labour-value concept provides a fascinating object lesson in how social relations of production and class interest may intrude on the delineation of 'science' and 'ideology,' and determine the relative fortunes of each.

Classical political economy emerged as a specialized field of inquiry some three hundred years ago. Its rise was inextricably bound up with the break-down of the feudal system, the proliferation of simple commodity production, the spread of European colonialism, and the articulation of national and international markets. Intellectually, it was part of the Enlightenment 'great awakening' that characterized the last phases of monarchical absolutism and the mercantilist trade system. From its inception, political economy was associated, as Therborn (1980: 89) notes, with 'perhaps the two most important currents of thought of the emergent bourgeoisie in its ideological struggle against the established feudal society – utilitarianism and (mainly in the case of the physiocrats) natural law.' Practically, it was concerned with the economic affairs of *the state*, as distinct from the management of a family household or individual business enterprise. More specifically, the political project of most of the early political economists was to influence the state to adopt policies favouring the interests of the bourgeoisie – interests that they took to embody the well-being of the great mass of the population, save the most recalcitrant and backward-looking elements of the landed aristocracy. As Simon Clarke (1982: 13) observes, the economic theories of classical political economy 'established the viability of capitalist society and showed that such a society could be ruled by reason and not by custom, as social order and class harmony were achieved on the basis of action oriented by enlightened self-interest.'

In France, the program of political economy found an early expression in attacks on the tax system of the *ancien régime*: that is, in opposition to the immunization of nobles and clergy, and in the proposal for a single tax on land. In England, it found a more advanced expression in the ideas of 'laisser-faire' and free trade, against which were arrayed not only significant sections of the aristocracy but also mercantilist elements of the bourgeoisie with an interest in preserving existing trade monopolies. As Robinson notes, 'Adam Smith's main argument ... was directed against mercantilism,' while 'Ricardo's theory of rent led up to the abolition of the corn law' (1968: 61).

The early popularity of the labour theory of value among the classical political economists needs to be situated within this general intellectual and programmatic context. While inklings of a labour-value theory are traceable to medieval canonist tracts, its first systematic elaboration was at the hands of the economic and philosophical thinkers of ascendant capitalism. Both Thomas Hobbes and John Locke subscribed to theories of labour-value, and both integrated the notion into their broader political philosophies. In particular, Locke sought to use the idea of labour-value as a premiss for his argument against the alienation (coerced separation) of property – as a *product of labour* – from those who produce it. The object of this critique was the transparently exploitative set of relations existing between the landed aristocracy and the actual cultivators of the land under feudalism: 'Whatsoever then [a man] removes out of the state that nature hath provided and left it in, he hath mixed his labour with, and joined to it something that is his own, and thereby makes it his property' (1968: 340). Here a labour theory of value is invoked to support the notion of a 'natural right' to property, a right violated by the feudal order but enshrined by the rising bourgeoisie.

If Locke used a labour-value theory in support of his political theory of possessive individualism, the notion of labour-value found an altogether different status and use in the writings of Adam Smith and David Ricardo, the two pre-eminent figures of classical political economy. In Smith's writings, the theory appears as an adjunct to his case for a free trade policy as a means of encouraging productivity gains and the accumulation of capital stock. What is distinctive about Smith's ruminations on labour-value, however, is that he acknowledges embodied labour as the determinant of the exchange-value of commodities only in an 'early and rude society' preceding 'the accumulation of stock and the appropriation of land' – that is to say, preceding the emergence of social classes. In other words, for Smith, the labour theory of value has full validity only where class divisions do not yet exist. Once economic theory allows for the existence of ground rent and profit (corresponding to the incomes of landowners and capitalists), then land and capital must be considered along with labour as factors determining market prices. Even so, Smith regarded labour as not only the *principal source* of value, but also as its *sole measure*: 'The real value of all the different component parts of price ... is measured by the quantity of labour which they can, each of them, purchase or command. Labour measures the value not only of that part of price which resolves itself into labour, but of that which resolves itself into rent, and of that which resolves itself into profit' (Smith 1970: 153). Hence, Smith's theory of labour-value is confused to the extent that he 'mixes notions of labour commanded (the amount of labour that can be employed) with the labour expended' (Fine 1982: 76).

David Ricardo's conception of economic value was similarly shaped by an understanding of society as divided into social classes; but unlike Smith, Ricardo saw the analysis of the distribution of national income among these classes as the key task of political-economic theory. In *Principles of Political Economy and Taxation*, he writes: 'The produce of the earth – all that is derived from its surface by the united application of labour, machinery and capital, is divided among three classes of the community; namely, the proprietor of the land, the owner of the stock of capital necessary for its cultivation, and the labourers by whose industry it is cultivated ... To determine the laws which regulate this distribution, is the principal problem in Political Economy' (1951: 5). It was in order to disclose the laws governing the distribution of this social wealth that Ricardo confronted the problem of its *measurement*, and it was precisely in this connection that he felt obliged to move beyond the sphere of relative commodity prices to the *social origin* of the value constituted by this wealth.

While Ricardo distinguished between 'natural prices' and 'market prices,' and anticipated Marx's distinction between labour expended and 'necessary' labour, his theory of labour-value failed to make any rigorous distinction between value and price. The consequence was that, in observing that even 'natural prices' are constituted by influences independent of (necessary) labour time, Ricardo arrived at a '93 per cent' labour theory of price: the idea that while labour is the dominant determinant of commodity prices under normal conditions, it can never be the sole determinant.

Ricardo was the last of the major classical political economists to enunciate a labour theory of value, and since his time, the great majority of economists within capitalist societies have decisively rejected the notion of labour-value. The prevailing attitude of mainstream economists is well captured in Joseph Schumpeter's assertion that 'for economics as a positive science [as distinct from a 'social philosophy'] ... it is important to ask how the labour theory of value works as a tool of analysis, and the real trouble is that it does so very badly' (1962: 24). Schumpeter neglects to add, however, that the worth of any analytical tool can only be judged by how well it serves a specific analytical agenda, as well as the practical project with which that agenda is associated. In this light, it could easily be argued that the main reason for the repudiation of the theory of labour-value by mainstream economists was that, after Ricardo, the concept of labour-value had quite simply lost its ability to contribute to the project to which conventional economists have always been devoted, namely, the elaboration of ideas useful to the legitimation and/or the 'fine-tuning' of the existing capitalist order. As Clarke (1982: 106) has put it: 'The essential ideological weakness of the Ricardian system is that it does not provide a very satisfactory basis on which to defend profit.'

Such an argument acquires cogency when it is appreciated that economics, as a vocation, is subject to ideological as well as scientific determinations, and that its leading theorists have generally been committed to the promotion and perpetuation of capitalist economy (whether through fiscal tinkering or substantive reform). Accordingly, it is by no means a tendentious exercise to point out that John Locke was secretary to the British Council on Trade and invested in the silk and slave trades; that Ricardo was a successful stockbroker and contractor of loans who made an enormous fortune during the Napoleonic Wars; that Eugen Von Boehm-Bawerk was finance minister of the Austro-Hungarian Empire as well as the author of the definitive marginalist critique of Marx's economics; that Joseph Schumpeter had been a minister of finance and the president of an Austrian bank before entering academic life; and that John Maynard Keynes enriched himself as a jobber in currency, securities, and primary commodities (Therborn 1980: 89–90). Nor is it irrelevant to point out that two of the English pioneers of marginal-utility theory, Stanley Jevons and Alfred Marshall, were virulent academic antagonists of organized labour. Jevons attacked trade unions for promoting the 'delusion' of a 'supposed conflict of labour with capital,' and Marshall, outraged by a strike of engineering workers, wrote: 'I want these people to be beaten at all costs; the complete destruction of unionism would be as heavy a price as it is possible to conceive, but I think it is not too high a price' (quoted in ibid.: 93–4).

Given the decidedly pro-capitalist profile of the economics profession throughout modern history, it is hardly surprising that when a 'popular economics' made its appearance at the beginning of the nineteenth century, establishment economists were quick to appreciate the potential threat it posed. One of the more influential and original exponents of this new economics was a partisan of working-class self-organization, a fierce critic of capitalism, and subsequently a socialist. His name was Thomas Hodgskin, and the titles of his two main works bear eloquent testimony to his anti-establishment heresy: *Popular Political Economy* (1827) and *Labour Defended Against the Claims of Capital; or, The Unproductiveness of Capital Proved, With Reference to the Present Combinations Against Journeymen, By a Labourer* (1825). Importantly, Hodgskin was also a Ricardian – more specifically, an exponent of Ricardo's labour theory of value, which he had fashioned into a weapon for the critique of capitalism. After Hodgskin, the labour theory of value was never again to be favourably entertained by respectable economists. The tradition of 'classical political economy' began to falter, challenged on the one side by Ricardian socialism and later Marxism, and on the other by what Marx termed 'vulgar economy,' an approach that sought to dispense with a theory of value entirely.

To the extent that classical political economy retained a theory of value, it was Mill's 'cost of production' theory. But while Mill's theory restored a semblance of rigour and coherence to the classical approach, it was unable to provide a clear picture of the relations of determination between profit, rent, and wages – precisely the problem that had most exercised Ricardo. Still, unlike vulgar economy, Mill's Ricardian political economy minus a labour theory of value commanded a real authority by virtue of its continuing – and ideologically appealing – focus on the problem of distribution (Clarke 1982: 108).

Meanwhile, the project of refining and further developing the labour-value formulation was being passed on from the Ricardian socialists to Marx. Unlike Ricardo, who was interested in labour quantities as a *numéraire* – as a means of measuring heterogeneous use-values in terms of a common yard-stick, and unlike Hodgskin, who regarded Ricardo's theory as a ready-made basis for identifying labour as the source of society's wealth, Marx was concerned with the issue of how economic value and its various forms express the contradictory *social relations* of capitalism as a historically determinate socio-economic order. Fundamental to Marx's reformulation of the labour-value problematic was the distinction he drew between value and exchange-value (and therefore price). Whereas the concept of exchange-value is concerned with a price system whose function is 'to put on the market the quantity of commodities that is required to fulfil the social need, i.e. the quantity for which the society is able to pay the market value' (Marx 1981b: 289), Marx's purpose in analysing the more abstract concept of value was to expose the *hidden nexus* that exists between individuals operating in a society in which private labours are not immediately recognizable as social. The invisibility of this nexus and the implications of this invisibility are at the heart of Marx's analysis of the value-form and his critique of commodity fetishism; indeed, they constitute the pillars of a labour-value theory that is fundamentally different, in content and in purpose, from those espoused by the classical political economists.

By identifying the inherent contradictions of the value relation in its fully developed capitalist form, Marx claimed to have discovered the basic economic laws of motion of the capitalist mode of production. We need to be clear on this point: Marx did not claim to have 'proved' that labour is the sole source of new value. In his view, once the essence of value is appropriately defined, the basis of value in labour is an incontestable fact. What he claimed to have accomplished was the analysis of the *implications* of this fact for the 'real history' of the capitalist mode of production. In a famous letter to Kugelmann, Marx mocked the 'vulgar' criticisms of his labour-value formulation:

Even if there were no chapter on 'value' in my book [*Capital*], the analysis of the real relations which I give would contain the proof and demonstration of the real value relations. All that palaver about the necessity of proving the concept of value comes from complete ignorance both of the subject dealt with and of scientific method. Every child knows that a nation which ceased to work, I will not say for a year, but even for a few weeks, would perish. Every child knows, too, that the masses of products corresponding to the different needs require different and quantitatively determined masses of the total labour of society. That this *necessity* of the *distribution* of social labour in definite proportions cannot possibly be done away with by a particular *form* of social production but can only change the mode of its *appearance*, is self-evident. No natural laws can be done away with. What can change in historically different circumstances is only the *form* in which these laws assert themselves ... The vulgar economist has not the faintest idea that the actual everyday exchange relations *can not* be directly identical with the magnitude of value. The essence of bourgeois society consists precisely in this, that *a priori* there is no conscious social regulation of production. The rational and naturally necessary asserts itself only as a blindly working average. And then the vulgar economist thinks that he has made a great discovery when, as against the revelation of the interconnection, he proudly claims that in appearance things look different. (Marx and Engels 1965: 209–10)

It is the theoretical potency of arguments such as this – pointing unmistakably to Marx's preoccupation with a problematic different from that entertained by all versions of bourgeois political economy – that has forced the more sophisticated of Marx's critics to argue, as Schumpeter did, that 'it is incorrect to call the labour theory of value ''wrong,'' ' even while, in the next breath, announcing that 'it is dead and buried' (1962: 24–5). Schumpeter's seemingly contradictory assessment is actually highly revealing of the ideological complexion of his and many others' dismissals of Marx's theory of labour-value. The point does not seem to be whether the theory is right or wrong. The point is rather that it constitutes a bad 'tool of analysis' for 'economics as a positive science.'

The 'marginalist revolution' sought to provide the analytical tools necessary to transform economics into just such a 'positive science' and to transcend the impasse created by the breakdown of the classical system. To be sure, neoclassical marginalism owed more both in theory and in method to the vulgar tradition than to the classical one, despite its success in acquiring that scientific aura that always eluded vulgar economy. But it is important to emphasize that the 'rigour' of the marginalist theory of value was dependent on a dual theoretical movement: the adoption of vulgar economy's theoretical focus on micro-economic phenomena (in particular, *individual* producers, *individual* consumers, and *individual* commodity prices), and the elaboration of a 'positive' theoretical account of price formation (going beyond vulgar economy's simple disavowal of the labour theory of value). This dual movement defined the contours of the marginalist revolution in relation to classical and vulgar political economy as well as Marxism. As Ronald Meek observes: 'The new starting-point became, not the socio-economic relations between men as producers, but the psychological relation between men and finished goods' (1973: 235).

Marginalism *displaced* the analysis of the social origins of economic value with an entirely different agenda of analysis: an inquiry into the *subjective* basis of the market determination of commodity prices. Indeed, in asserting that '*rareté* is the cause of value in exchange' and that 'the theory of exchange based upon the proportionality of prices to intensities of the last wants satisfied ... constitute the very foundation of the whole edifice of economics,' Leon Walras (1954: 145) succinctly expressed the key insights of what was essentially a 'demand-side' theory of price formation. Marginal-utility theory undoubtedly generated a number of techniques that are useful to describing and predicting the phenomena of a market economy. Of equal importance, however, was its *ideological* function: the elimination of the analytical agenda of classical political economy, which had been inherited, refined, and to some significant degree transformed by Marx.

Joan Robinson, a determined critic of Marx's theory of labour-value but no apologist for the neoclassical system, argued that the 'marginalist revolution' in economic theory was hardly the triumph of science over 'metaphysics' that its adherents pretended, but was principally an ideological reaction to the 'disagreeable smell' of the labour theory (1968: 48). Not only, asserted Robinson, was 'utility' a 'metaphysical concept of impregnable circularity,' it also served as a justification for 'laisser faire': 'Everyone must be free to spend his income as he likes, and he will gain the greatest benefit when he equalizes the *marginal utility* of a shilling spent on each good. The pursuit of profit, under conditions of perfect competition, leads producers to equate marginal costs to prices, and the maximum possible satisfaction is drawn from available resources' (ibid.: 53)

Interestingly, however, Robinson's assessment of marginalism as an 'ideology to end ideologies' is much less balanced than that of Marxists. As a champion of Keynesian macro-economics and a leading figure of the Cambridge School, which has sought to revive interest in the concerns of classical political economy, Robinson had a keen insight into the very real deficiencies of marginalist micro-economics. Moreover, as a critic of all notions of economic value, she was apt to dismiss a utility-based theory of value no less forcefully than a labour-based one. Perhaps owing to this frame of reference, Robinson missed one of the most salient features of marginalism – that it not only served to ideologically sanction laisser-faire but also to determine the *limits* of the 'free market' and the scope for *economic reform* at a time of flagging confidence in the ability of the market economy to reproduce spontaneously the conditions of social harmony. As Clarke points out, neoclassical marginalism arose in response to a felt need to ground *evaluative* judgments concerning the 'proper' prices of commodities upon a scientific theory of price, so that price levels could achieve an optimal allocation of resources, especially scarce resources. 'The solutions that were reached would ... serve as the basis of policy prescriptions about the proper role of state intervention in the formation of prices in order to achieve such an allocation' (1982: 149).

The reluctance of neoclassical economists to engage the Marxist theory of value is, in view of such preoccupations, entirely understandable. They are the continuators of a theoretical and ideological tradition that has always been primarily concerned with finding practical arguments on behalf of policies perceived as *beneficial* to the growth and extension of the capitalist economy. The theoretical agenda of Marxist political economy has always been quite different: to disclose the barriers and limits to capitalist production; to demonstrate the inevitability of economic crises and disequilibria under capitalism; and to point the way forward to a socialist society in which the growth of human productive capacities and the full flowering of the human personality will no longer be impeded by the structural constraints of capitalism.

The fact that the 'destiny' of the labour theory of value was to pose questions and come up with answers that are injurious to the project of perpetuating the capitalist order is undoubtedly the fundamental reason that it fell out of favour with the theoretical defenders of that order and that it was inherited, and subsequently transformed, by capitalism's socialist critics. By itself this statement establishes very little about the scientific merit of the theory. However it should alert us to the need to understand science *in relation to* specific programmatic orientations and social interests – and not as an 'absolute' standard of truth unconnected to the practical goals of human action.

The precise dividing line between 'science' and 'ideology' is often well concealed, and it may be that most theoretical production will contain ideological elements in combination with scientific ones. Given this, it may be tempting to conclude that both marginalism and the Marxian labour-value formulation will contain some measure of truth as well as certain blind spots. But if science is identifiable with that body of knowledge and that methodological strategy that permits the generation of the greatest number of reliable answers to the largest number of pertinent questions about reality, there would seem to be excellent grounds for adjudging Marx's theory as scientifically superior to marginalism. For there is nothing in Marx's theory of value that prevents us from generating a theory of *market price* informed by marginalist insights. Indeed, Marx's own discussion of 'market value' in the third volume of *Capital* leaves the door wide open to a 'demand-side,' and even marginalist, account of individual price formation. Marx never dismissed the questions posed by neoclassical economists as 'irrelevant' or 'non-scientific'; he merely regarded them as *less significant* than the ones that he broached for the specific purpose of disclosing and explaining capitalism's historical laws of motion.

A similar intellectual generosity is conspicuously absent from the stance of the neoclassical economists. Paul Samuelson, a well-regarded examplar of the breed, attributes Marx's 'stubborn' adherence to the labour theory of value to the fact that 'it provided him with a persuasive terminology for declaiming against "exploitation of labour," ' even though it 'constituted bad scientific economics' (1968: 32). But how Samuelson can expect his own scientific commitments to be taken seriously when he egregiously *misrepresents* Marx as having said that 'the price ratios of goods can be predicted from labour costs alone' (ibid.: 819) can only remain a mystery to those with any familiarity with Marx's value theory. Samuelson not only fails to acknowledge the legitimacy of the questions that Marx sought to answer on the basis of his theory of value; following Boehm-Bawerk and others, he assumes that Marx was concerned with the same theoretical issue that he is (that is, the 'prediction' of price ratios). Surely the *minimum* criterion for distinguishing between what is ideological and what is scientific in a particular discourse is *a concern for the facts*, including the facts about what one's own putative 'ideological' opponent has actually said. Yet, on this elementary criterion, Samuelson, not Marx, is exposed as the 'bad scientist.'

Charles McKelvey, in an original attempt to reconstruct Marx's concept of science in light of the cognitional theory of Bernard Lonergan, has pointed out that what pre-eminently distinguished Marx as a scientist was his refusal to subordinate his 'desire to know' to 'the desire for prestige, power, material possessions, and material comfort' (1991: 155). While Marx acknowledged the scientific achievements of Smith and Ricardo, he also knew that their analyses were necessarily flawed by their historical and social standpoints. Only by adopting the standpoint of the working class and accepting as given the latter's objective conditions was Marx able to theoretically, methodologically, and programmatically surpass the bourgeois 'horizon' of classical political economy. More precisely, by encountering the working-class movement, taking seriously its conditions and questions, and transforming its insights in light of the prevailing knowledge of bourgeois culture (in philosophy, science, and political economy), Marx was able to formulate a theoretical knowledge that was *less partial* (if not less partisan) and therefore *more objective* in its grasp of concrete realities than anything produced by professional economists who limit themselves to the narrow horizon of bourgeois class interest. In this, it may be said, he fulfilled the most demanding – and personally courageous – requirement of an authentically scientific analysis of the capitalist socio-economic order.

4 Marx's *Capital* and Its Critique

Elements of Marx's Theory of Value

If it is possible to reduce the several thousand pages of the many books and manuscripts comprising Marx's 'critique of political economy' to a single theme, it is surely this: for Marx, the capitalist mode of production (and, inter alia, its 'law of motion') is not 'eternal' but subject to specifiable historical limits that it is a task of science to disclose. On one influential and eminently plausible interpretation of Marx, these limits are precisely those of the *capitalist law of value*, as a historically specific expression of a more general 'law of human labour-time' (Marx 1973: 173; Colletti 1972: 91–2), to bring about a systematic increase in the productive capacities of humankind and therewith progress in the development of human culture. In other words, Marx's project in his critique of political economy is to specify, *on the basis of his theory of value*, how and why capitalist relations of production (principles of social organization) must become fetters on the development of the forces of production (human productive and creative capacities).

Marx's 'Concept' of Value

Marx provides what is perhaps the clearest statement of the *distinctive procedure* he followed in elaborating his theory of value in *Notes on Adolph Wagner*, a short polemical work written late in his career:

Herr Wagner forgets that neither 'value' nor 'exchange value' are my subjects, but *the commodity* ... In the first place I do not start out from 'concepts', hence I do not start out from the 'concept of value', and do not have 'to divide' these in any way. What I start out from [in *Capital*] is the simplest social form in which the labour-product is presented in contemporary society, and this is the 'commodity'. I analyze it, and right from the beginning, in the *form in which it appears*. Here I find that it is, on the one hand, in its natural form, a *useful thing*, alias a use-value; on the other hand, it is a *bearer of exchange-value*, and from this viewpoint, it is itself 'exchange-value'. Further analysis of the latter shows me that exchange-value is only a *'form* of appearance', the autonomous mode of presentation of the *value* contained in the commodity, and then I move on to the analysis of the latter ... Hence I do not divide *value* into use-value and exchange value as antitheses into which the abstraction 'value' splits, rather [I divide] the *concrete social form* of the labour-product; '*commodity*' is, on the one hand, use-value, and on the other hand, 'value', not exchange-value, since the mere form of appearance is not its proper *content*. (1989: 41–2)

This brief passage possesses the greatest methodological significance for an appreciation of Marx's theory of value. On the one hand, Marx emphasizes his concern with the question of 'forms' and their analysis – as well as with the relationship between forms and their 'content.' On the other hand, he insists that the starting-point of his theory is not conceptual (an ideal abstraction), but something *real*, something that evidently can be regarded as having both a 'natural form' and a 'social form' – the *individual commodity*, considered as a 'real abstraction.'

If the concepts of use-value and exchange-value are determined by the abstract qualities of a real object, however, it cannot be said that they are themselves entirely *determinant* of what must *follow* in the analysis of the commodity. Classical political economy, no less than Marx, recognized that a commodity is characterized by both 'value in use' and 'value in exchange'; but this recognition did not lead the classical economists to the same conclusions regarding the commodity-capitalist economy that Marx drew. Indeed, even the Marx of *The Contribution to the Critique of Political Economy* of 1859 had yet to break with that tradition's conceptual conflation of 'value' and 'exchange-value.' What, then, led him to do so?

Consider the following passage from Marx's 1868 letter to Kugelmann: 'the form in which [the] proportional distribution of labour asserts itself [as a "natural law" stemming from "the *necessity* of the *distribution* of social labour in definite proportions"], in a state of society where the interconnection of social labour is manifested in the *private exchange* of the individual products of labour, is precisely the *exchange*-value of these products' (1968: 209). The concept of exchange-value in this passage is unmistakably that of a specific social *form* of a general human imperative to distribute aggregate social labour in definite proportions – a form peculiar to a society where the medium of 'interconnection' amongst different units of social labour is the *indirect* one of private exchange.

However, exchange-value is also a concept derived from the analysis of the 'individual commodity,' which, according to the opening sentence of *Capital I*, is itself the 'elementary form' of 'the wealth of societies in which the capitalist mode of production prevails' (1977: 125). Thus, while the individual commodity has characteristics that are readily observable, it is also the elementary form of something greater than itself: the 'immense collection of commodities' that is the 'appearance' of wealth in a capitalist society.

Taking stock, the concept of exchange-value arises from the analysis of the *individual commodity*, as a form-characteristic of what turns out to be both a concrete object with a real (natural and social) content and an 'elementary form' of something larger than itself. The form-content distinction in this context is unmistakably aligned with – and a special case of – the distinction between the general (or universal) and the particular. As a particular incarnation of a general class of objects called commodities, the individual commodity is both a real concrete object and a manifestation of the abstract characteristics of *all* commodities.

Once the focus of analysis moves from the individual commodity to the mutual interconnections existing within the world of commodities, it becomes necessary to deploy a different 'concept' from that of exchange-value – a more 'general' or 'universal' concept that captures the characteristics of commodities no longer perceived as discrete things-in-themselves, but as a collection of products of labour, whose existence is necessarily a *collective* one.

Marx derives the concept of *value* from exchange-value by noting that a 'common element' must stand behind the myriad representations that an individual commodity can have as an exchange-value. For example, the exchange-value of a quarter of wheat can be represented by x boot-polish, y silk, z gold, or varying quantities of other physically incommensurable commodities. When a commodity is exchanged with another type of commodity, its exchange-value finds expression in varying quantities of different use-values. As a consequence, exchange-value necessarily appears as 'accidental and purely relative,' as 'the quantitative relation, the proportion, in which use-values of one kind exchange for use-values of another kind' (1977: 126).

Having made this point, Marx then implies that it furnishes something like a logical proof for the existence of a common factor capable of rendering physically heterogeneous commodities commensurable in exchange. For Marx, 'abstract utility' cannot play this commensurating role, since it is precisely the different use-values of commodities that *qualitatively* distinguish them from one another and impose the need for a means of commensuration that abstracts from utility: 'As use-values, commodities differ above all in quality, while as exchange-values they can only differ in quantity, and therefore do not contain an atom of use-value' (ibid.: 128).

Marx's solution to the problem of commensuration proceeds as follows: 'Let us now take two commodities, for example corn and iron. Whatever their exchange relation may be, it can always be represented by an equation in which a given quantity of corn is equated to some quantity of iron, for instance 1 quarter of corn = x cwt of iron. Both are therefore equal to a third thing, which in itself is neither the one nor the other. Each of them, so far as it is exchange-value, must therefore be reducible to this third thing' (127).

As is well known, Marx identifies this 'third thing' as the circumstance that these commodities are products of labour. But this is logically insufficient. The reduction of all commodities to a 'common element' must entail abstraction from the useful characteristics of the product of labour, and these characteristics are shaped by the 'useful character of the kinds of labour embodied in them' (128). For true abstraction from utility to occur, the labour embodied in commodities that serves to render them commensurable in exchange must be conceived as 'human labour-power expended without regard to the form of its expenditure,' as 'congealed quantities of homogeneous human labour' characterized by 'phantom-like objectivity' (ibid.). Marx refers to this 'human labour in the abstract' as a 'social substance' and to the products of labour abstracted from their utilities as 'crystals of this social substance,' as 'commodity values.' The upshot is that 'the common factor in the exchange relation, or in the exchange-value of the commodity, is therefore its value' (ibid.).

Much has been said about the supposed weakness of this argument as a 'logical proof' of the labour theory of value. But what should be noted at this point is that the burden of Marx's argument is not to 'prove' that the substance of either value or exchange-value is labour (abstract or otherwise), but rather that the exchange-value of a commodity stands in a specific relation to its value: as form to content.

Form and Content

As a material expression and individual manifestation of a social division and distribution of labour carried out 'unconsciously,' behind the backs of private commodity producers, the commodity is unavoidably implicated in 'value relations' and is, in this sense, a 'crystal' of value, understood as a 'social substance.' But the 'form of appearance' of the commodity's value (that is to say, of its relationship to the larger social process of forcibly articulating a division and distribution of labour between various branches of production) is necessarily its forms of exchangeability with other products, that is, its exchange-value(s). As a 'value' the commodity is conceived in abstraction from its use-value, as the embodiment of a definite fraction of the aggregate social labour employed in the production of all commodities; and it is this that makes 'value' the *common factor* underlying the *different* exchange-values that the individual commodity can manifest.

Depending upon the angle from which one approaches the problem, then, value can be conceived as the 'content' or 'substance' of exchange-value, or as the 'form' assumed by the division of labour under determinate social relations of production. Value may be defined as 'a representation in objects, an objective expression, of a relation between men, a social relation, the relationship of men to their reciprocal productive activity' (Marx 1978, 3: 147) or as 'a definite social mode of existence of human activity (labour)' (Marx 1978, 1: 46), which must assume the phenomenal form of exchange-value. As Rubin puts it: 'value is "reified," "materialized" *labor* and simultaneously it is an expression of production *relations among people*' (1973: 153). Rubin explains this apparent contradiction as follows: 'The two definitions of value contradict each other if one deals with physiological labor; but they perfectly supplement each other if one deals with *social* labor. Abstract labor [the *substance* of value] and value have a social and not a material-technical or physiological nature' (ibid.).

The Significance of Marx's Method

What Rubin points to here is the necessity for an adequate specification of the *method* underlying Marx's 'forms analysis.' As he rightly insists, '[the] process of development of forms in their various phases' can only be properly explored through a *genetic-dialectical* method, which considers the developmental and contradictory relations among things. Crucially, such an approach is associated with an 'internal' conception of *the form/content relation*:

One cannot forget that on the question of the relation between content and form, Marx took the standpoint of Hegel and not of Kant. Kant treated form as something external in relation to the content, as something which adheres to the content from the outside. From the standpoint of Hegel's philosophy, the content is not in itself something to which form adheres from the outside. Rather, through its development, the content itself gives birth to the form which is already latent in the content. Form necessarily grows from the content itself. (1973: 117)

The point of all this is that the 'dividing line' between form and content is not at all a clear-cut issue. To understand how value can be *both* the 'social content' of exchange-value and the 'objective (or material) expression' of the social relations existing between the productive activities of people requires an analysis of *the form and the substance of value*; and this is precisely the way in which Marx proceeds. We shall return to these questions in due course, but first we need to consider the specific character of capitalist social relations and their role in defining the content of the law of value.

Capitalism and the Law of Value

The law of value is a *regulatory principle* of an economy in which the products of labour are produced for the purpose of private exchange. The social production relation that is fundamental to such 'commodity production' is the *social equality of commodities and commodity producers* as well as *the social equality and homogeneity of commodity-producing labour*. The 'egalitarianism' of this principle no more presupposes the abolition of vertical social differentiation or 'ranking' than it obviates the technically heterogeneous and differentially skilled character of concrete 'utility-shaping' labours. What it does point to, however, is the idea of the 'exchange of equivalents' – that is, to the *normative* aspiration of maintaining a 'level playing field' in the sphere of exchange.

Under conditions of generalized (that is, capitalist) commodity production, however, two other social production relations profoundly affect the concrete operations of the law of value. These are (a) the *exploitative relation* existing between capital and wage-labour, and (b) the *competitive relation* that exists amongst individual private capitals (the latter relation encompassing a tendency toward 'monopolization' or 'oligopolization' as a necessary outcome of competition).

If, following Rubin (1973), it is correct to view 'value under capitalism' as expressing the *ensemble* of these social production relations, then it should be apparent that the capitalist law of value must lead the capitalist mode of production to 'move in contradiction.' The 'contradictions' of Marx's theory are *real contradictions*, not 'logical' ones: they are conceptual reflections of the contradictory relations comprising the object under investigation, namely a mode of production based on three distinct principles of social organization.

What then does Marx's law of value refer to? Unfortunately, Marx's own explicit definition of this law is not particularly enlightening: 'Whatever the manner in which the prices of various commodities are first mutually fixed or regulated, their movements are always governed by the law of value. If the labour-time required for their production happens to shrink, prices fall; if it increases, prices rise, provided other conditions remain the same' (1978: 177). So formulated, it is hard to imagine anyone disagreeing with such a 'law of labour-value.' But the substantive content of Marx's law is actually both more contentious and far more interesting than this quotation suggests. A weak version of it is expressed in Morishima's 'Fundamental Marxian Theorem,' which states that positive surplus value (or a positive rate of surplus value) is a necessary and sufficient condition for the existence of positive profits and a positive rate of profit (Morishima 1973: 6). Foley, among others, has furnished a stronger definition, according to which '*the source* of the value added of the mass of commodities produced is the labor expended in producing them' (1986: 14; emphasis added). Couple this with Hilferding's insistence that value exists as an 'objective, quantitatively determined magnitude' (1975: 159) and we arrive at the propositions that *living labour is the sole source of all new value* and that *value exists as a definite quantitative magnitude* at the level of the capitalist division of labour (or economy) as a whole.

These 'fundamental postulates' of Marx's theory of value, which are *shared* by the apparently contradictory analyses of volumes 1 and 3 of *Capital*, are the basis of Marx's delineation of the 'economic law of motion' of the capitalist mode of production. Marx's theory of value as an analysis of the developmental tendencies of capitalism stands or falls with these postulates; so it is in respect to them that the controversy surrounding this theory needs to be clarified and assessed.

Marx's Value-Magnitude Analysis in Capital I

In chapter 1 of *Capital I*, Marx identifies the 'substance' of value as 'abstract labour,' defined as labour abstracted from its concrete utility-shaping characteristics and conceived as an aspect of the homogeneous mass of social labour entering into the production of commodities. The *measure* of this value-creating substance is socially necessary labour-time, defined as 'the labour-time required to produce any use-value under the conditions of production normal for a given society and with the average degree of skill and intensity of labour prevalent in that society' (1977: 129). It follows from this that 'the value of a commodity is related to the value of any other commodity as the labour-time necessary for the production of the one is related to the labour-time necessary for the production of the other' (130). Note that Marx speaks here of the *value* of commodities, not their exchange-values. There is nothing in this statement, or in any of Marx's other statements in *Capital*, to suggest that the quantitative ratios (or proportions) in which particular commodities actually exchange is determined solely by the way in which they relate to one another as embodiments of abstract socially necessary labour time.

The concept of socially necessary labour stands in contrast to the concrete and individual labours expended under varying conditions of technical efficiency in different productive enterprises. Just as a given commodity is produced through an expenditure of concrete labour that is also an allocation of abstract social labour, so the individual labour-time expended in the production of that commodity stands in a particular relation to the socially necessary labour-time required for its production. In measuring the *value* represented by a particular commodity, then, it is necessary to approach this measurement at the social – or, at least, the industry-wide – level, not at the individual level. The labour-time actually expended on the production of a commodity is determinant of its value only insofar as that labour-time enters into the determination of the *average* conditions of production of all such commodities. In Marx's words: 'The value of a commodity ... varies directly as the quantity, and inversely as the productivity, of the labour which finds its realization within the commodity' (ibid.: 131).

Marx's Analysis of the Value-Form

Having derived the concept of value from that of exchange-value and having defined both the substance and magnitude of value in terms of abstract labour and socially necessary labour-time, Marx proceeds to a demonstration of how value gives rise to its various forms of appearance. It should first be emphasized that the term 'value-form' may be understood in two distinct senses. The first pertains to value as a specific *historical form* of the social division of labour – a social form that predominates in capitalist but not precapitalist societies. The second sense pertains to value conceived as an objectification or materialization of abstract social labour, that is, as the *content* of exchange-value (the value-form within commodity-producing societies). Our concern here is with the 'value-form' in this second sense, that is, with how value is represented through *its* forms of appearance.

Since value has a purely social existence, its form can only appear in the mutual relations existing between commodities. Prior to his logico-historical derivation of it, this form is identified by Marx as the 'money-form,' for this is universally known as the 'common value-form' of commodities 'which contrasts in the most striking manner with the motley natural forms of their use-values' (1977: 139). The *necessity* of the money-form, Marx seeks to show, is implied by even the simplest expression of the value 'contained in the value relation of commodities.' But what is the *origin* of the money-form, and how does it develop as 'the expression of value'?

Marx begins by considering 'the simple, isolated, or accidental form of value,' in which *x* units of commodity A are equal to or worth *y* units of commodity B. In this expression, commodity A plays an 'active role' while commodity B plays a 'passive' one. 'The value of the first commodity is represented as relative value, in other words the commodity is in the relative form of value. The second commodity fulfils the function of equivalent, in other words it is in the equivalent form' (ibid.). What this means is that the value of commodity A finds expression in commodity B, while commodity B is the standard by which the value of commodity A is expressed. 'Whether a commodity is in the relative form or in its opposite, the equivalent form, entirely depends on its actual position in the expression of value. That is, it depends on whether it is the commodity whose value is being expressed, or the commodity in which value is being expressed' (140).

Further reflection on the relative form yields the insight that while commodity B is a material representation of A's value, they are equated not by virtue of their natural forms as products of concrete labour, but rather because commodity A's value must possess an existence *distinct from* its status as a product of concrete labour. Accordingly, the physical form of commodity B becomes the value form of commodity A, or 'the physical body of commodity B becomes a mirror for the value of commodity A' (144). But this is possible only because commodity A has entered into a 'relation with commodity B as an object of value, as a materialization of human labour' (ibid.). The expression of equivalence between physically distinct commodities thereby discloses the specific character of abstract labour as value-creating labour. It also reveals that it is the process of exchange that reduces all individual, utility-shaping labours as these are embedded in commodities to their common aspect as instances of social labour in general.

Moving on, Marx considers the three peculiarities of the equivalent form of value as these have emerged from the preceding analysis. First, 'use-value becomes the form of appearance of its opposite, value' (148). The physical body of commodity B expresses the value of commodity A and is the objectification of the latter's abstract labour content. It follows from this that the *concrete labour* that went into the production of commodity B's physical body stands in a relation of equivalence to the abstract labour embodied in commodity A: 'The equivalent form therefore possesses a second peculiarity: in it, concrete labour becomes the form of manifestation of its opposite, abstract human labour' (150). This leads directly to a third peculiarity, namely that the equivalent form demonstrates that 'private labour takes the form of its opposite, namely labour in its directly social form' (151). This follows from the fact that while the labour that produced commodity B is the labour of private commodity producers, it 'possesses the characteristic of being identical with other kinds of labour' (150). Indeed, 'it is precisely for this reason that it presents itself to us in the shape of a product which is directly exchangeable with other commodities' (ibid.).

The 'reversals' suggested in this analysis of the value-form are of central importance to Marx's whole value theory. Within value relations, Marx asserts, *use-value appears as value, concrete labour as abstract labour, and private labour as social labour.* The commodity is a unity of use-value and value, but this dual character of the commodity is only expressed when its value has a form of appearance distinct from its natural (use-value) form. This form of appearance is its exchange-value; and it is *through exchange* that the internal opposition of use-value and value is given external expression. One might say that exchange-value furnishes a ground of unity between value and use-value, just as exchange relations provide the framework for a resolution of the contradictions arising from the value/use-value opposition.

The next stage of Marx's analysis is his development of the 'total or expanded form of value' out of the simple form. Marx observes that commodity A exchanges not only with commodity B, that is, with one other commodity, but with a whole *series* of other commodities whose individual identities are irrelevant to their role as equivalents. The expanded relative form of value, unlike the simple form, reveals that the relations existing between commodities are not contingent or accidental. Since the individual commodity is now perceived as a 'citizen' of the whole world of commodities, its value appears unaltered in magnitude 'whether expressed in coats, coffee, or iron, or in innumerable different commodities belonging to as many different owners' (1977: 156).

Despite its advantages over the simple form, the expanded relative form of value evinces a serious defect: 'the relative form of value of each commodity is an endless series of expressions of value which are all different from the relative form of value of every other commodity' (ibid.). This poses the need for a 'single, unified form of appearance' of the abstract human labour constituting the commodity's value.

The problem is resolved, however, when Marx inverts the total or expanded form of value and derives the 'general form of value.' Since the value of commodity A is expressed in an innumerable series of other commodities, it follows that these latter commodities express their value through commodity A. Thus, a single commodity, here commodity A, may be set aside to represent the value of all other commodities. The generic name for such a commodity is 'the universal equivalent,' and its 'natural form is the form assumed in common by the values of all commodities.' Since this commodity is directly exchangeable with all other commodities, the 'physical form [it assumes] counts as the visible incarnation, the social chrysalis state, of all human labour' (159).

It is theoretically conceivable for any commodity to assume the universal equivalent form of value; however, 'a commodity is only to be found in the universal equivalent form ... if, and in so far as, it is excluded from the ranks of all other commodities, as being their equivalent' (162). Once a particular commodity is so excluded it becomes the *money commodity* (in 'the money form of value'), and this completes the separation of the commodity's expression of value from the commodity itself.

Marx notes that 'the only difficulty in the concept of the money form is that of grasping the universal equivalent form, and hence the general form of value as such' (163). Any derivation of the money form of value that does not begin with the simple form and follow its transformation into the general form of value must proceed ahistorically, through an idealist dialectic of concepts. Thus, Marx's 'manner of presentation' of the money form in *Capital* differs from that of the *Grundrisse* in that the former work provides a historical as well as a logical derivation of the categories of analysis. Nevertheless, the following brief passage from the *Grundrisse* serves to clarify the main conclusions of Marx's value-form analysis:

[Each commodity's] value must ... have an existence which is qualitatively distinguishable from it, and in actual exchange this separability must become a real separation, because the natural distinctness of commodities must come into contradiction with their economic equivalence, and because both can exist together only if the commodity achieves a double existence, not only a natural but also a purely economic existence, in which the latter is a mere symbol, a cipher for a relation of production, a mere symbol of its own value. (1973: 141)

The historical development of commodity production and exchange constitutes also the emergence of the money form of value. With the advent of capitalist 'generalized commodity production,' money becomes the singular form of expression of value. Marx makes this point unequivocally clear in *Capital*: 'Money as the measure of value is the *necessary* form of appearance of the measure of value which is immanent in commodities, namely labour-time' (1977: 188).

Value and Commodity Fetishism

Marx follows up his analysis of the value-form in *Capital* with his famous discussion of 'The Fetishism of the Commodity and Its Secret.' This section contains at least part of the explanation for Marx's insistence upon founding his analysis of the capitalist mode of production on a properly specified 'labour theory of value.'

It is by no means 'obvious' that commodities contain value in the specific sense that Marx attaches to this concept. Indeed, the forms of appearance of value *lead us away* from the recognition that commodities both reflect and give expression to definite social production relations existing between commodity producers. The value-form, in this sense, contributes to a *false* understanding of the realities of commodity-producing societies and of the social relations existing within them.

The 'mysterious' or 'enigmatic' character of the commodity-form of the product of labour stems fundamentally from the fact that 'the commodity reflects the social characteristics of men's own labour as objective characteristics of the products of labour themselves, as the socio-natural properties of these things' (1977: 164–5). The consequence is that the commodity-form 'reflects the social relation of the producers to the sum total of labour as a social relation between objects, a relation which exists apart from and outside the producers' (165). But in what sense are these reflections amenable to an analysis informed by the idea of 'fetishism'?

Marx notes that fetishism refers to a situation in which 'the products of the human brain appear as autonomous figures endowed with a life of their own, which enter into relations both with each other and with the human race' (ibid.). In the 'misty realm of religion,' such figures are purely illusory products of the human imagination, their relations both with each other and with human beings wholly fantastic projections. Yet in analogizing the 'world of commodities' to this mystical religious realm, Marx asserts that the commodity-form 'is nothing but the definite social relation between men themselves which assumes here, for them, the fantastic form of a relation between things' (ibid.). This can easily be interpreted to mean that it is a 'fantasy' to believe that social relations between people are reducible to a relation between things. But commodity fetishism is not linked to any such 'belief'; to the contrary, it is linked to the *denial* that a relation between things can express social relations between people, and that the products of labour 'relate' to one another as they do because they are 'bearers' of definite social production relations.

When Marx refers to the 'socio-natural properties' of commodities, he means to suggest that the commodity-form of the product of labour, as a *thing*, renders obscure the distinction between the natural and social aspects of the commodity. Indeed, prior to rigorous scientific investigation, the social and natural characteristics of the commodity are indistinguishable in that they present an amalgamated face in the *natural form* of the commodity as a physical object or effect. Thus, the most salient feature of the fetishism that attaches to commodities is the *denial* of the 'sociality' of commodities, *not* the denial that social relations are reduced to relations between things under conditions of commodity production and exchange. The *social* dimension of commodities, for those bewitched by commodity fetishism, seems to be unrelated to their conditions of production and appears to spring entirely from their mutual relations of exchange. As a result of this (mis)perception, the value of the individual commodity appears to be *externally related* to its status as a product of labour – just as the process of exchange appears as externally associated to the process of production. The upshot of all this is explained in the following crucial passage:

Objects of utility become commodities only because they are the products of the labour of private individuals who work independently of each other. The sum total of the labour of all these private individuals forms the aggregate labour of society. Since the producers do not come into social contact until they exchange the products of their labour, *the specific social characteristics of their private labours appear only within this exchange.* In other words, the labour of the private individual manifests itself as an element of the total labour of society only through the relations which the act of exchange establishes between the products, and, through their mediation, between the producers. To the producers, therefore, the social relations between their private labours appear *as what they are*, i.e. they do not appear as direct social relations between persons in their work, but rather as material [*dinglich*] relations between persons and social relations between things. (1977: 165–6; emphasis added)

Marx's basic proposition in this passage is that value relations refer to the *indirect* and *hidden* relations established between private producers through the act of commodity exchange. Within these relations, social production relations are manifested *in fact* through commodity exchange relations: 'private labours appear ... as material [*dinglich*] relations between persons and social relations between things.' But this appearance is *not illusory*; indeed, private labours appear here 'as what they are.' The mediation between private labours and the aggregate labour of society is provided by the exchange of privately produced commodities; and, consequently, persons *do* relate to one another through the mediation afforded by 'things.'

Still, as *commodity producers*, persons stand in a relation of formal equality to one another; their social production relations are predicated on the actuality of their socially equal status. This point too bears stressing: the 'free' exchanges characterizing commodity relations are the basis for 'the products of labour [acquiring] a socially uniform objectivity as values, which is distinct from their sensuously varied objectivity as articles of utility' (1977: 166). This social uniformity is not a function of the equality of concrete labours, for concrete labours are only exceptionally 'equal'; rather, it is a function of the social equality of producers whose labour is concretely or technically heterogeneous but *socially homogeneous*. As Marx insists: 'Equality in the full sense between different kinds of labour can be arrived at only if we abstract from their real inequality, if we reduce them to the characteristic they have in common, that of being the expenditure of human labour-power, of human labour in the abstract' (ibid.). Such a reduction is inconceivable, however, except where exchanges are conducted on the assumption of the social equality of the private producers.

The above considerations provide a necessary basis for interpreting the following well-known passage: 'Men do not therefore bring the products of their labour into relation with each other as values because they see these objects merely as the material integuments of homogeneous human labour. The reverse is true: by equating their different products to each other in exchange as values, they equate their different kinds of labour as human labour. They do this without being aware of it. Value, therefore, does not have its description branded on its forehead; it rather transforms every product of labour into a social hieroglyphic' (166–7). Note what Marx is asserting here: it is *because* people equate their products as values through the act of exchange that they unconsciously equate their different kinds of labour as well. Exchange, as the *social form* of commodity production, both gives expression to and conceals the regulative role of labour in the determination of commodity values. It gives expression to it in the sense that free exchange is the institutional presupposition of commodity production and valuation; it conceals it by permitting quantitative variance between a commodity's value and its exchange-value. Marx sums up some of these themes as follows:

The production of commodities must be fully developed before the scientific conviction emerges, from experience itself, that all the different kinds of private labour (which are carried on independently of each other, and yet, as spontaneously devel-

oped branches of the social division of labour, are in a situation of all-round dependence on each other) are continually being reduced to the quantitative proportions in
which society requires them ... The determination of the magnitude of value by labour-
time is therefore a secret hidden under the apparent movements in the relative values
of commodities. Its discovery destroys the semblance of the merely accidental determination of the value of the products of labour, but by no means abolishes that
determination's material form. (168)

And further:

The forms which stamp products as commodities and which are therefore the preliminary requirements for the circulation of commodities, already possess the fixed
quality of natural forms of social life before man seeks to give an account, not of
their historical character, for in his eyes they are immutable, but of their *content and
meaning*. Consequently, it was solely the analysis of the prices of commodities which
led to the determination of the magnitude of value, and solely the common expression
of all commodities in money which led to the establishment of their character as
values. It is however precisely this finished form of the world of commodities – the
money form – which conceals the social character of private labour and the social
relations between the individual workers, by making those relations appear as relations between material objects, instead of revealing them plainly. (ibid.)

   This latter passage contains the key to differentiating between the classical
and Marxian labour-value formulations. Whereas classical political economy
was concerned with the magnitude of labour-value as this related to the
formation of money prices, Marx was concerned with the 'content and meaning' of 'the forms which stamp products as commodities.' But this content
and meaning, pertaining to 'the social character of private labour and the
social relations between the individual workers,' is obscured – concealed –
by the 'finished' money form of value. Unlike the classical political economists, therefore, Marx does not proceed from the magnitude of value as
labour-time to the money-price of commodities. Instead, he looks for the
reasons for the successive transformations of the value-form, while establishing value theory as the basis for disclosing the economic laws of motion
of the commodity economy in aggregate. The *relevance* of such an investigation, however, can only be grasped by those who are prepared to see that
commodity production is but one (perishable and transcendable) socio-
historical form of production – in other words, by those prepared to dispel
the mystifying influences of commodity fetishism: 'The whole mystery of
commodities, all the magic and necromancy that surrounds the products of

labour on the basis of commodity production, vanishes therefore as soon as we come to other forms of production' (169).

Marx elaborates his critique of classical political economy on this basis more fully at the conclusion of chapter 1 of the first volume of *Capital*:

Political economy has indeed analyzed value and its magnitude, however incompletely, and has uncovered the content concealed within these forms. But it has never once asked the question why this content has assumed that particular form, that is to say, why labour is expressed in value, and why the measurement of labour by its duration is expressed in the magnitude of the value of the product. These formulas, which bear the unmistakable stamp of belonging to a social formation in which the process of production has mastery over man, instead of the opposite, appear to the political economists' bourgeois consciousness to be as much a self-evident and nature-imposed necessity as productive labour itself. (173–5)

Value, Capital, and Exploitation

In approaching Marx's analysis of capital, it is important to recognize that Marx regards capital as *both* a form of value and an expression of social production relations that are specific to the capitalist mode of production. As a form of value, capital encompasses, as a social production relation, the *equality* of commodity producers and of commodities. As a *metamorphized* form of value, however, capital also encompasses and expresses two other social production relations: an *exploitative* relation between capitalists and workers, and a *competitive* relation between different 'individual' capitalists.

By stating that Marx sees the category of capital as encompassing (at least) three social production relations, we are acknowledging a profound difference between Marx's concept of capital and that found in non-Marxian economics. Against those who defined capital simply as a 'factor of production,' as a stock of producer goods, or as an investable fund of monetary wealth, Marx insisted that capital is pre-eminently a *social relation in process*. Two passages from *Capital* serve to clarify this notion:

Capital is not a thing, it is a definite social relation of production pertaining to a particular historical social formation, which simply takes the form of a thing and gives this thing a specific social character ... [Capital] is the means of production monopolized by a particular section of society, the products and conditions of activity of labour-power, which are rendered autonomous vis-à-vis this living labour-power and are personified in capital through this antithesis. (1981b: 953–4)

[In capitalist circulation] value suddenly presents itself as a self-moving substance which passes through a process of its own, and for which commodities and money are both mere forms ... Value therefore now becomes value in process, money in process, and, as such, capital. (1977: 256)

Marx's definition of capital as 'value in process' is the culmination of his discussion of the 'general formula' for capital, where he considers the transformation of money into capital. Denoting commodities by C and money by M, Marx contrasts two possible series of transactions that can occur within the sphere of circulation: the sale of commodities followed by the purchase of different commodities (C-M-C), and the buying of commodities with the aim of realizing an enlarged magnitude of money through sales (M-C-M'). According to Marx, M-C-M' is 'the general formula for capital, in the form in which it appears directly in the sphere of circulation' (1977: 257). But this formula appears to embody a contradiction: How is it possible to purchase commodities and then resell them at a price permitting an increment on the original money-capital investment? Several possible explanations present themselves – the presence of trade monopolies, a non-universalized market, and so on – but each of these appeals to a suspension of the normal operation of the law of value. The law of value is not inconsistent with the idea of a 'redistribution' of value among commodities, such that individual commodities will be sold at prices diverging from their (abstract) labour-value; but it is most certainly inconsistent with the idea that value can be *created* in the act of exchange. 'Buying cheap and selling dear' – the watchword of merchant capital and mercantilist economics – is predicated either on unequal exchange in an international market, or on the possibility of a real transfer of commodity value from productive to commercial capitals before the sale of these commodities at prices approximating their value. Assuming equal exchange in the aggregate (that is, the conservation of value in exchange), it is impossible to see how – through exchange alone – a net increase in value can be realized in the form of M'. Yet the existence of this 'surplus-value,' which Marx initially defines as the difference between M' and M, is the only possible value-theoretic explanation for the realization of profits, interest, and other readily observable phenomenal forms of augmented value.

Marx explains the origin of this surplus-value in the unique capacity of one particular commodity to create more value than it embodies. This commodity is *labour-power* – the ability to labour. The money-price of labour power is the wage paid to its seller, the worker. But the value of the commodities produced by workers will normally exceed the value of all inputs. Thus, the value of output commodities exceeds the value of input commodities simply because one of the input commodities, labour power, imparts more value to the output commodities through its *activity* than it represents as a mere 'ability.'

The apparent contradiction contained in the formula M-C-M' is resolved by establishing that this circuit encompasses a phase of *production*, without which surplus-value could not be produced and the circuit could not be successfully completed. Within this circuit, commodities are bought not with a view to their resale at a higher price, but with a view to producing *new* commodities embodying a magnitude of value exceeding the original investment.

The centrality of production to the process of creating surplus-value is illustrated in the following diagrammatic representation of the general formula for capital:

$$M - C \, (LP \, \& \, MP) \ldots P \ldots C' - M'$$

where LP denotes labour-power, MP the means of production, P the productive process that transforms input commodities C into output commodities embodying greater value C', and M and M' money capital as before. The key point in this expanded version of the circuit of capital is that, through the purchase of commodities constituting inputs to production, money capital is transformed into productive capital capable of yielding the commodity capital C'. The realization of the value embodied in C' involves the transformation of C' into M' through the successful sale of the output commodities. Thus, the circuit of capital embraces two overlapping phases of activity: the circulation of money and commodity capital, and the process of production, which transforms inputs into new outputs while also imparting to these outputs a quantity of new value derived from living labour.

Let us reconsider the C-M-C circuit, which appears to well describe the economic activity of petty commodity producers like small-scale farmers or fishermen. The law of value may be said to be operating here in a situation of perfect equilibrium: that is, where individual commodity prices and values completely coincide. One commodity (say grain) is taken to market where it is sold at a price reflecting its value (that is, its socially necessary labour input). The money derived from this sale is then taken by the petty commodity producer and used to purchase other commodities (say, clothing or farm machinery), which represent a magnitude of value equivalent to that of the grain. The point is that this circuit is equally applicable to the sale of the commodity labour-power. For the wage-labourer, money earned though the sale of labour-power is not capital but simply the means to purchase those commodities necessary to the reproduction of one's ability to work. The circuit ends in consumption, in 'use,' rather than in the augmentation of value (profit).

Yet the circuit C-M-C, in so far as it applies to labour-power sold for a wage, is also a necessary *presupposition* of the circuit M-C-M'. Unless the commodity labour-power is sold for a money-wage that is used to purchase articles of consumption, it is not possible for money capital to be transformed into the productive capital necessary for its self-expansion. This is why the distinction that Marx makes between labour-power (as a commodity) and labour (as a value-creating activity) is so pivotal to his analysis. This distinction renders intelligible not only the compatibility of C-M-C and M-C-M' but the decisive dependence of the latter upon the former. At the same time, this distinction makes it possible for Marx to reconcile theoretically two seemingly antithetical social relations of production as these exist under capitalism: the equality of commodity producers and commodities, and the exploitation of labour by capital.

The commodity labour-power has an altogether unique status as an input to production in that it is neither the product of a capitalist production process nor a commodity with a 'fixed' or 'constant' influence on the valorization (value-expansion) process of capitalist production. Unlike all other commodity inputs to production, labour-power expresses a social relation of production between owners of the means of production and non-owners. Indeed, this is why Marx's characterization of capital as 'the means of production monopolized by a particular section of society' is so important to his analysis. For it is the *class inequality* inherent in this monopolization of the means of production that makes it possible to understand how relations of exploitation can *interpenetrate* relations of equal exchange. It is only when we abstract from production, and focus solely on the sphere of circulation, that the principle of equality among commodity producers appears to predominate within capitalist society. The formal equality of the market-place cannot and does not obviate the social inequalities and exploitation inherent in a situation where the means of production are owned and controlled by a tiny minority while the direct producers are dispossessed of means of production and compelled on pain of starvation to sell their ability to work to the highest bidder. It is the class inequality between workers and capitalists that compels workers to sell their labour-power at a price reflecting its cost of reproduction rather than at a price reflecting the actual contribution of their labour to the value of the newly produced commodities.

The sale and purchase of labour-power occurs entirely within the sphere of circulation and commodity exchange. The consumption of labour-power, however, occurs within production, where it is put to use by capitalists in the creation of *surplus value*. The 'equality' of the sphere of commodity-exchange is thus succeeded by the 'despotism' of the sphere of production; relations of formal equality are displaced by relations of exploitation. None of this involves a 'logical' contradiction, merely the depiction of a contradictory reality in which the law of value comes to lend a particular and historically specific form to class inequality and to the extraction of a social surplus product from the direct producers.

In its incarnation as capital, value is sometimes referred to as 'self-expanding' or 'self-valorizing.' This is the burden of the idea that capital is value in process: *capital is an exploitative relation of production operating through value relations*. Hence, under capitalism, exchange is the social form not only of the reproduction of the 'material content' of society but also of the exploitative relation between a class of appropriators and a class of direct producers.

Capital analysed from the point of view of its relation to wage-labour is termed the 'social capital' by Marx, and it is precisely through the analysis of this relation that Marx develops the fundamental categories of his 'economics': the constituent categories of value making up the commodity, and the basic quantitative relationships underlying the capitalist economy's 'laws of motion.'

Let us begin by considering the total value of the commodity product. In the process of its production, the commodity receives value from both 'living' and 'dead' sources: from living labour, on the one hand, and from various elements of the means of production, on the other. In furnishing these sources of value, both of which are required for a physical production process that is also a valorization process, capital appears in two forms: as constant capital and as variable capital. Within production, constant capital takes the material form of means of production (machinery, raw materials and fuel, and so on) that can impart to the new commodity product no more value than they represent. In other words, the elements of constant capital can only transfer *previously existing* value to the newly produced commodity. They cannot create *new value*.

Marx attributes the role of creating new value to the variable capital 'invested' in the acquisition of labour-power. Labour-power is the only commodity input to production that releases *living labour*, the sole source of new value. The value newly created by living labour in production is considered by Marx to account for both the value embodied in the wages received by productive workers and the surplus-value created by these workers during the 'unpaid' portion of their working day.

The total value of the commodity product may therefore be represented as

$P = c + v + s$, where c represents the value objectified in those embodiments of 'dead labour' that contribute indirectly to the value-expansion process (that is, through a transfer of value effected by living labour); v represents the value embodied in the wage bill of productive workers (whose labour-power itself assumes the social form of variable capital within production); and s represents the surplus-value created by the surplus-labour of productive workers (surplus-labour being the difference between the length of the working day and the labour time necessary for the production of the value embodied in wages).

By dividing the working day into two periods – one during which the worker creates the value equivalent of the day's wages and another during which surplus-value is created – Marx provides a convenient way of considering the first of his fundamental quantitative relationships or ratios: the rate of surplus-value. Marx represents this relationship as s/v, the ratio of the two flows of new value created by living labour.

The rate of surplus-value exerts its influence within a capitalist economy through its impact on the *rate of profit*, which may be defined as the rate of valorization of the total capital 'advanced' for the purpose of capitalist production, or, more simply and conventionally, as the rate of return on invested capital. The rate of profit may be represented in a number of ways consistent with Marx's meaning, but Marx usually defined it as the ratio of surplus-value to 'total capital' ($s/c + v$) for purposes of simplified theoretical exposition. This ratio occupies a central place in Marx's analysis because it is the decisive regulator of capitalist accumulation and growth.

For the social capital as a whole, if not for individual capitalist enterprises, the rate of profit is 'co-determined' by the rate of surplus-value and the *composition* of the capital applied to production. The composition of capital refers to the proportions in which 'living' and 'dead' labour appear in the total process of production and reproduction, and may be expressed in several different ways. For the moment, however, the composition of capital will be represented as the ratio c/v – the ratio that Marx uses in his discussion of the 'transformation' of commodity values into prices of production. This brings us to the third social production relation encompassed by capital: the competitive relation existing between the many 'individual capitals' that make up the social capital as a whole.

Value, Capitalist Competition, and the General Rate of Profit

In defining capital as an exploitative social relation of production operating through value relations, I have so far stressed the exploitative aspect of capital while slighting the issue of what it means to say that capital operates through value relations. But implicit in the notion of value relations is the existence of *many* private commodity-producers supplying a market-place and seeking a livelihood through the sale of their commodity products. Not surprisingly, then, Marx states that capital 'exists and can only exist as many capitals' and that consequently 'competition is nothing other than the inner *nature of capital*, its essential character, appearing in and realized as the reciprocal interaction of many capitals with one another, the inner tendency as external necessity' (1973: 414).

Individual capitals do not face uniform prospects of an accretion of their value. Owing to a host of factors, they enjoy quite different profit margins and rates of profit. However, capitals that earn less than the average rate of profit cannot be expected to survive indefinitely; hence, there exists a strong tendency for all capitals to seek out the most favourable possible conditions of valorization. This tendency presupposes that capital is *mobile*: that it can move from one sector of the economy to another in search of higher profits. Capital mobility – which is never 'perfect' owing to the perennial difficulties of rapidly transforming productive and commodity capital into the more easily investable money form – is the mechanism for the equalizing tendency of the various rates of profit and for the (tendential) formation of a 'general' rate of profit. And it is the appearance of this general rate of profit that underlies a crucial transformation of the value-form: the transformation of commodity values (understood as 'monetized values' or 'direct prices' dictated solely by the commodity's socially necessary labour content) into (tendentially uniform) *prices of production.*

Prices of production are not market prices, so we are not considering the transformation of value into a final 'monetized' exchange-value but into an intermediate form. The specificity of this form pertains to the influence of a single mechanism on the process of price formation: the 'redistribution' of surplus-value that is effected by the equalization of profit rates through competition.

In Marx's theory individual capitalists do not directly appropriate the surplus-value produced by 'their own workers.' Rather, the appropriation of surplus-value is conceived as a process of collective class exploitation, while the distribution of the aggregate (social) surplus-value among different capitals is seen as the effect of inter-capitalist competition in the sphere of circulation and the tendential formation of a general rate of profit.

In view of all this, it should be apparent that the equalization of profit rates will tend to produce a divergence between the surplus-value 'represented' by a particular commodity and the actual profit that can be realized through its sale. While at the aggregate level total profit 'should' equal total surplus-value, and total value 'should' equal total prices of production, the differing conditions of production will mean that a divergence between value and price of production will be the norm for individual commodities. But what is meant by 'different conditions of production' in this connection?

As we have already seen, different capitals have varying compositions – that is, they are *heterogeneous* with respect to their ratios of dead to living labour. Although the variable portion of the capital is solely capable of creating surplus-value, it is apparent that enterprises that invest a relatively greater portion of their capital in labour-power than in objectified means of production will not automatically realize more surplus-value than those that are more 'capital-intensive.' Instead, a portion of the *socially produced* aggregate surplus-value will become a constituent of the production price of a given commodity *in the form of profit* and *in proportion to the capital invested in its production.*

Accordingly, the individual capitalist will *tend* to receive as an increment to his invested capital not the magnitude of surplus-value produced by his own workers but the profit that is due in accordance with the general rate of profit calculated on the capital investment. Hence Marx's *theoretical formula* for the transformation process: 'When a capitalist sells his commodities at their price of production, he recovers money in proportion to the value of the capital consumed in their production and secures profit in proportion to his advanced capital as the aliquot part of the total social capital' (1978b: 159).

Both the adequacy of Marx's conceptualization of the transformation process and the consistency of the production price theory with the theory of value have been disputed by a long list of critics, including many who were otherwise sympathetic to Marx's theoretical project. In the next two sections, the 'traditional' criticisms of Marx's value theory will be considered, together with various 'alternative' solutions to the transformation problem.

Traditional Criticisms and Orthodox Responses

The first phase of the controversy surrounding Marx's theory of value, characterized principally by a confrontation between neoclassical marginalism and the 'orthodox' understanding of Marx's *Capital* prevalent among the classical Social Democratic theorists, took the form of a clear-cut Marxist/anti-Marxist cleavage. While complete unanimity never existed among the neoclassical critics of Marx's value theory, nor among the Social Democratic guardians of Marxist orthodoxy, the terms of debate between the two camps were relatively straightforward, as were the class and political loyalties of virtually all the participants in the debate. This makes the task of summarizing the first phase of the controversy a relatively simple one.

With the publication of the third volume of *Capital* in 1894, the floodgates of debate between Marx's neoclassical critics and his defenders were fully opened. True, many criticisms of Marx's theory of value had already appeared in the 1870s and 1880s following the publication of the first volume of *Capital*; indeed, Marx had himself responded to one of them – Adolph Wagner's polemic – shortly before his death in 1883. Two circumstances, however, served to slow the critical response. First, during the quarter of a century between the publication of the first and third volumes of *Capital*, most professional economists were attempting to put their own house in order by establishing a solid theoretical framework that could stand as a cogent alternative to Marx's theories. Second, the professional economists most concerned with answering Marx's critique of political economy had been frustrated by the unavailability of the long-promised conclusion to Marx's analysis in *Capital III*, which, like *Capital II*, was drawn together from Marx's unfinished notes under the editorship of Friedrich Engels.

Among the many critiques of Marx that appeared after 1894, Eugen von Boehm-Bawerk's *Karl Marx and the Close of His System* ranks as the most influential. Most of the criticisms of Marx's value theory advanced by Loria, Wicksteed, Pareto, Croce, Schumpeter, and other representatives of neoclassical economics and early modern sociology find expression there, and, just as important, in a cogent, systematic, and comprehensive fashion. Accordingly, Boehm-Bawerk's critique remains a touchstone of the value controversy, as do the responses that it elicited from Marxist theorists in the early years of the twentieth century.

On Boehm-Bawerk's interpretation, Marx's law of value 'states and must state ... that commodities are exchanged in proportion to the socially necessary working time incorporated in them.' But in the third volume of *Capital*, Marx argues that the price ratios of commodities in exchange are decisively influenced by a phenomenon that is independent of embodied labour-time: the tendency for the profit component of price to be determined by the general rate of profit as calculated on the cost-price of the commodity. According to Boehm-Bawerk, these two positions are logically incompatible. Having exposed this contradiction in Marx's theoretical system (as between the accounts of the first and third volumes of *Capital*), Boehm-Bawerk then shows that it arises from a confrontation between a palpably real phenomenon (the general rate of profit and its influence on commodity exchange ratios) and Marx's false theory regarding the determination of commodity price.

In building his case against Marx, Boehm-Bawerk cites the following passage from *Capital III*, which seems to suggest that Marx was well aware of a contradiction in his theoretical system:

At a given rate of surplus-value it is only for capitals of the same organic composition – assuming equal turnover times – that the law holds good, as a general tendency, that profits stand in direct proportion to the amount of capital, and that capitals of equal size yield equal profits in the same period of time. The above argument is true on the same basis as our whole investigation so far: *that commodities are sold at their values*. There is no doubt, however, that in actual fact ... no such variation in the average rate of profit exists between branches of industry, and it could not exist without abolishing the entire system of capitalist production. The theory of value thus appears incompatible with the actual phenomena of production, and it might seem that we must abandon all hope of understanding these phenomena. (Marx 1981b: 252; emphasis added)

Triumphantly, Boehm-Bawerk concludes: 'To speak plainly his solution is obtained at the cost of the assumption from which Marx has hitherto started, *that commodities exchange according to their values*. This assumption Marx now simply drops' (1975: 21).

What Boehm-Bawerk conveniently neglects to add is that the 'assumption' that 'commodities are sold at their value' is *just that*: an *assumption* that Marx posits at different points in order to lay bare specific features of the capitalist mode of production. Moreover, it is an assumption that is posited as part of a procedure of *theoretical abstraction* from certain other features of capitalism that are in no way regarded by Marx as incidental to a concrete theoretical reconstruction of the capitalist totality. But what this 'assumption' most emphatically *is not* is a necessary or constitutive postulate of Marx's value theory.

Why then does Marx speak of an apparent incompatibility between the 'theory of value' on the one side and 'the actual phenomena of production' on the other? As we have seen, capitalist reality for Marx constitutes a contradictory unity of three social production relations: between independent and socially equal commodity producers, between capitalists and wage-labourers, and between different competing capitals. The *appearance* of an incompatibility between Marx's labour-value formulation and the equalization of profit rates among capitals of different composition corresponds to a *real contradiction* that is a constitutive element of capitalist social reality. This contradiction has nothing at all to do with the notion that commodities exchange at their value from one conceptual perspective and that they exchange at their prices of production from an alternative perspective: that is, nothing to do with a *theoretical* contradiction, as Boehm-Bawerk asserts. Rather, this 'contradiction' arises from the fact that the theory of value maintains that living labour is the sole source of new value, while empirical observation conclusively discloses that capital invested in 'dead labour' (such as machinery and building structures) can establish the same rate of profit as capital invested in living labour.

The real contradiction that gives rise to the apparent incompatibility between the law that only living labour can produce surplus-value and the observable tendency toward uniform rates of profit among capitals of varying composition is this: within capitalist society, capital simultaneously expresses an exploitative relation between social classes and an equalitarian relation between competing individual capitals. The *production* of surplus-value presents itself as a process of class exploitation operating through value relations, while the *realization* of profits appears as a life-and-death struggle among individual 'socially equalized' capitals for their rightful share of total profits (a struggle also operating through value relations). By acknowledging the real-life tendency toward a general rate of profit, Marx reveals that the social production relations of capitalist society inevitably result in a real contradiction between the valorization process and the realization process, a contradiction that is 'resolved' in reality through the tendency of capitals of equal magnitude to realize equal profits, *regardless* of their compositions. But the fact that this contradiction is resolved in this way does *not* entail a renunciation on Marx's part of the *fundamental* postulate of his theory of value: that living labour is the sole source of all new value, including surplus-value.

As for the 'assumption' that 'commodities exchange according to their values,' this can be dropped as soon as the focus of analysis shifts from the exploitative class relation between capital and labour manifest in the sphere of production to the competitive relation between individual capitals manifest in the sphere of circulation/realization.To further underline the point: the 'withdrawal' of the assumption of commodities exchanging according to their values in no way entails the abandonment of the 'value postulate' *shared* by the first and third volumes of *Capital*, namely that, irrespective of how the exchange ratios of particular commodities are determined, and irrespective of how the aggregate social surplus-value is 'shared out' to individual capitals in the form of profit, the magnitude of surplus-value is decisively determined by the socially necessary labour-time expended by productive living workers.

Hilferding makes much the same sort of argument in his response to Boehm-Bawerk: '[His] entire train of reasoning is utterly beside the point. Marx is inquiring about the total value, and his critic complains because he is not inquiring about the value of the individual commodity' (1975: 158).

But the idea of 'total value' produced can only be incomprehensible to an economist who reduces the idea of value to an exchange relation between discrete commodities. As Hilferding observes: 'Boehm-Bawerk overlooks the fact that value in the Marxist sense is an objective, quantitatively determined magnitude. He overlooks it because in reality the concept of value as determined by the marginal utility theory lacks this quantitative definiteness' (ibid.: 159–60).

Boehm-Bawerk's criticism of Marx is not wholly concerned with the alleged contradiction between the first and third volumes of *Capital*. He is also concerned to expose Marx's faulty logic in identifying 'labour' as the common factor underlying the exchange-values of different commodities. According to Boehm-Bawerk, 'Marx searches for the "common factor" which is the characteristic of exchange value in the following way: He passes in review the various properties possessed by the objects made equal in exchange, and according to the method of exclusion separates all those which cannot stand the test, until at last only one property remains, that of being the product of labour. This, therefore, must be the sought-for common property' (1975: 69).

Boehm-Bawerk's first substantive point of criticism is that Marx deliberately excluded goods that are *not products of labour* from his analysis, and even defined such goods as non-commodities. Such 'gifts of nature,' however, constitute 'important objects of property and commerce,' and it would be preposterous to assume that the prices attaching to these goods are established arbitrarily or by accident simply because they are devoid of labour content. How then are the prices of this undeniably important class of economic goods determined? This question obliges us to consider non-labour candidates for the designation of 'common factor.' In Boehm-Bawerk's view there are several properties shared in common by *all* exchangeable goods, products of labour as well as gifts of nature, among them: scarcity in relation to demand, regulation by the law of supply and demand, causing expense to their producer, and being subject to apportionment. What all these properties point to however is the concrete *utility* of all exchangeable goods. Thus, for Boehm-Bawerk – a leading exponent of the marginal utility theory – the 'common factor' shared by all exchangeable goods and accounting for their value in exchange is the circumstance that they all possess a *use*.

Responding to this argument, Hilferding reminds us first that Marx derives his concept of value not through a formal-logical process of 'eliminating' everything but labour as the substance of value, but rather by starting with the material form assumed by social labour in capitalist society: the individual commodity. The real object of Marx's investigation is not the determinants of price in a commodity-capitalist economy, but the forms of appearance and modes of distribution and apportionment of *social labour* under conditions of commodity exchange. In Hilferding's words:

[Marx] starts from labour in its significance as the constitutive element in human society, as the element whose development determines in the final analysis the development of society ... [Capitalist] society has, as it were, assigned to each of its members the quota of labour necessary to society; has specified to each individual how much labour he must expend. And these individuals have forgotten what their quota was, and rediscover it only in the process of social life. It is therefore because labour is the social bond uniting an atomized [commodity-producing] society, and not because labour is the matter most technically relevant, that labour is the principle of value and that the law of value is endowed with reality. (1975: 133–4)

This passage demonstrates, unmistakably in my opinion, that the 'orthodox Marxism' of the turn of the century was, contrary to the asseverations of some contemporary Marxists, not entirely blind to what Diane Elson has referred to as Marx's 'value theory of labour.' Indeed, on Hilferding's interpretation, the value theory of labour was nothing less than the true starting-point, if by no means the sole content, of Marx's theory of value.

Hilferding points out that a good becomes a commodity in Marx's sense only to the extent that it becomes a 'bearer of social labour' and the 'material expression' of a social relationship of production. By the same token, however, goods that are not products of labour can acquire the 'character' of commodities 'as the expression of derivative relationships of production' (1975: 134). The gifts of nature can have exchange-value, then, to the extent that they are subsumed under the dominant relations of production of a commodity-capitalist society. An illustration of this is the changing status of land in history and the process whereby land 'acquires the characteristics of a commodity as a condition requisite to the production of commodities' (135).

The second aspect of Boehm-Bawerk's criticism – concerning the status of labour as the common factor underlying commodity values – is no stronger than the first. As Ernest Mandel points out: 'Marx nowhere ... declares that the *only* property common to commodities is that they are products of human labour' (1968 2: 711). Moreover, Marx has no need to 'prove' that labour is such a singular property of commodities. The significance of Marx's discussion concerning labour as the *relevant* common factor underlying commodity exchange is that it suggests the need for 'a *social* property which makes it possible to weave a fabric of relationships between all these producers' (ibid.: 712). This point reinforces Hilferding's crucial observation that Boehm-Bawerk's catalogue of 'common properties' shared by all ex-changeable goods 'continually confuses the natural and the social' (1975: 135) – the hallmark of economic fetishism.

Boehm-Bawerk's attempts to logically confute Marx's labour-value for-mulation are not convincing in themselves; however, they acquire a certain power when they are joined to his attempted demonstration of the superiority of the marginalist approach to value. His argument on this terrain proceeds as follows:

Labour and value in use have a qualitative side and a quantitative side. As the value in use is different qualitatively as table, house, or yarn, so is labour as carpentry, masonry, or spinning. And just as one can compare different kinds of labour according to their quantity, so one can compare values in use of different kinds according to the amount of value in use ... If Marx had chanced to reverse the order of the examination, the same reasoning which led to the exclusion of value in use would have excluded labour; and then the reasoning which resulted in the crowning of labour might have led him to declare the value in use to be the only property left, and therefore to be the sought-for common property, and value to be 'the cellular tissue of value in use.' (1975: 76–7)

In response, Hilferding makes the point that Boehm-Bawerk proceeds from 'the error of attempting from the subjective individual relationship, where-from subjective estimates of value are properly deducible, to deduce an objective social measure' (1975: 133). This error follows from a theory of value that, by starting with the natural qualities of commodities as use-values, focuses upon 'the individual relationship between a thing and a human being instead of starting from the social relationships of human beings to one another' (133).

Geoffrey Kay presses beyond such general methodological points by estab-lishing that the 'logical structure' of Marx's argument can in no way accom-modate the simple substitution of the concept of utility for that of labour as the common property rendering different commodities commensurable in exchange: 'To insist with Boehm-Bawerk that use-value is not only the reason for exchange ... but also its basis and its measure, posits among other things the category of general utility. But as such a category is incapable by its nature of achieving any form of existence, it is doomed to unreality, and any theory based upon it must be a contentless abstraction' (1979: 53).

The same sort of argument can be made against the category of 'abstract labour,' however, if concrete labour is conceived as its sole form of appear-ance: 'If we constitute abstract labour as the common property of concrete labour – the expenditure of muscles, brains, etc. – we are inventing a mental abstraction and not discovering the real abstraction that Marx was after ... [A]bstract labour defined simply as the common property of concrete labour is not distinguishable at all. It can no more be distinguished from concrete labour than the quality of being a mammal can be distinguished from the feline body of a cat or the canine body of a dog. It cannot be distinguished quite simply because there is nothing to distinguish, because it does not exist' (ibid.: 55).

In what sense, then, can we speak of abstract labour as existing independently of the concrete manifestations of human labour? If concrete labour is not the necessary form of appearance of abstract labour, what is? Kay reminds us that the answer to these questions is to be found in Marx's analysis of the value-form – an analysis that is slighted by Hilferding and entirely ignored by Boehm-Bawerk. As Kay puts it: 'in searching for the form of existence of abstract labour we are merely looking for the value-form ... [Money] is the medium through which concrete labour becomes abstract labour. In a word it is money that is the form of existence of abstract labour' (ibid.: 58).

The failure of Hilferding and many other orthodox Marxist theorists of the Second International, such as Bukharin (1972), to highlight Marx's value-form analysis in their critiques of marginalist economics both reflected and reinforced a tendency on their part to underestimate the *methodological* divide between Marx and his neoclassical critics. For example, according to Bukharin, 'the methodological difference between Karl Marx and Boehm-Bawerk may be summarized concisely as follows: objectivism-subjectivism, a historical standpoint – an unhistorical standpoint, the point of view of production – the point of view of consumption' (1972: 32). Bukharin's set of contrasts is germane as far as it goes, but does this really constitute an *adequate* 'concise summary' of the methodological differences existing between Marx and the marginalists? It seems doubtful, and our suspicions on this score can only be strengthened if we recall that the orthodox theory of the Second International attempted, in numerous ways, to accommodate itself to the prevailing positivism of the era (Colletti 1972).

Bukharin's critique of Menger's and Boehm-Bawerk's 'methodological atomism' is certainly instructive and important, as is his larger argument that a scientific analysis of economic phenomena should begin with economic subjects as these appear as members of a 'social economic system,' not as isolated individuals. Yet Bukharin, along with other leading Social Democratic theorists, failed to specify the truly distinctive features of Marx's method. Consequently, their defence of Marx left many important issues unexplored, many significant questions unanswered, and many opportunities open for a reinterpretation of Marx's political economy in ways that were quite consistent with the limited methodological strictures that they specified, yet inconsistent with the more demanding, if elusive, principles of Marx's own theory of scientific knowledge.

The Controversy Surrounding the 'Transformation Problem'

During the 'first phase' of the value controversy, the most significant critique of Marx's procedure for transforming commodity values into prices of production was that made by the Prussian statistician and Ricardian economist Ladislaus von Bortkiewicz, a critique that was made largely outside the terms of debate between Marxism and neoclassical marginalism. The technical-mathematical character of Bortkiewicz's critique anticipated much of the later discussion surrounding the transformation problem and value theory as this was to unfold among Marxist economists. Paradoxically perhaps, this Ricardian's sympathetic criticisms of Marx's engagement with the 'transformation problem' contributed more to a dissension among Marxist economists than did any of the hostile polemics that emanated from the marginalist camp. Indeed, it was precisely Bortkiewicz's relative proximity to Marx's own problematic that made his critique and alternative 'solution' to the value-price transformation problem a significant pole of attraction for a number of academically trained Marxists, in particular Paul Sweezy, the Marxist economist who did the most to popularize Bortkiewicz's contributions and to legitimize them within Marxist economic discourse (Sweezy 1975, 1968 [1942]).

For reasons that will become clear shortly, it is useful to approach Marx's transformation procedure as this is illustrated by his example involving three capitals (or branches of production) rather than the five-capital model that Marx describes in greatest depth in chapter 9 of *Capital III* ('Formation of a General Rate of Profit [Average Rate of Profit] and Transformation of the Values of Commodities into Prices of Production').

Once again, the individual value of a commodity is calculated as the sum of c (constant capital expended) + v (variable capital expended) + s (surplus value produced), while the commodity's price of production is calculated as the sum of cost price (c + v = k) and profit (p), where p is calculated as the product of k multiplied by the average rate of profit (p'). Marx's three-branch example is represented in table 1.

Like his earlier example, Marx's illustration as reproduced in this above table leads us to conclude that the phenomenon of profit-rate equalization between branches of production with different compositions (c/v ratios) poses

TABLE 1

	c	v	s	p'	Value	P.P.	Value–P.P. deviation
I	80	20	20	20%	120	120	0
II	90	10	10	205	110	120	+10
III	70	30	30	20%	130	120	−10
	240	60	60	20%	360	360	0

SOURCE: Karl Marx, *Capital Volume Three* (1981b), 264

no special problem for the two equalities that his theories of value and exploitation jointly posit: the equality of values and prices of production (in aggregate) and the equality of profits and surplus-value (in aggregate). Like his earlier five-capital example, therefore, this three-branch illustration of the transformation process sustains Marx's theoretical formula: 'When a capitalist sells his commodities at their price of production, he recovers money in proportion to the value of the capital consumed in their production and secures profit in proportion to his advanced capital as the aliquot part of the total social capital' (1978: 159).

Bortkiewicz's point of departure is that Marx failed to consider how his theoretical formula for the transformation of commodity values into prices of production can be reconciled with the model of 'simple reproduction' of a capitalist economy that he outlines in the second volume of *Capital*. Assuming the existence of three 'departments of production' that encompass the total social capital of a given economy, Bortkiewicz reconstructs Marx's transformation scheme in terms of a series of equations positing the conditions of simple reproduction. The three departments of production are Department I, which produces means of production (the elements of constant capital), Department II, which produces workers' consumption goods, and Department III, which produces capitalists' consumption ('luxury') goods. The conditions of simple reproduction in such a three-department model are represented in the following system of equations:

(1) $c_1 + v_1 + s_1 = c_1 + c_2 + c_3 =$ total value, Dept. I
(2) $c_2 + v_2 + s_2 = v_1 + v_2 + v_3 =$ total value, Dept. II
(3) $c_3 + v_3 + s_3 = s_1 + s_2 + s_3 =$ total value, Dept. III,

where the numerical subscripts refer to the three departments of production, and where it is assumed that demand equals supply.

For Bortkiewicz, the challenge is now to transform this 'value' expression of the conditions of simple reproduction into a 'production price' expression, while simultaneously maintaining the equality of the social aggregates at the heart of Marx's theory (s = p and total value = total production prices) and conforming to 'the law of the equal rate of profit.' Marx's own solution to this problem is considered unacceptable by Bortkiewicz because 'it excludes the constant and variable capitals from the transformation process, whereas the principle of the equal profit rate ... must involve these elements' (1975: 201). To 'correctly' transform commodity values into prices of production, the values of the input commodities c and v need to be transformed along with the magnitude of surplus-value produced.

The reason this correction seems necessary is ascertainable once Marx's own mathematical illustrations are replaced by an illustration reflecting the conditions of simple reproduction. Operationalizing Bortkiewicz's procedure, Sweezy divides a hypothetical capitalist economy into three departments of production, each with its own unique composition of capital. Applying Marx's transformation procedure to this model, he finds that a discrepancy arises between the quantity of constant capital produced in Department I and the total quantity of constant capital consumed in production by all three departments. A similar discrepancy arises with respect to the variable capital produced and consumed. Thus, *assuming variance in capital compositions as between departments of production*, Marx's solution to the transformation problem appears to be flatly inconsistent with an equilibrium model of simple reproduction.

The 'correction' to Marx's transformation procedure recommended by Bortkiewicz and Sweezy proceeds in two steps. First, as already noted, the general rate of profit is to be applied to c and v as well as s. If this is done, and if the 'unit of account' of both value and production price is unity, then a result is obtained in which a direct correspondence between the output of each department (expressed in price terms) and the income of each department (again in price terms) is achieved. As Sweezy puts it: 'The output of Department I equals the constant capital used up; the production of Department II equals wages paid out; and the output of Department III is sufficient to absorb the total surplus-value accruing to the capitalists' (1968: 120). This procedure also allows for total value equalling total production prices, and total surplus-value equalling total profits. (A mathematical example of the procedure is furnished by Sweezy, but not by Bortkiewicz.)

All appears well until the assumption that the unit of account of the price and value expressions will be the same is dropped. Sweezy's example of the 'corrected' transformation procedure then appears to be a 'special case.' In general, *gold*, as the 'common measure' of value and price, will not have the *same* price and value. That is to say, the price of gold and the value of gold (as the 'money commodity') will diverge from one another whenever the capital composition of the gold industry rises higher or falls below the composition of the social capital as a whole (the socially average capital composition). The consequence will be that the accounting measure of both value and production price will no longer equal '1' in both the value and price schemes, meaning that the specific capital composition of the gold industry will unavoidably affect the entire transformation process (Sweezy 1968: 121–2). The upshot is that the Bortkiewicz/Sweezy alternative to Marx's transformation procedure restores the conditions of simple reproduction (equilibrium), allows for the identity of total surplus-value and total profits, but requires that total value deviate from total price (at least whenever the capital composition of the gold industry diverges from the social average).

In assessing the significance of the Bortkiewicz/Sweezy handling of the transformation problem, we need to be clear on how it differs from Marx's own transformation procedure. It should first be noted that Sweezy *does not use* Marx's three-capital illustration of the transformation process but constructs his own. The data in table 1 cannot be reconciled with a model of simple reproduction even if Bortkiewicz's method of transforming cost price along with surplus-value is applied. The reason is straightforward: Marx's own mathematical illustrations of the transformation process never assume the conditions of simple reproduction or interdepartmental equilibrium. Marx is solely concerned with establishing the effects of variant capital compositions as these influence individual production prices, not as they influence whole departments of production. In short, Marx did not attempt to confront his transformation procedure with the model of simple reproduction elaborated in *Capital II.*

Bortkiewicz and Sweezy, by contrast, begin by assuming simple reproduction and then proceed to the further assumption that the problem of variant capital compositions needs to be understood in relation to the 'departments of production.' The problem is that Bortkiewicz and Sweezy nowhere provide a theoretical rationale for their postulate of variant capital compositions as between whole departments of production.

One possible rejoinder to Bortkiewicz and Sweezy on this question is to suggest that departments of production will likely mirror the composition of the social capital as a whole. Since the assumption of interdepartmental divergence of capital compositions is fundamental to Sweezy's critique of Marx's transformation procedure, this line of argument is a perfectly relevant one, and the onus is really on Sweezy to establish *why* unequal compositions as between departments should be postulated. This point has been pursued by Shane Mage (1963: 238).

Another possible line of response to the Bortkiewicz-Sweezy 'correction' was formulated by J. Winternitz (1948: 276–80). Winternitz argued that it was arbitrary to hold the ratio of prices and values in Department III equal to 1 in order to ensure the equivalence of gold's price and value expressions. To select *this* as the 'invariance postulate' could only lead to the conclusion that values and prices of production will generally diverge just as soon as the postulate is relaxed. Winternitz maintained that a different invariance postulate should be selected, one more consistent with Marx's basic theoretical assumptions. Accordingly, he recommended the addition of a further equation to the transformation formula: one that would ensure the equality of aggregate values and aggregate production prices. The result – once 'cost price' was transformed in accordance with Bortkiewicz's method – was a discrepancy between the magnitude of total profit and the magnitude of total surplus-value.

Winternitz's challenge to Bortkiewicz was of a genus that was to be repeatedly attempted by participants in the transformation-problem debate. For a considerable period of time, Bortkiewicz's 'correction' of Marx was interrogated primarily on his own terrain of formal mathematical models, with only his 'secondary' premises receiving the sort of scrutiny that should have met his more fundamental theoretical assumptions. Consequently, the debate tended to bog down in arguments concerning the plausibility of assorted invariance postulates and their unique effects on a model that appeared congenitally resistant to maintaining both of Marx's aggregate equalities along with equilibrium conditions of simple reproduction – all of which only served to underscore Seton's observation that 'there does not seem to be an objective basis for choosing any particular invariance postulate in preference to all the others, and to that extent the transformation problem may be said to fall short of complete determinacy' (1957: 153).

Rather than quarrel over which invariance postulate is most appropriately plugged into a Bortkiewicz-type model of value-price transformation, it would seem more fruitful to question some of the basic presuppositions of that model: the *need for* 'simultaneous valuation' of cost price and surplus-value, and the appropriateness of seeking to establish a theoretical space in which the conditions of simple reproduction (relating to the turnover of the total social capital) *encounter* the problem of value-price transformation (which concerns the results of the interactions of *many individual capitals*). Since such an examination must return us to some of the fundamental issues posed by Marx's theory of value, and since the transformation problem continues to figure prominently in the contemporary value controversy, I shall defer further discussion of these points to the next chapter.

5 The Contemporary Value Controversy

The origins of the contemporary controversy surrounding Marx's theory of labour-value are easily specified. First, by the 1960s, the critique of neo-classical economic theory undertaken by the Cambridge School of Piero Sraffa, Joan Robinson, Nicholas Kaldor, et al. had constituted itself as a major 'neo-Ricardian' challenge to some central tenets of marginalism and was doing much to encourage the rehabilitation of some characteristic concerns of classical and Marxian political economy: in particular, the problem of the source, measurement, and distribution of an economic surplus. Second, the renewed interest in Marx's thought resulting from the New Left/student radicalization of the 1960s focused increasingly upon Marx's 'economics' as the world capitalist economy experienced worsening dislocation after 1970 (the collapse of the Bretton Woods monetary agreement, falling rates of profit in several of the advanced capitalist countries, and the world-wide recession of 1974–5). Third, interest in Marx's theory of capitalist crisis was spurred during the 1970s by the apparent exhaustion of Keynesian macro-economic policy, which had manifestly failed to anticipate the specific features of the emerging economic crisis of Western capitalism as popularly encapsulated in the notion of 'stagflation.'

These economic, political, and intellectual developments provided the socio-historical backdrop to the contemporary value controversy. By way of introduction to the controversy's principal themes, a brief characterization of each of its main camps will serve to specify further the context and significance of this 'second phase' of debate surrounding Marx's theory of value.

Main Camps of the Contemporary Value Controversy

Neo-Ricardianism

Contemporary neo-Ricardianism encompasses both a 'left wing,' which considers itself Marxist in some circumscribed sense, and a right wing, which is primarily concerned with what Sergio Latouche (1976) has aptly called the 'reswitching of dominant ideologies' within the economics profession. Our concern here will be strictly with 'left neo-Ricardianism,' that is, with the varied attempts of Marxist or neo-Marxist economists either to reconcile Piero Sraffa's (1960) critique of neoclassicism with Marxian political economy or to revise the latter substantially in light of the former.

This characterization of left-wing neo-Ricardianism already suggests a certain tension within its ambit that should be noted. Neo-Ricardian Marxism *began* as an attempt to employ Sraffa's system to resuscitate a rather moribund 'orthodox' understanding of Marx's political economy. To Ronald Meek and Maurice Dobb, two of the stalwarts of this orthodoxy during the darkest days of the Cold War, Sraffa's system was in no sense a threat to Marx's fundamental ideas. Rather, it was a welcome ally in the project of analysing economic phenomena (in particular, the distribution of net income, inclusive of a 'surplus') in a fashion that takes into account the existence of an *antagonistic class structure*. But the fact that both of these eminent Marxist scholars *ended* by touting the potential superiority of Sraffa's framework over Marx's attests to more than a weariness in upholding a logically untenable orthodoxy; it also suggests that both men – in common with many of their 'orthodox' colleagues – may well have had an essentially Ricardian appreciation of Marx's economics all along. Hence, it might legitimately be inferred that *one* of the streams leading into modern neo-Ricaradian Marxism is a certain tradition of Marxist orthodoxy itself. Indeed, the collapse of this 'Ricardian-Marxist' orthodoxy was an important formative influence in the development of this school.

If Meek and Dobb emphasized the importance of a friendly encounter between Sraffian and Marxian economics, a younger generation of radical neo-Ricardians sought a substantial overhauling of Marxian political economy on the basis of Sraffa's model. Indeed, it was the Sraffa-based critique of Marx's value theory as articulated by Ian Steedman, Geoff Hodgson, and others that came to define the neo-Ricardian position within the contemporary value controversy – and it is this strain of neo-Ricardianism that will principally concern us.

Neo-Orthodoxy

The second camp within the value controversy is constituted by what I call the 'neo-orthodox' school. Far more than the neo-Ricardian Marxists, the neo-orthodox theorists encompass a substantively heterogeneous range of opinion, although they are united by a strong emphasis on 'value-form' analysis and by a commitment to specifying the distinctive methodological underpinnings of Marx's political economy. The general indifference of the neo-orthodox theorists to the analysis of the magnitude of value, as well as their understanding of Marx's project as essentially a *critique* of political economy rather than a development of it, invites a characterization of neo-orthodox Marxism as a 'sociologizing' or 'philosophizing' current within the value controversy.

In part, the neo-orthodox school is a reaction to the collapse of the Ricardian-Marxist orthodoxy and the rise of neo-Ricardianism, in part a relatively autonomous development owing its origins to an encounter between the humanist philosophical preoccupations of the early New Left (Hegel, Lukács, Marcuse, alienation theory, and so on) and Marx's critique of political economy in *Capital I.* The theoretical result of this encounter – a commitment to the analysis of the value-form and a reassertion of the critique of *economic fetishism* as fundamental to Marx's critical project – has led some to identify this school with the work of Isaac I. Rubin, although it is at least arguable that Rubin's general approach is equally consistent with that of the Marxist 'fundamentalists.'

Fundamentalism

The fundamentalist camp within the value controversy is an inchoate and somewhat amorphous group that shares certain positions in common with both the Ricardian-Marxist orthodoxy and the neo-orthodox school. Since the term 'fundamentalist' has often been used to refer to *all* adherents of Marxian economic orthodoxy, I should make clear that I reserve the designation to those who are more concerned with the over-all coherence of Marx's political economy than with the 'letter' of Marx's analysis. In particular, the fundamentalist project involves a commitment to reviving interest in Marx's analysis of the value-form at least in part in order to *enrich* his value-magnitude analysis, rather than to abandon it in the neo-orthodox fashion. This orientation also decisively distinguishes the fundamentalists from orthodox Ricardian-Marxists, who are almost exclusively concerned with the magnitude of value and indifferent to its form. The term 'fundamentalist' seems appropriate in that it indicates a return to *both* aspects of Marx's fundamental theoretical program: the analysis of the form *and* the magnitude of value. (Needless to say, none of this implies a *dogmatic* stance of the type associated with religious fundamentalism.)

The goal of what follows is to highlight some of the more distinctive theoretical and methodological positions of each of these schools of thought by drawing upon and critically interrogating the work of some of the more prominent participants in the contemporary value controversy.

The Neo-Ricardian Challenge

There are some very substantial reasons for labelling the ostensibly Marxist followers of Sraffa's economics as 'neo-Ricardians' – even though the term post-Sraffians would probably do just as well. These reasons have less to do with the *specific* positions of Ricardo and the neo-Ricardians as with certain methodological and theoretical considerations pertaining to a broadly common 'problematic' – a problematic quite distinct from Marx's, yet one that has recurrently been suppressed and revived within the boundaries of bourgeois economics: the complex of issues surrounding *the distribution of income* conceived at least in part as a distribution of surplus. Without anticipating too much of what will be discussed later, it should be observed that such a problematic differs from Marx's in two decisive respects: in its focus on the distribution rather than the production of a surplus, and in its disregard of the socio-historical form of surplus production and economic reproduction in general. These Ricardian features are very much in evidence both in Sraffa's work and in the neo-Ricardian Marxists' critique of Marx's value theory. We begin with a consideration of Sraffa's project as it relates *indirectly* to Marx's.

Sraffa and Marx

Whatever his followers might believe about the wider implications of his theoretical model, Sraffa apparently had a well-defined and quite limited objective in mind when he wrote *The Production of Commodities by Means of Commodities*. This objective was not at all to undermine the credibility of Marx's critical analysis of capitalism, but to develop an 'internal' or 'immanent' critique of several marginalist propositions that had long served as pillars of the neoclassical system, as well as to adumbrate some ideas suggestive of an 'external' critique of general equilibrium analysis.

Sraffa develops his critique on the basis of a series of models that illustrate how 'prices of production' are constituted. Throughout his analysis he abstracts from the marginalist problem of 'demand-side' determination of market prices. His concern is rather with the influence of such distributional variables as the wage rate and the rate of profit on commodity prices as commodities emerge from a production process in which they appear as the products of other commodities (namely, the commodities constituting the physical means of production and the wage-bundle).

Sraffa constructs his central economic model by successively considering: (1) a subsistence economy in which the same commodities appear as inputs and outputs; (2) a surplus-generating economy that obeys the principle of the equalization of profit rates; (3) an economy in which the wage varies according to labour's 'share' of the surplus; and (4) the economic conditions of existence of a 'standard' or composite commodity that can be used in the analysis of income distribution over a given period of time.

The central equation of Sraffa's 'standard system' is

$$r = R(1 - w),$$

where r is the rate of profit; R, the ratio of net product (Sraffa's surplus) to the means of production; and w, the wage per unit of labour (or the wage component of national income). After demonstrating that the standard system is unique, Sraffa employs his equation for a variety of theoretical purposes. The underlying premiss of all of these investigations is that once either of the distributional variables is fixed (that is, either the wage or profit rate), we can then 'determine' – meaning, calculate – both prices and the real level of the other distributional variable. Accordingly, within Sraffa's system, either the wage rate or the profit rate can function as the 'independent variable' for the system as a whole.

It would be tangential to our purpose to explore the implications of Sraffa's economic model for the critique of marginalist theory. However, it is important to identify some of the ways in which the Sraffa model diverges from Marx's approach to the analysis of capitalism:

1 Sraffa does not define commodities as socio-historically specific manifestations of social labour (that is, as the *social form* of the product of labour under determinate conditions), but rather as *things* – as physical inputs or outputs of a production process that is regarded entirely from a 'technical' point of view. Accordingly, Sraffa's conception of commodity production is *fetishistic*.
2 Intimately related to this fetishism is the divergence between Marx's and Sraffa's respective *objects of analysis*. Marx is concerned with analysing

the role of *social labour* in generalized commodity production (that is, with the capitalist production of commodity-values *by means of labour*), while Sraffa's economic model is given historical specificity only through his assumption of the operation of a 'uniform rate of profit' – an assumption that necessarily refers to the operations of a capitalist economy. Yet, in Sraffa's model of capitalism, labour is represented only by a proxy: the wage goods that enter into the reproduction process. Let us be clear on this point: the problem with Sraffa's model from Marx's standpoint is *not* that it allows for the complete elimination of living labour from production (conceived as a technical process of producing goods), for Marx clearly envisaged the possibility of a more-or-less complete automization of the material production process. The problem is that such a possibility is present in a model that involves such phenomena as profits, wages, prices of production, and equalized rates of profit – that is, phenomena that suggest the institutional presence of capitalist relations of production. From Marx's standpoint, the presence of such social relations demands that the production process be approached not only in respect of its technical or physical aspects, but first and foremost in respect of its *social* aspects (that is, production as valorization and as exploitation). A social production system that requires the class appropriation of surplus labour cannot dispense with labour as an input to production. Yet Sraffa sidesteps this crucial issue by banishing all considerations of class relations to the sphere of distribution.

3 Sraffa's concept of the 'surplus' is a purely physical aggregate, the origins of which remain unspecified and the magnitude of which is coextensive with Marx's 'net product' (the sum of variable capital and surplus-value expressed in use-values). In a very rough sense, this surplus refers to what is available for human consumption and reinvestment after the consumed material inputs have been 'replaced.' It is true that Sraffa acknowledges alternative ways of treating the *wage*. Indeed, in his simplest model, he treats the wage – or, more specifically, the bundle of wage goods – as a *necessary* input (subsistence for workers). The ideal procedure, according to Sraffa, would be to treat a portion of the wage as subsistence (a necessary input) and a portion as a share of surplus. But in order to abstract from the *social* or *cultural* determinants of subsistence, Sraffa ends up treating the *entire wage* as a component of the surplus.

By treating wages as part of the surplus, Sraffa places himself decisively at odds with Marx. Implicitly, this procedure denies that labour is a 'necessary' input to production in an economy based on generalized commodity production and oriented toward profit-maximization. The

significance of labour and of labour's income, the wage, is reduced to its
role in limiting capital's 'share' of the surplus within the realm of distribution. By definition, the role of labour *in creating surplus value* is
denied. Again, the problem with this is *not* that in all conceivable production systems or economies living labour is indispensable to the creation of a physical surplus; the problem is that Sraffa's physical surplus
can be and is expressed in terms of production prices divisible into profits and wages, and is therefore constitutive of a 'uniform rate of profit.'
And, once again, this can only mean that Sraffa's physical surplus par-
takes of a *capitalist* social form. Hence, Sraffa moves *directly* from a
surplus conceived as a physical aggregation to a 'price-form' (profits and
wages), while effectively denying the *necessary* role of social labour in
mediating this transformation.

As we shall soon see, the neo-Ricardians regard this direct movement
as a positive advantage of Sraffa's system. But from Marx's standpoint,
whatever 'technical' advantage is gained in this way is more than offset
by the enormously misleading implications of treating price as a direct
and immediate external form of 'physical products' rather than as the
money-form of the social labour that enters into their production. To put
the matter bluntly, the assumption built into Sraffa's system is that one
can speak of prices, profits, and wages without reference to social labour,
whereas in Marx's view these phenomena could have no existence whatsoever except in an economy founded upon the class appropriation of
surplus labour.

These fetishistic features of Sraffa's system are, of course, just as consistent with neoclassical notions as they are inconsistent with Marx's
conceptions. Arguably, Sraffa can be excused for employing them as part
of an 'internal critique' of the neoclassical system; but there would seem
to be altogether less justification for regarding his models as a ready-
made basis for an 'internal critique' of Marx's theory. And yet this is
precisely the way many neo-Ricardians have treated it.

4 Although attempts have been made by some neo-Ricardians (notably
Hodgson) to develop a theory of exploitation consistent with Sraffa's
system, the phenomenon of exploitation really does not belong to a
world in which commodities are produced by 'things.' It is therefore
strictly incorrect to state that in Sraffa's system the phenomenon of
exploitation belongs to the sphere of distribution; the *most* that one can
say is that *if* exploitation occurs in Sraffa's system, it can only occur
externally to production. This *follows* from the fact that living labour is
in no sense an essential ingredient of Sraffa's system and from the fact

that Marx's 'labour-power' is *not* among the commodities that appear as means of producing other commodities. Accordingly, the production of the surplus is in no way conceived as a result of exploitation.

5 For Sraffa, a surplus-generating economic system is one experiencing what Marx would have called 'expanded reproduction.' But for Marx the existence of a surplus must be understood in social as well as physical terms. Expanded reproduction can occur with or without exploitation; but, under capitalism, a surplus product can only result from the *coercive* extraction of *surplus labour* within the sphere of production. Furthermore, the appropriation of surplus-labour under capitalism, as a market economy, must take the form of the appropriation of *surplus-value* as realized profit. None of this is captured in Sraffa's system, but none of it becomes 'redundant' or 'inessential' on this account either.

In light of these divergencies between Marx and Sraffa, it is quite remarkable that the once-orthodox Marxist economist Ronald Meek could have concluded a discussion of Sraffa in the following way:

Our Sraffa-type sequence of models does essentially the same set of jobs which the Marxian labour theory was designed to do; it starts, as Marx's system did, with a 'prior concrete magnitude' which limits the level of class incomes; it is based on the same view about the order and direction of determination of the variables as Marx's was; it is just as well suited to the application of a 'logical-historical' method of approach; and it has the great additional advantage that it contains a built-in solution of the 'transformation problem.' (n.d.: xlii)

The idea that Sraffa's system 'contains a built-in solution of the "transformation problem"' certainly explains much of its appeal to Marxists who had grown exasperated with this issue. However, it should be clearly understood that Sraffa does not furnish a solution to Marx's transformation problem except by supposedly demonstrating that value and surplus-value can be ignored, or treated as 'redundant,' in the derivation of prices of production and profits from 'physical data.'

Ian Steedman's 'Sraffa-Based' Critique of Marx

The starting-point of Steedman's study is the traditional one: the transformation problem. His handling of this issue is, however, far from traditional. After reaffirming the standard Bortkiewiczian criticism of Marx's transformation procedure (that Marx failed to transform the prices of inputs), Steedman presses a somewhat different criticism: that Marx's solution of the transformation problem 'is internally incoherent, even when input prices are transformed' (1981: 35). This assertion rests upon what is a central proposition of Steedman's critique, namely that Marx's value magnitudes are 'redundant,' as well as 'irrelevant' to the degree that they deviate from their price correlatives.

Steedman correctly argues that in Marx's own theory the value rate of profit and the money rate of profit must diverge once prices diverge from values. But if this is so, the question then becomes, *which* of these 'distinct' rates of profit is the 'relevant' one? It is no good to say that they have relevance at 'different levels.' For Steedman, only the money-rate of profit can affect the concrete microeconomic decisions of real capitalists, and therefore only the money rate will influence capital mobility, evince a tendency to equalize, and constitute a uniform rate of profit. Consequently, it is the uniform *money* rate of profit that is the *significant* rate of profit in capitalism.

Steedman's argument requires response at two levels. First, while Steedman accepts the notion that an 'abstraction' (the uniform rate of profit) can have a real bearing on the business decisions of capitalists, he is insistent that only the uniform money rate will exercise this influence. But the problem is that capitalists do not in fact calculate either a money or a value rate of profit, at least not on a 'uniform' basis. The uniform rate of profit can only be a *tendential* phenomenon that exerts its influence not as a calculable guide to wise microeconomic investment decisions, but as a limiting factor – a 'parametric determinant' – on the amount of profit a given capital can earn. Second, it can be shown that Steedman's understanding of the relationship between the value and money rates of profit is problematic. Steedman specifies this relationship in a way that owes much more to Ricardo than it does to Marx, since it is predicated on a rather crude understanding of value as *embodied* labour.

The real core of Steedman's book, however, is not his revelation of the supposed 'inconsistency' or 'incoherence' of Marx's value-price transformation. Rather, it is his thesis that Marx's value magnitude analysis is *redundant* to the Sraffian method of deriving price phenomena from physical factors and that it cannot meet the challenge posed by the problem of 'joint production' – a problem that Sraffa exploited to much effect in his critique of neoclassical capital theory.

It is unnecessary to reproduce Steedman's own model in detail. Suffice it to say that Steedman's Sraffa-like 'physical' depiction of a simple capitalist economy is rendered in terms of 'units' of labour and of raw materials like iron, gold, and corn, and that this 'physical data' is the basis for specifying

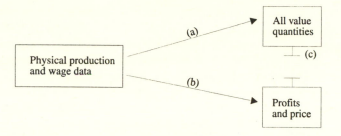

Figure 1 Steedman's illustration of the 'redundancy' of values

the same economy in terms of value (by which Steedman means the 'socially necessary labour' directly and indirectly consumed in production). The upshot is that 'from knowledge of the physical conditions of production and the real wage, one can determine values, the value of labour power and surplus-value,' as well as such quantitative relationships as the rate of surplus-value (Steedman 1981: 41-2).

Steedman's argument may be summarized as follows. The physical data of an economy determines both the value magnitudes of Marx's analysis and the price magnitudes that find phenomenal expression. But since value magnitudes are generally inconsistent with price magnitudes (as the debate around the transformation problem has presumably conclusively established), calculation in value terms is redundant and irrelevant. One does not *need* to specify economic phenomena in value terms in order to derive (calculate) prices and profits. This is illustrated by figure 1, which Steedman comments on as follows:

The solid arrow labelled (a) shows that from the physical data all the value quantities can be explained ... Arrow (b) shows that from the same data one can explain profits and prices, etc. ... The dashed and 'blocked off' arrow (c) represents the fact that one cannot, in general, explain profits and prices from value quantities as set out in the usual value schema, that S/(C + V) is not the rate of profit, etc. We thus have to picture our theoretical structure as having a 'fork-like' character, with a 'value prong' arrow (a), and a 'profit-price prong', arrow (b). *There is*, in general, *no way from one prong to the other.* (1981: 49)

Although Steedman provides no corresponding figure to represent what he understands to be Marx's 'theoretical structure,' it seems likely that figure 2 captures the essence of Marx's model of price and profit determination on

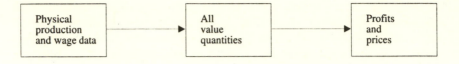

Figure 2 An illustraion of Steedman's account of Marx's theory

Steedman's view. At this point we need only note that much of the cogency of Steedman's charge of 'redundancy' depends on the adequacy of the account of Marx's theory represented by this figure.

The *fundamentals* of Steedman's critique are set out above, and all refinements to it rest upon a common set of theoretical assumptions. This is important because, as Steedman himself insists, if one wishes to contest what is essentially an 'argument in logic,' one must do so 'either by finding a logical flaw in the argument or by rejecting explicitly and coherently one or more of the assumptions upon which it is based' (1981: 49).

The second pillar of Steedman's critique of Marx concerns the compatibility of Marx's theory of value with the 'real-world' problem of 'joint production.' Steedman tries to show that in cases where some production processes result in joint products (for instance, mutton and wool), commodity values, calculated as quantities of embodied labour-time, may well be indeterminate. Further, Steedman suggests that when values *are* determinable such cases can give rise to situations in which *negative* values and *negative* surplus-value appear alongside positive prices and a positive rate of profit. Both of these claims, particularly the latter one, appear to strike a fatal blow to the analytic integrity of a labour-value theory of price and profit determination.

Further consideration of Steedman's argument can be pursued later in connection with the responses that it has provoked.

The Neo-Ricardian Challenge to Marx in Perspective

Many years have now passed since the original publication of Steedman's *Marx After Sraffa*. Contrary to the expectation of many of its enthusiasts, however, this work failed in its stated purposes – to end the debate surrounding Marx's value-magnitude analysis, and to redirect the energies of Marxists to the construction of a new materialist political economy on a post-Sraffian basis. It did, however, mark the culmination of a particular stage of the contemporary value controversy by clearly establishing the full implications of adopting Sraffa's 'physical magnitudes' approach. There was henceforth no longer a question of 'reconciling' Sraffa and Marx, or of 'reading' Sraffa as 'complementary' to Marx; the question became one of *choosing* between them. Whether or not Steedman's critique of Marx holds up, it was his great achievement to have sharpened the lines of demarcation within the value controversy and forced its participants to more rigorously clarify their positions.

While Steedman's critique had the appearance of originality, it was largely an extremely able and concise rehearsal of old complaints about Marx's treatment of a number of issues – the value-price transformation, the reduction of heterogeneous to simple labour, and so forth – as seen through the eyes of a follower of Sraffa. Despite his avowal that he was aware of the 'qualitative' or 'value-form' aspects of Marx's theory, Steedman never allowed his appreciation of them to influence – he might say 'confuse' – his portrayal of Marx's analysis in its quantitative dimensions. Steedman's Marx is theoretically and methodologically very close to Ricardo, a Marx whose analysis in the third volume of *Capital* appears, at best, as unrelated to his analysis in the first volume.

This appraisal raises an important consideration pertaining to the 'periodization' of the controversy. Up to the mid-1970s, students of Marx's *Capital* tended to focus their attention on *either* the 'value-form' analysis of *Capital I* or the 'value-magnitude' analysis of *Capital III*. Neo-Ricardians like Steedman, Hodgson, Lippi, and others tended to engage a range of issues in Marxist political economy as these had been represented by the Ricardian-Marxist orthodoxy. And what the orthodox tradition had in common with neo-Ricardianism was a preoccupation with value-magnitude analysis: with the mathematical quantification and modelling of Marx's value categories with a view to addressing several narrowly conceived 'economic' problems (that is, problems that mainstream economists would recognize as germane to their 'positive' analytical agenda). Most of the Marxist economists who distanced themselves from the old orthodoxy and neo-Ricardianism were otherwise occupied – primarily with the qualitative aspects of Marx's theory as developed in the value-form analyses of *Capital I*.

Between these two currents of 'Marxian political economy' there was little real communication. As Ben Fine has aptly observed: 'Each strand subscribed to a different method, each addressed a different problem, making little if any contribution to that of the other side, and each engaged on textual terrains that were not only distinct but which were also separated by the vast majority of both Volumes I and II of *Capital*. At the same time, the situation was described as a dialogue of the deaf (even if it was hardly a dialogue of the dumb)' (1986: 7). This general configuration of theoretical interests and analytical partisanship appeared to shift with the successive contributions of Yaffe (1975), Gerstein (1976/1986) and Shaikh (1977) to the discussion of the value-price transformation. Despite their differences, each of these pieces was characterized by an attempt to engage the value-magnitude issues on the basis of a 'truer' appreciation of Marx's concept of value than that recapitulated in Steedman's notion of value as 'embodied socially-necessary labour time.'

Neo-Orthodoxy and the Rediscovery of the Value-Form

Although the modern neo-orthodox school took shape in part as a *reaction to* the post-Sraffian critique of Marx, it is important to recognize that it was also inspired by a desire to transcend the 'Ricardian' reading of Marx popularized by such prominent Marxist economists as Dobb, Meek, and Sweezy. From its earliest formative days, the school has taken a quite consistent stand with respect to what has traditionally been the central issue of the value controversy: Marx's value-price transformation. The neo-orthodox tack on this matter has been to (a) deny that this is a real 'problem' for Marx's overall theoretical structure, once this is *properly* understood, and (b) affirm the 'correctness' of Ricardian or neo-Ricardian criticisms of the orthodox understanding of Marx's handling of the transformation of values into prices of production. Thus, Ira Gerstein (1986/1976), in a seminal neo-orthodox article, concedes that 'the point made by Bortkiewicz [concerning the transformation of inputs] is valid (although his conclusions from it are not) and must be confronted' (1986: 72), while Diane Elson, writing in a later stage of the controversy, allows that 'there is no doubt that within its own terms [Steedman's] critique of the theory of value, as an explanation of equilibrium prices in terms of labour quantities, is quite correct' (1979: 121).

Concessions of this sort may seem to be an odd way to defend Marx's theory of value, but they need to be understood as one aspect of the neo-orthodox school's attempt to *redefine* the central issue of the value controversy. In this respect, the neo-orthodox project has been to challenge the notion that Marx subscribed to a Ricardo-style theory of value as *embodied labour* and to show that Marx's concept of abstract labour is inconsistent with any such theory. From this standpoint, the traditional debates surrounding the 'transformation problem' can be dismissed as substantially irrelevant to any development within Marx's theory of value and as germane only to those trapped within the (mistaken) framework of an embodied-labour theory of value.

The most distinctive features of the neo-orthodox approach to the theory of value may be disclosed by examining three interconnected sets of questions: the neo-orthodox critique of the old (Ricardian-Marxist) orthodoxy; the neo-orthodox opposition of abstract to embodied labour; and the neo-orthodox response to neo-Ricardianism.

Critique of the Old Orthodoxy

The period 1972–3 was something of a turning-point for the modern value controversy. It saw the publication in English of Rubin's *Essays on Marx's Theory of Value* for the first time, as well as the appearance of Geoffrey Pilling's seminal article on 'The Law of Value in Ricardo and Marx' (1972/ 1986). As we have already noted, Rubin's work constituted an early attempt to specify the relationship between Marx's theory of value and the fundamental principles of historical materialism. Pilling's aim was similar, if more narrowly focused: to distinguish clearly Marx's and Ricardo's respective problematics while demonstrating that many influential Marxist economists had developed an unacknowledged Ricardian appreciation of Marx's work. Maurice Dobb was a case in point. According to Pilling, Dobb's view that 'Marxism is superior in an "operational" sense in that "labour" provides ... a constant to which all the other entities in his model can be reduced' betrayed an elementary misunderstanding of Marx. Not only was Marx's method inconsistent with the notion of 'model-building,' it was not *reductionist* in the way suggested by Dobb: 'The task of Marx's critique of political economy was *not* one that involved him finding a "constant" in terms of which everything could be quantified but of establishing the laws of mediation through which the "essence" of phenomena manifested itself as "appearance" ' (1986: 21).

Ricardo had regarded labour as a 'numeraire' for the measurement of social wealth (including the value of individual commodities). But, says Pilling, Marx's theory of value was guided by a quite different method and purpose: All Ricardo's weaknesses reflect [an] empiricism and resolve themselves into this: that while he starts correctly from the law of value he attempts *immediately* to deal with all the phenomena which conflict with this law ... What is lacking in [Ricardo's] *Principles* is any treatment of the process of *mediation* by which the 'forms of appearance' in bourgeois society are connected to the source of their origin, the law of value' (1986: 30–1). This 'process of mediation,' in Marx's view, served both to express and obscure the relationship between commodity-producing labour and the price structure constituting the immediate regulating mechanism of economic reproduction.

Gerstein further concretized a distinctive theme of the emerging neo-orthodox school by noting that the old orthodoxy had tended to identify the value of a commodity with the *concrete* labour producing the commodity, thereby failing to see the real significance of Marx's concept of 'abstract labour.' While 'vulgar Marxists' entertained Ricardian preoccupations, Marx himself regarded the value-creating aspect of labour as abstract and 'emphasizes that [abstract labour] has a purely social reality' (1986: 51). This point leads directly to a contrast with Ricardo's 'labour theory of price': 'The reason that Marx's theory of value is not a theory of price is that there is no way to reduce observable concrete labour to social abstract labour in advance, outside of the market which actually effects the reduction' (52). As for the *measurement* of value, this cannot be done by analysing the conditions of production, that is, through a reckoning of units of socially necessary labour-time. Abstract labour, as the substance of value, 'can be "measured" only when it takes the independent form of money, a form that poses it against the bodily form of the commodity in which it is embodied' (53).

Gerstein's emphasis on the money-form as the only possible measure of abstract labour and value is a recurring theme of the neo-orthodox school – but his reference to the abstract labour 'embodied' in commodities is not. Increasingly, neo-orthodox theorists have argued that the concept of abstract labour should be regarded as wholly incompatible with *any* 'embodied-labour' theory of value.

Abstract Labour versus Embodied Labour

The starting-point of the neo-orthodox attempt to contrapose 'abstract labour' and 'embodied labour' is a critical re-examination of Marx's own handling of the idea of 'value-creating labour.' Neo-orthodox theorists perceive at best an equivocation and at worst a contradiction in Marx's argument. Much of the problem hinges on the following passage from *Capital I*: 'On the one hand, all labour is an expenditure of human labour-power, in the physiological sense, and it is in this quality of being equal, or abstract, human labour that it forms the value of commodities. On the other hand, all labour is an expenditure of human labour-power in a particular form and with a definite aim, and it is in this quality of being concrete useful labour that it produces use-values' (1977: 137). Elsewhere in his discussion of the dual character of commodity-producing labour, Marx refers to concrete or 'useful' labours as 'qualitatively different productive activities' that share the quality of being 'a productive expenditure of human brains, muscles, nerves, hands, etc.,' thereby implying that *this* is what is meant by 'human labour in general' (134–5).

Such a 'physiological' conception of abstract labour appears, however, to be at odds with Marx's insistence (at the beginning of his discussion of the value-form) that 'not an atom of matter enters into the objectivity of commodities as values' (1977: 138). Indeed, Marx goes on to assert that 'commodities possess an objective character as values only in so far as they are all expressions of an identical social substance, human labour, that their objective character as values is therefore purely social' (138–9).

It is important to note that neo-orthodox theorists have tended to associate a 'physiological expenditure of human labour' *exclusively* with 'concrete labour.' In their view, the actual expenditure of labour on a commodity can *only* bear on that commodity's concrete characteristics as a use-value. In contradistinction, abstract labour is creative of 'social values,' but not of physical use-values. Accordingly, concrete labour can find 'embodiment' within a commodity while abstract labour cannot. One can speak of 'embodied concrete labour' but not of 'embodied abstract labour.'

The essential problem with the notion of embodied abstract labour has been well stated by the fundamentalist theorist Anwar Shaikh: 'It is clear in Marx ... that it is not the historical cost of a commodity in labor time, but rather its current cost of reproduction, which determines the magnitude of a commodity's Value. As such, it is not a question of the labor-time "embodied" in a commodity but of the social cost which the current production of the commodity entails' (1977: 113). For this reason Shaikh prefers to use the expression 'abstract labour represented' rather than Marx's 'abstract labour embodied' – even though Marx makes it sufficiently clear that the term 'embodied' should not be taken literally. Does all this boil down then to an arid terminological dispute? The answer is probably yes – even though both neo-orthodox and fundamentalist theorists are right to insist that Marx's notion of 'embodied abstract labour' is theoretically imprecise and potentially misleading. However, when Shaikh refers to the 'abstract labour *time*' required for the production of a given output, he sides with Marx on a substantive theoretical point that many neo-orthodox theorists appear perplexed by: the idea that value is created *entirely* within the sphere of production through the expenditure of labour that, under conditions of commodity production, is *both* abstract and concrete.

Let us consider the influential neo-orthodox argument of Himmelweit and Mohun:

The process of the theoretical discovery of abstract labour is not merely a process of mental generalization, but has a real existence in the reality of the exchange process. The equalization of products of labour on the market occurs every day, standardized by money, the universal equivalent of value. Since individuals alienate their products as commodities in exchange, so too do they alienate the labour producing those commodities. Abstract labour is a real activity, a social reality, whereby individuals alienate their labour-power from themselves. (1981: 235)

Several points in this passage deserve highlighting. First, Himmelweit and Mohun emphasize that 'abstract labour' refers to a *real activity* inserted within a specific socio-historical dimension – an activity pertaining to production for exchange. Second, and more problematically, the real activity to which abstract labour refers does not appear as an activity grounded in production, but appears to involve market exchange at least as much as it involves the actual production of commodities. The 'real abstraction' underlying abstract labour is identified with the activities of individuals in *alienating* 'their products as commodities in exchange.' Accordingly, 'abstract labour' has a purely 'social' existence. It is not conceived as an aspect of *productive* labour – the other aspect being the *concrete* one. Instead, it is conceived as a 'social reality' springing from the act of commodity exchange – or, at least, from the *interaction* of production and exchange.

Himmelweit and Mohun are certainly correct to suggest that Marx's concept of abstract labour is a real abstraction, while the Ricardian notion of commensurable embodied concrete labour is an 'anomalous assumption.' However, by following Rubin in identifying a 'physiological expenditure of labour' entirely with the concrete aspect of labour, they effectively sever the concept of abstract labour from its *general* basis in the production of commodities. Once this is done, there is a strong tendency to associate concrete labour with the production process and abstract labour with the exchange process. Since abstract labour is conceived as both the creator and the substance of value, such reasoning can only attenuate the proposition basic to Marx's theory that value is *created* in production.

Yet one does not need to deny that values are 'purely social' or that 'not an atom of matter enters into the objectivity of commodities as values' in order to affirm that a 'physiological' expenditure of human labour is value-creating *provided* that this expenditure is subject to a process of real abstraction, *occurring in production* even though framed and conditioned by exchange. It is precisely *because* exchange effects a process of 'equalization of products of labour on the market' (that is, involves a real abstraction) that production oriented toward exchange must take account of the fact that 'physiological labour' is both utility-shaping and value-creating – that is, both concrete and abstract at one and the same time. To deny this is to invite De Vroey's peculiar thesis that value is created 'not in production but at the articulation of production and circulation' (1981: 173) – a notion replete with circular reasoning and requiring the most robust of mental gymnastics.

The Transformation Problem and the Response to the Neo-Ricardians

Himmelweit and Mohun's conception of abstract labour represents *one possible* direction of a value-form analysis: one that sublates the problem of the 'magnitude of value' by exalting money as the only possible measure of abstract labour. No doubt, the appeal of this approach is amplified by the apparent ease with which its exponents are able to stave off the neo-Ricardian assault on Marx's labour-value formulation. In this way, the 'value-form analysis' – or what Diane Elson calls the 'value theory of labour' – becomes a refuge from the formidable theoretical challenge of articulating the qualitative and the quantitative aspects of Marx's value theory.

The problem with this approach is that once it is accepted that 'abstract associated labour has no substantial existence apart from the value form, money' (Eldred 1984: 136), then commodity values appear to be severed entirely from any determination in the conditions of their production, and the way is paved for an effective *identification* of value and price. This result draws the neo-orthodox theorist as close to neoclassicism as the embodied-labour concept draws the old orthodoxy to Ricardianism and neo-Ricardianism. The ultimate 'banality' of a 'value theory of labour' that denies the exclusive role of productive labour in the creation of *values* (conceived as distinct from and regulative of production and market prices) is well stated by Gleicher (1985: 152): 'When stripped of its Hegelian garb, the [value theory of labour] reduces to the assertion ... that the allocation of labour between industries is determined in the context of generalized commodity circulation by the formation of market prices. As such, however, neither the Sraffian, classical Marxist or for that matter neo-classical theorists would deny the validity of this assertion.'

In Gleicher's view, the valid insights of the 'value-form analysis' or of a 'value theory of labour' can be put to good use only if they are presented in a fashion that is consistent with Marx's 'labour theory of value.' Yet it is just this theory that many neo-orthodox theorists abandon in their haste to avoid a confrontation with the neo-Ricardians on the traditional terrain of the value-magnitude analysis.

Let us examine in turn the responses given by the neo-orthodox school to the transformation problem and to the Steedman critique of Marx.

Gerstein approaches the transformation problem as follows: 'The theory of value belongs to the level of production, considered in abstraction, and the general rate of profit to the level of the complex unity of production and circulation. The question then is not how to reconcile the two sides of a contradiction, but how to move or 'transform' from one level of analysis to another' (1986: 67). And further: 'The transformation from Volume I to

Volume III is not a transformation from value to price, but from value and price considered purely from the point of view of production to value and price as modified by circulation and capitalist competition' (68).

Gerstein's notion that not only the forms of value but values themselves are 'modified' by circulation and competition should be especially noted since it anticipates the *indeterminacy* of the neo-orthodox school's treatment of the *source* of value. However, Gerstein also addresses the traditional debates surrounding the transformation problem *on the basis* of the form-analytic insights. In other words, he wrestles with the transformation problem and seeks to 'solve' it in a way consistent with 'forms-analysis' – *while also providing himself with an escape route from the value-magnitude analysis.*

Appearing after the publication of Steedman's *Marx After Sraffa*, the approach of Himmelweit and Mohun is less equivocal. They locate the central problem in Marx's solution to the transformation problem in his notion of surplus-value *redistribution*:

Surplus-value is not redistributed between capitals so as to equalize the rate of profit, because there is no state *from* which this *re*distribution occurs. At no stage in the circuit of capital is surplus-value attributed to capitals in proportion to the labour-power they consume. A parable of the sale of the commodity leading to a redistribution until each capital's share of surplus-value is proportional to the total capital advanced is as misleading as parables of redistribution through history. Redistribution is meaningful only if one can specify a state from which it occurs and a state prevailing after the redistribution. (1981: 240–1).

Once the notion of surplus-value redistribution is dropped, then the traditional frame of reference for discussion of the transformation problem is itself transformed. No longer is there a question of developing a mathematical model that assumes a process of *re*distribution (as all the traditional 'solutions' and 'corrections' do); rather the question becomes one of recognizing the real contradictions of capitalism and giving them a theoretical reflection: 'The transformation ''problem'' is therefore a necessary result of the contradictory nature of capitalist production relations: it is a contradiction in reality, and not at all a problem with Marx's theory, which simply conceptualizes this reality' (ibid. 241). *Not* a problem, in other words, for the value-form analysis of *Capital I*, even if it *is* a problem for Marx's attempt to solve the Ricardian dilemma of reconciling an embodied-labour theory of value with the process of profit-rate equalization! Once again, if one *begins* with the premiss that value is formed in exchange and is only vaguely related to the activity of labour within the sphere of production, then one does not need to concern oneself with value transfers or redistributions amongst different firms or branches of production. The transformation issue becomes a purely 'qualitative' problem of specifying the ways in which the value-form is influenced by circulation and capitalist competition: 'Competition distributes aggregate surplus-value according to total capital advanced, but there is no *re*distribution' (248).

It is curious that Himmelweit and Mohun speak at one point of the need to conceive 'the value *produced in production* first in abstraction from competition, and second while allowing for the effects of competition' (ibid. 248). For if value is 'produced in production,' it must be produced at particular sites and in definite magnitudes. This would seem to mandate the introduction of some notion of 'redistribution' in order to explain the process whereby particular capitals are able to 'realize' values that have been produced by *other* capitals. By rejecting the notion of redistribution, Himmelweit and Mohun are forced to either adopt a 'parable' according to which capitals 'realize' only those values that they have produced (which really negates the role of competition and profit-rate equalization) or embrace the idea that values are 'produced in production' but 'formed' (in the sense of 'quantitatively determined') in exchange. We already know, of course, that the latter is the real tendency of the neo-orthodox school. And we also know that such a position can only be construed as antithetical to the theoretical postulates that Marx was trying to *sustain* with his transformation procedure, in particular the idea that new value is quantitatively determined by the application of living labour in production. This returns us to an earlier point: that the neo-orthodox school's handling of the transformation problem reflects a typically neoclassical preoccupation with the value of *individual* commodities (that is, with the metamorphoses of the value-form as these pertain to microeconomic exchange relations).

It is in light of all this that Himmelweit and Mohun's response to Steedman's post-Sraffian critique of Marx should be approached. With respect to Steedman's argument regarding the 'redundancy' of values, Himmelweit and Mohun concede the point so long as 'values' are understood in terms of an 'embodied-labour' concept. The significance of value as a theoretical category does not relate to its utility in calculating what is more accurately calculated on the basis of physical data and a specified wage rate. Rather it concerns the 'specification of what is produced (the composition of output) and how (the technical co-efficients of production),' in relation to 'the way in which the labour process is organized and from the way in which production, as a social activity through the market's universal commensuration of what is produced, determines both what is produced and how it is produced' (ibid. 255).

Himmelweit and Mohun also concede that Steedman is right to argue that the 'established methods of calculating values' lead to indeterminate or negative results in some cases. But again, these results are deemed relevant only to the critique of an *embodied-labour* concept of value. Joint production and similar 'anomalous' cases appear as real contradictions because the law of value 'operates through the distorted form of capitalist competition' and 'the capital that set in motion some production processes which are "wasteful" of social labour may still be validated by that competition, and hence produce a portion of the total surplus-value' (ibid.: 262–3).

Many of the 'qualitative' considerations adduced by Himmelweit and Mohun in their responses to Steedman are valid and important. But, in advancing these considerations, they offer up as a kind of sacrificial lamb to neo-Ricardianism all of the quantitative elements in Marx's value theory that endow it with deterministic force. Moreover, the excision of these elements is accomplished by equivocating on the key question of the relationship between production and exchange within Marx's theory, as well as by drawing close to the neoclassical conception of an effectively autonomous role for market exchange in the determination of both value and price. Not only does this approach render a value-magnitude analysis impossible; it also calls into question the primacy of production in a social-ontological sense. Hence, where the old orthodoxy subordinated the value-form to the value-magnitude analysis, the neo-orthodox theorists have done precisely the reverse; the only continuity is in the *dissociation* of the 'quantitative' and 'qualitative' aspects of Marx's theory of value.

An important consequence of the neo-orthodox preoccupation with the 'form of value' over the 'magnitude of value' is a tendency to go beyond the correct perception that 'interaction' occurs between production and the other moments of economic reproduction (circulation, exchange, consumption) to the conclusion that, under capitalism, exchange emerges as the *predominant* moment. Such an approach is not at all the same as saying that market exchange is the *social form* of a commodity-producing economy (Rubin 1973). Indeed, by implicitly rejecting the social-ontological primacy of *production*, it involves a complete evacuation of Marx's problematic and a major concession to neoclassical marginalism as well as neo-Ricardianism. In fact, through its 'qualitative' focus on microeconomic exchange relations, the neo-orthodox school draws dangerously close to the conventional economic identification of value and price. This drift is particularly evident in statements by Gerstein and De Vroey quoted above, but the logic of such an identification is also evident in the work of Elson, Eldred, and Himmelweit and Mohun, despite occasional references to 'value produced in production' and the like. In this connection, Alain Lipietz's balance sheet of the French neo-orthodox experience should be noted: the French school's 'failure to deal with the problem of [the] magnitude [of value] had an unexpected result: they abandoned the pole of substance and slipped irresistibly towards a purely formal and subjectivist theory of value' (1985: 158).

The 'autonomous role' of exchange in modifying or forming values appears much less autonomous once the focus of analysis shifts from the value formation of discrete commodities (whose values must be brought into correspondence with the values of similar commodities in the market) to the mechanisms of value creation conceived from the ontologically fundamental standpoint of the material-production process, from whence *all* commodities emerge and where *total value* is defined.

Fundamentalist Value Theory

Like the neo-orthodox school, the fundamentalist value theorists recognize that the old orthodoxy issued in the dead-end of neo-Ricardianism because of its failure to come to terms with the profound theoretical and methodological differences between Marx's and Ricardo's respective legacies. But unlike that school, the fundamentalists have sought to develop a response to the neo-Ricardians capable of preserving and further developing the value-magnitude analysis – an analysis that they regard as indispensable to a scientific investigation of the 'laws of motion' of the capitalist mode of production.

In what follows we will be concerned with (a) fundamentalist approaches to the transformation problem; (b) the fundamentalist critique of neo-Ricardianism; and (c) fundamentalist responses to the 'joint-production' and 'choice of technique' arguments. Throughout we will be particularly concerned with the contributions of Anwar Shaikh, perhaps the most consistently interesting and provocative of the fundamentalist theorists.

Fundamentalist Approaches to the Transformation Problem

As we have seen, the Bortkiewicz-Sweezy criticism of Marx's transformation procedure is that Marx failed to 'transform' the inputs along with the outputs in his transformation model. Furthermore it is alleged that Marx was *aware* of this 'logical inconsistency,' as the following passage from his discussion of prices of production appears to show:

It was originally assumed that the cost price of a commodity equalled the *value* of the commodities consumed in its production. But for the buyer of a commodity, it is the price of production that constitutes its cost price, and can thus enter into forming the price of another commodity. As the price of production can diverge from its value, so the cost price of a commodity, in which the price of production of other commodities is involved, can also stand above or below the portion of its total value that is formed by *the value of the means of production going* into it. It is necessary to bear in mind too that if the cost price of a commodity is equated with *the value of the means of production* used up in producing it, it is always possible to go wrong. (1981b: 264–5; emphasis added)

When Marx states that 'it is always possible to go wrong' when cost price is equated with the value of the *means of production* consumed, it would seem that he is contradicting what he says in his 'transformation formula,' according to which the capitalist 'recovers money in proportion to the value of the *capital* consumed' (ibid.: 259).

A proto-fundamentalist attempt to dispute the Bortkiewicz-Sweezy contention of a 'logical inconsistency' in Marx's transformation procedure was carried out as early as 1963 by Shane Mage. The starting-point of Mage's response to this Ricardian criticism is that 'the value of *the means of production* consumed' and 'the value of the *capital* consumed' are by no means interchangeable formulations. It is a *fetishistic* error to equate capital – including constant capital – with physical things, that is, with means of production. It *follows* from this that the value of the *capital* consumed in production is not necessarily the same as the value of the means of production consumed. Moreover, this observation seems to be supported by what Marx says immediately following the passage quoted above: 'The cost price of the commodity is a *given precondition* independent of his, the capitalist's production, while the result of his production is a commodity that contains surplus-value, and therefore an excess value over and above its cost price' (1981b: 265).

As a 'given precondition' the cost price of a given commodity input to a capitalist's production process should be regarded as a form of value that has *already* been subject to the transformation process. Since it is the *value of the capital* exchanged with input commodities that is consumed in production, and not just the physical commodities themselves, a value expression of cost price must take into account the status of means of production as commodities whose values are subject to transformation. In other words, input commodities have *already* been subject to the influence of the general rate of profit (and, for that matter, other sources of determination in the sphere of circulation) and have been purchased at a 'market price.' But this 'market price' corresponds to the *value* of the capital that has been exchanged with it for the purpose of consuming that input commodity in production. The market price of an input commodity finds a renewed *value* expression in the value of the money capital invested in its purchase. As Mage puts it: 'The difference between the value created by its production and its price of production has *already* been transferred to other capitalists through the average rate of profit ... Accordingly, in the Marxian formulas c + v + s and c + v + p, c and v are indeed value expressions: they express the value of the capital consumed' (1963: 243).

Referring to the same passages from Marx, Ernest Mandel makes a similar point: 'The extract cited does not imply that prices of production of inputs should be calculated within the same time-span as prices of production of outputs' (1981: 22–3). If this is the case, then it is not valid to assume that Marx anticipated, but ignored, the so-called 'feedback problem' that the Bortkiewicz method of 'simultaneous transformation' tries to meet. For Mandel, 'inputs in current cycles of production are *data*, which are given at the start of that cycle, and *do not have* a feedback effect on the equalization of the rates of profit in various branches of production during that cycle. It is sufficient to assume that they are likewise calculated in prices of production and not in values, but that these prices of production result from equalization of rates of profit during the *previous* cycle of production, for any inconsistency to disappear' (ibid.: 23). Operationally, Mandel's point has the same result as Mage's argument: inputs – whether conceived as values, prices of production, or market prices – should *not* be transformed *along with* outputs. Rather, the assumption should be made that these inputs have already been subject to a transformation process in a previous period.

Guglielmo Carchedi also arrives at this conclusion, basing himself upon a somewhat more complex line of argumentation: 'While c [the elements of constant capital] must be bought and sold at the same price, this price is at the same time its social value as an output ... of the previous period and its individual (but not embodied) value as an output of the present period' (1986a: 229).

Shaikh has attempted a 'form-theoretic' approach to the transformation problem from a different angle, arguing that Marx's transformation procedure does not literally concern the transformation of values into prices of production, but rather 'transforming one form-of-Value, direct prices, into another form, prices of production' (1977: 134). By 'direct prices' Shaikh means a money price equal to a commodity's value relative to the value of the unit of money; or, more simply put, a monetized expression of value that still allows the assumption that exchange occurs in proportion to the *value* of commodities. This conception has the merit of underlining that commodity-values have undergone a form change *before* they are subject to the transformation wrought by the equalization of profit rates. Unfortunately, this form change is systematically concealed in the traditional 'algebraic' attempts to find a 'correct solution' based upon simultaneous valuation of inputs and outputs. For this reason Shaikh eschews the use of linear equations in selecting a method with which to demonstrate Marx's own correct, if incomplete, procedure. Shaikh, building on an idea independently suggested by Morishima (1974), proposes an 'iterative' solution in which Marx's 'perfectly general' procedure can be extended (successively applied) to arrive at 'correct' prices of production.

What all of these approaches have in common is a desire to demonstrate that there is no inconsistency in Marx's transformation procedure – no 'error in logic.' But the problem is not simply one of understanding Marx's procedure/solution in its own terms, as important as this may be; it is *also* one of reconciling it with some notion of economic equilibrium. As we have seen, all the algebraic attempts to solve the problem on the basis of a model involving three departments of production have had to rely on arbitrarily selected 'invariance postulates' or 'normalization conditions' that are in general incompatible with one or the other of the aggregate equalities posited by Marx. Even Shaikh's non-linear iterative solution (which assumes the standard three-department model) does not allow for the simultaneous results: total values = total prices, and total surplus-value = total profit. The conclusion is plain: *neither* Marx's transformation procedure nor the alternative procedures based on the Bortkiewicz principle of simultaneous valuation can accommodate the two aggregate equalities without violating the conditions of simple reproduction.

In light of this, only two possibilities remain open to the fundamentalists: either to dispute the importance of reconciling the value-price transformation process with the presuppositions of simple reproduction, or to redefine 'what is at stake' in the transformation process itself. The first strategy has been most fully explored by Yaffe (1975) and Carchedi (1986a). The latter argues as follows:

[The reproduction] schemes concern themselves with 'the reconversion of one portion of the value of the product into capital and the passing of another portion into the individual consumption of the capitalist, as well as the working class' [Marx, *Capital II*]. In other words, these schemes concern themselves with the redistribution of the social product (in terms of use and exchange value) *after* that product has been realized through sale, in such a way that the *equilibrium* conditions of simple (or expanded) reproduction are met ... Both inputs and outputs are commodities whose value has already been produced and realized so that – obviously – a commodity must be sold (as output) and bought (as input) at the same price (market price). To consider constant and variable capital as inputs in an input-output sense means to have already left the transformation problem behind, to deal with *already realized* values. (1986a: 220–1)

The second fundamentalist strategy has been to call into question the *necessity* of sustaining *both* of the aggregate equalities. If the conservation of value through exchange is somehow built into the transformation procedure (by positing the value-price equality as a normal condition), then there is a problem in explaining how total profit can diverge from total surplus-value. Shaikh has offered a novel and rather convincing explanation for this process, which will be considered later in connection with his response to Steedman.

One other possible rejoinder to the traditional critiques of Marx's transformation procedure has been articulated recently. This involves the *abandonment* of the 'uniform rate of profit' concept. Strictly speaking, this is inconsistent with a 'fundamentalist' position, since it not only rejects the framework of Marx's critics, but of Marx himself. However, as the proponents of this position have sought to show, profit-rate uniformity plays a far less significant role in Marx's theoretical system than it does in neo-Ricardianism and neoclassicism. Indeed, for Marx, the uniform rate of profit is an abstract concept flowing from a *tendential* law – the equalization of profit rates – rather than a 'real condition.' We shall examine this line of argument more closely at the end of this section.

Shaikh's Critique of Neo-Ricardianism

The strength of the neo-Ricardian critique of Marx appears to reside in its logical rigour and mathematical precision. But neither logic nor mathematics is a substitute for good theory, and neither can yield reliable conclusions if the theoretical presuppositions of an argument are faulty. As we have seen, Steedman himself acknowledged this point in *Marx After Sraffa*, and this is precisely the basis of Shaikh's response to Steedman and neo-Ricardianism in general:

The analysis of Marx is, I claim, vastly superior in its overall structure to anything imaginable within the flat conceptual space of the neo-Ricardians. Indeed, it is their vaunted algebra, on which they base so many of their claims to rigor, that is in fact their greatest weakness. This is so, as we shall see, precisely because their algebra goes hand in hand with a series of concepts taken directly from what Marx calls vulgar economy: equilibrium, profit as *cost*, and worst of all, perfect competition and all that it entails. It is not the algebra but rather these concepts, whose apologetic and ideological roots are well known, that generate the basic conclusions. This will become immediately apparent when it is shown that exactly the same algebra generates very different conclusions, once it is 'asked' different questions. And these questions, in turn, are different exactly because the method and the system of concepts in Marx, his scientific analysis of the law of value, is so unlike that of vulgar economy. (1981: 268–9)

Shaikh begins with a lucid and concise presentation of his own interpretation of Marx's theory of value. Drawing upon Marx's famous letter of 1868 to Kugelmann, he shows that the foundation of Marx's theory is the historical-materialist thesis that *'labour-time is fundamental to the regulation of the reproduction of society*: the performance of labour produces both use-values and social relations; the performance of surplus labour reproduces both the surplus product and the class relation; and a particular distribution of the "social labour in definite proportions" results in the production of "the (specific) masses of products corresponding to the different needs" of society' (ibid.: 270). However, since capitalist production is based on generalized commodity production, 'the vast bulk of the products that constitute the material basis of social reproduction are produced without any direct connection to social needs' (ibid.). This means that production is directly for exchange and that the private independent labour processes making up the social division of labour need to be 'forcibly articulated' with one another. But it also means – and this is crucial to Shaikh's subsequent argument – that each of these private independent labour processes is 'dominated by the profit motive' (ibid.). What all this suggests is that these production processes are informed and animated by the knowledge that their commodities must 'measure up' to certain *social* standards if they are to be sold *at a profit*. This circumstance establishes a particular *relation* between production and exchange:

Exchange is the sphere in which the contradiction *internal to production itself*, the contradiction between private labour and the social division of labour, is made visible. It is here that each capitalist first gets the good or bad news, through the medium of prices and profits. But at the same time, because this contradiction is internal to the social division of labour itself, its resolution implies the *domination* of the outcome of exchange, of prices and profits, by social labour-time. The outcomes of exchange are 'the form in which this proportional distribution of labour asserts itself' [Marx to Kugelmann, 1868]. (ibid.: 271)

Shaikh does not deny the 'relatively autonomous' role of exchange in economic reproduction; indeed, it is precisely *because* exchange is the sphere in which the contradictions of commodity production are both 'exposed and resolved' (to quote Marx) that the process of exchange 'reacts back' upon the sphere of production and lends a particular form to the results of a given 'proportional distribution of labour.' However, Shaikh refuses to lose sight of the fundamental historical-materialist principle that what transpires in exchange *must be* regulated and dominated by the way in which social labour-time has been allocated in the sphere of production. This permits him to see 'abstract labour' – the substance of value – as the reflection in thought of 'a real social process': a process rooted not in exchange, as it appears to the neo-orthodox theorists, but rather in the conditions whereby commodities are produced for the purpose of sale and the realization of profit. Accordingly, abstract labour and value are, for Shaikh, the results of commodity *production*. Both are *created* through the real activity of producing commodities before they can enter into the realm of exchange. Once in exchange, of course, commodity-values must then be *realized* in money form. But this process of realization is *distinct* from the creation, production, or formation of values in much the same way that the sale of a commodity is conceptually distinct from its production.

By refusing to conflate the concepts of 'value production' and 'value realization' into a muddled notion of 'value formation' in the manner of the neo-orthodox school, Shaikh preserves a fundamental distinction that is apparently better understood by the neo-Ricardians than it is by the neo-orthodox theorists. This distinction concerns the measurement of value and abstract labour. For the neo-orthodox school *money* is the sole measure of abstract labour. But since money is incapable of measuring 'labour-time,' the 'abstract labour' that it measures is necessarily far removed from any concept of the socially necessary labour-time required for the reproduction of a given commodity. The process of exchange is given *full* autonomy to 'determine' the aliquot share of the 'total abstract labour' that is to be assigned (in some 'social accounting sense') to that commodity. While the structure of production might influence the exchange process in some measure, it is far from dominating it in the neo-orthodox account.

Shaikh *reinstates* the notion of 'socially necessary labour-time,' which is central to Ricardian and neo-Ricardian interpretations of Marx. At the same time, however, he links it to a concept of how commodities 'represent' value rather than 'embody' abstract socially necessary labour, while recognizing the importance of the 'value-form' to Marx's theory. For Shaikh, abstract labour (as the *substance* of value) serves to *link* the value-form and value-magnitude analyses and consequently is measurable in *two* senses: at the level of exchange or circulation, *money* appears as its sole measure and form

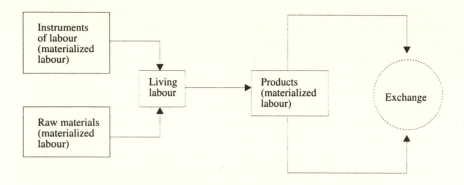

Figure 3 Marx's account of labour-value regulated reproduction according to Shaikh

of appearance; but at the level of production, the concept is conceptually apprehended/measured in terms of *labour-time*.

By denying that 'abstract labour' can be measured at the level of production in terms of 'socially necessary labour-time,' the neo-orthodox school renders consistent their theoretical revision according to which value is created, if only in some 'final' sense, in exchange. Shaikh and the fundamentalists overturn this revision by explaining how the 'form of value' and the 'magnitude of value' are contradictory in the sense that they are conceptual reflections of the real contradictions of commodity production: '*labour involved in the production of commodities produces value, while exchange merely realizes it in money-form.* It is only because of this that Marx can distinguish between the amounts of value and surplus-value created in commodity production, and the generally different amounts realized through exchange' (Shaikh 1981: 274).

Having summarized Shaikh's understanding of Marx's theory of value, we may now consider his critique of Steedman. As an accompaniment to the figures used in our earlier discussion of Steedman's argument concerning the redundancy and irrelevance of a value analysis, it is useful to consider Shaikh's diagrammatic conceptualization (in figure 3) of Marx's account of economic reproduction as determined by labour-values.

As can readily be seen by comparing figure 3 with figure 2 (on page 92), Shaikh's conceptualization of the role of labour-values in economic reproduction is very different from the one that Steedman imputes to Marx. Indeed, Shaikh's figure captures the essential points of both his understanding of Marx and his critique of Steedman's redundancy argument:

It is human productive activity, the actual performance of labour, that transforms 'inputs' into 'outputs,' and it is only when this labour is successful that we have any 'physical production data' at all. Moreover, if the labour process is a process of producing commodities, then it is one in which value is materialized in the form of use-values. Thus both 'inputs' and 'outputs' are the use-forms of materialized value, and we can then say that in the *real* process it is values that determine the 'physical production data' ... [I]t is *values that also determine prices*, in a double sense: prices are the forms taken by values in exchange, and the magnitudes of these values dominate and regulate the movements of their price forms. (ibid.: 280)

It can scarcely be said that Shaikh and Steedman have an equal claim to a correct interpretation of Marx's understanding of the process whereby labour-values dominate capitalist economic reproduction. For although he does not explicitly acknowledge it, Shaikh has provided a faithful diagrammatic representation of one phase of the *circuit of capital* as Marx defines it in the formula: $M - C ... P ... C' - M'$. By comparison, Steedman's representation of Marx amounts to little more than a crude caricature.

Shaikh next turns his attention to Steedman's argument that there is an irremediable *inconsistency* in Marx's analysis of prices of production and the transformation process. Shaikh starts by taking up from where his own treatment of the transformation problem had left off: 'The question is, given that circulation neither creates nor destroys values (assuming the whole product is sold), how is it that profits can differ from surplus-value?' (283). His answer is based on Marx's distinction between the circuit of capital and the circuit of capitalist *revenue*. It should be recalled that most of the attempts to develop a 'correct' scheme of transformation of values into prices of production have sought to do so without violating the 'equilibrium' conditions of reproduction. But such schemes are concerned exclusively with the circuit of capital, and they cannot by their nature take into account the effects of *value transfers* between the circuit of capital and the circuit of capitalist revenue.

To appreciate the significance of this distinction, consider first what happens when there is a value-price divergence with respect to means of production or workers' articles of consumption. In all such cases, the divergence can be explained in terms of a transfer of value within the circuit of capital: what one capitalist loses in capital values is gained by another, and in the end the value-transfers cancel one another out. Consider now what happens when there is a value-price divergence in capitalists' articles of consumption. Because the circuit of capitalist revenue originates in the circuit of capital, it might be expected that all of the value associated with this revenue will be 'fed back' into the circuit of capital once this revenue is expended by capitalists on articles of personal consumption. And indeed it will be. However, a 'social accounting' problem will appear as a result of any decline in the prices of such commodities relative to their value. Such price drops will entail an equivalent loss of profit in relation to surplus-value, *but* 'the loss in *capital-value* due to profits being below surplus-value ... appears as a gain in *revenue-value* to the capitalists who buy these articles of consumption' (285). The result is that the loss in capital-value is compensated by an equivalent gain elsewhere, but this compensation 'disappears from the purview of the circuit of capital and is therefore not "charged" ... against the fall in profit' (ibid.). Simply put, the capitalists get to have their cake – and to complain about *not* having it too!

The relevance of all this to the transformation problem is summarized by Shaikh as follows: 'It is this transfer of value between the circuit of capital and the circuit of revenue, through the process of exchange, that explains why price-value deviations can give rise to deviations between the sum of profits and the sum of surplus-values, *without violating the law of conservation of value through exchange*' (ibid.). This idea, which Shaikh notes is entirely absent from most Marxist discussions, finds support in the following passage from Marx: 'This phenomenon of the conversion of capital into revenue should be noted, because it creates the *illusion* that the amount of profit grows (or in the opposite case decreases) independently of the amount of surplus-value' (1978 3: 345). Or, as Shaikh puts it after some reflection on the form-of-value and the relative autonomy of the sphere of circulation: 'Profit ... depends not only on the mass of surplus-value but also on its specific mode of circulation' (1981: 286).

This argument is directly relevant to answering Steedman's general point that the money rate of profit, but not the value rate, has a significant bearing on the operations of a capitalist economy. Shaikh points out that such a conclusion is predicated on the correct observation that profit can diverge from surplus-value, but also on the *incorrect* notion that this divergence is not 'strictly limited.' Taking the concept of the relative autonomy of circulation from production as his starting-point, Shaikh demonstrates 'how value categories themselves provide the limits to the variations in their money-expressions' (ibid.). The value rate of profit is a 'significant' rate of profit in the capitalist economy because it provides an *axis* around which the money rate oscillates (just as value magnitudes are the 'centre of gravity' of production price magnitudes). Discrepancies arise between the value and money rates of profit as a result of a divergence between the mass of surplus-value and the mass of profit, a divergence determined by 'the extent to which the prices of capitalists' articles of consumption deviate from the values of these articles' and by 'the extent to which this surplus-value is consumed by capitalists as revenue' (286–7). None of this, however, vitiates the 'significance' of the value rate of profit; indeed, if anything, it *underscores* the importance of invoking the value rate of profit as a way of *demystifying* the money rate of profit.

The upshot of Shaikh's argument is as follows:

[In] the relatively autonomous mirror of circulation, the transformed rate of profit appears as a displaced image of the value rate of profit, essentially the same in determination but somewhat different in magnitude. The autonomy of the sphere of circulation is expressed in this displacement of magnitude; on the other hand, the limited nature of this autonomy manifests itself precisely through the fact that it is the structure of value categories (the pattern of organic composition, and the proportion of surplus-value that is converted into revenue) that provides the limits to this displacement effect. The variations in the form of value are thus shown to be conditioned and limited by the very structure of value itself. (290)

But what of Steedman's argument that a value rate of profit can have only a *conceptual* existence, while the uniform money rate of profit has a real and palpable existence reflected in the real behaviour of capitalists? Clearly, a uniform or general rate of profit can only be conceptualized on the basis of processes of *equalization* of profit rates occurring within the sphere of circulation. A general value rate of profit can only exist 'through' its circulation form, the money rate. But it does not follow from this that the money rate has primacy over the value rate. For the value rate of profit has a real existence not as a calculable ratio influencing capitalists' business decisions, but as a regulator and 'limiter' (parametric determinant) of the money rate of profit.

Shaikh makes the important point that Steedman's argument can be turned around and directed against the 'concept' of the *uniform* money rate of profit, a concept integral to all Sraffian models. For capitalists do not calculate a uniform rate of profit in order to price their commodities or transfer their capital. The uniform rate of profit is a purely tendential phenomenon operating behind their backs and imposing upon them certain decisions pertaining to price-setting, profit mark-up, and capital investment. But this imposition is a mediated and indirect one; the uniform money rate of profit can make its influence felt only through the far more 'concrete' market prices, stock-exchange indices, and individual profit rates upon which capitalists base their actual decision-making. The uniform money rate of profit, then, is no less an abstraction than the value rate of profit; moreover, the status of the latter as a 'real abstraction' may be far more secure.

The matter does not end here, however. Shaikh is prepared to accept that the concept of the uniform money rate of profit is a useful device in depicting real processes. The trouble is that Steedman understands and applies the concept in a neoclassical 'equilibrium' vein rather than in terms of tendential regulation. This relates to the charge that several Marxists have brought against Steedman according to which his analysis is infused with 'harmonistic' notions. Steedman's bias toward 'harmonism' finds its clearest expression in his treatment of prices of production and the uniform rate of profit as phenomena that 'obtain directly in circulation' – a notion that could only be entertained by a theorist who 'assumes that there is no contradiction between private independently undertaken labours and the social division of labour' (Shaikh 1981: 294). As Shaikh concludes: 'Once you replace the concept of tendential regulation with that of equilibrium, you have switched from abstraction as typification to abstraction as idealization. This is, of course, characteristic of vulgar economy, and is built into the basic mathematical foundations on which Steedman relies so heavily' (ibid.).

Fundamentalist Responses to the Choice-of-Technique and Joint-Production Arguments

Steedman's demonstration of how cases of joint production render value magnitude analyses either indeterminate or flatly contradictory is based upon a particular conception of how capitalists *choose* the techniques that they employ in production, as well as on a mathematical example of the results of a joint-production model. We shall consider Shaikh's argument concerning the 'choice of technique' issue first, and then turn to Emmanuel Farjoun's critical dissection of Steedman's joint-production model.

Steedman's 'choice of technique' argument is predicated on the correct observation that capitalists in a given industry are often confronted with the need to choose amongst several possible methods of production. Naturally, every capitalist wants to choose the method that will yield the highest possible rate of return on capital invested. But a contentious point arises when we consider *how* this can be accomplished. Steedman assumes that the method chosen will be the one that yields the highest rate of profit, as determined by existing prices and wages. Significantly, however, these prices are assumed to be exactly *equal* to prices of production, and all prevailing rates of profit are deemed to be *equal* to the 'uniform rate of profit.' A situation of 'perfect competition' and ideal equilibrium is also posited. Hence, if a *new* method of production is to be adopted, it *must* introduce a profit rate higher than the capitalist's existing rate of profit and therefore higher than the uniform rate.

The logical conclusion is that the new methods of production will only be adopted if they contribute to raising not only individual rates of profit but the uniform rate of profit as well.

Shaikh regards this argument, together with its implications for the 'logical ordering' of profit-rate determination and value-magnitude determination, as a 'resumé of the characteristic confusions of the neo-Ricardian school' (1981: 295–6). First, Steedman fails to consider the full significance of the fact that 'market prices and profit rates can never exactly equal prices of production and the uniform rate of profit' (ibid.: 296). Because this is so and because calculations are not being made in terms of prices that 'embody' the uniform rate of profit, it is quite possible for a new technique of production in a particular industry to raise the industry's profit rate while also *lowering* the average rate of profit: 'A production method that yields a higher than average rate of profit at one set of prices need not do so at some other set' (ibid.). This argument is a simple extension of Shaikh's earlier debunking of the vaunted 'significance' of the uniform money rate of profit as compared with the value rate of profit. Again, Shaikh does not wish to throw out 'prices of production' or the 'uniform rate of profit' as analytical devices; he merely wishes to underline their necessarily abstract and tendential character, while also exposing the false and misleading conclusions that can be generated with these concepts if they are employed in a different methodological spirit (one corresponding to notions of 'ideal equilibrium' and so on).

Emmanuel Farjoun, a charter member of the fundamentalist tendency that wishes to excise the notion of the 'uniform rate of profit' entirely from political economy, offers a detailed analysis of the conceptual assumptions and anomalous mathematical properties of Steedman's Sraffian model of joint production. However, while his attitude toward the uniform-rate-of-profit concept is certainly different – and more controversial – than Shaikh's, Farjoun's discussion of joint production is not entirely dependent on the rejection of profit-rate uniformity.

Farjoun takes Steedman's own example of joint production (Steedman 1981: 153) and alters it only by suggesting that Steedman's 'commodity 1' be machines and 'commodity 2,' cars. Following Steedman's, Farjoun's example is taken to represent an extremely simple capitalist economy with only two products: machines and cars. It is also assumed that there are two different industrial processes in use in the production of these two commodities, and that each of these processes produces both machines and cars jointly and simultaneously. The *material* flow of production for such an economy is represented in table 2.

Farjoun begins by noting that this *appears* to be a perfectly reasonable

TABLE 2

	Machines	Cars	Labour units	Machines	Cars
Process I	25	0	5	30	5
Process II	0	10	1	3	12

table and that, within the Sraffian framework, there is no reason to believe that such an economy could not function flawlessly. It is also quite apparent, after a little calculation, that if one tries to assign any reasonable numerical values to the concept of 'total socially necessary labour-time necessary to produce one machine' in the above table, then one cannot arrive at a positive solution. Some of the labour values will turn out to have negative numbers – a patently unacceptable result. Thus, Steedman's point that cases of joint production can be inconsistent with 'positive values' and that positive profits can coincide with negative surplus-value appears to be confirmed.

Farjoun agrees that the example shows that labour values are not well defined under arbitrary circumstances. But the question then becomes, Does this constitute a drawback or an advantage to a value-informed analysis? Farjoun considers it an advantage, arguing that the situation depicted by Steedman is *unreal* – not because it involves joint production, but because it posits two processes that *could not co-exist* in a real capitalist economy.

Consider first that the economy depicted in table 2 has a very peculiar characteristic: 'If one stops using the first process altogether and applies only the second process then one can increase all the outputs while using a smaller amount of total social labour, i.e. using less than six units of labour' (Farjoun 1984: 17). Consider also that Steedman's hypothetical economy is regarded as being in a state of equilibrium guaranteed by perfect competition and that capitalists are motivated by the rational goal of selecting technical processes that can maximize their rates of profit. Given such conditions, Farjoun asks, 'What company can long survive in the market if it uses process I while a competitor uses process II' (17)?

The problem with Steedman's example is that as a production table it is not 'on the frontier.' Farjoun elaborates:

Using exactly the same techniques as are used by other firms, each firm which has shares in process I can increase its output while reducing its input by moving even a small amount of labour to process II. In fact, for each unit of labour moved from process I to process II, we shall get a net product free of charge of two machines and one car. In other words, by a reallocation of labour and without introducing any new production techniques, in Steedman's counter-example one can increase the total net output (the total net product at the end of each production process). (ibid.)

We can also compare the *net output* per unit of labour for each production process, and if this is done it becomes clear that process I allows for (5 machines + 5 cars) / 5 units of labour = $(1M + 1C) / 1$ unit labour, while process II allows for $(3M + 2C) / 1$ unit labour. The upshot is that it is completely *unrealistic* to assume that any rational capitalist would use process I. And yet this example – involving such a patently unrealistic assumption – is used by Steedman to judge the 'consistency' of a value-magnitude analysis with cases of joint production!

These considerations suffice to establish Farjoun's fundamental point as against Steedman: 'Not every hypothetical production table is acceptable for economic matrix manipulations. Some tables must be regarded as either contradictory or incomplete' (1984: 19–20). This certainly applies to table 2, and for this reason the 'proof' it offers against the use of labour-values turns out to have no force whatever.

The combined effect of Shaikh's and Farjoun's critiques of Steedman is to expose how hidden theoretical assumptions can come to be disguised in apparently rigorous mathematical equations and reasonable-looking models. As Shaikh puts it, Steedman all too frequently 'takes refuge in algebra in order to obscure the profound silence on the question of method' (1981: 290).

Should the 'Uniform Rate of Profit' Be Abandoned?

It is fitting to conclude the discussion of fundamentalist value theory with a brief consideration of a question that has been entertained and debated *within* the fundamentalist camp: Should the concept of the uniform rate of profit be abandoned as a tool of analysis?

This question acquires an especial urgency to the extent that the discussion of Marx's value theory is couched in terms of a debate with the neo-Ricardian followers of Sraffa. For if the concept of 'value' is *fundamental* to Marxist political economy, the notion of a uniform rate of profit is no less fundamental to the Sraffian instrumentarium. In this connection we need only consider the testimony of Sraffa himself, who, after discussing a 'reasonable economy' that in his framework gives rise to infinite prices, remarks: 'It is perhaps as well to be reminded here that we are at all times concerned merely with the implication of the assumption of a uniform price [of production] ... and a uniform rate of profits on all the means of production' (1960: 91).

Farjoun is quite justified to note that in Sraffa's hands the concept of the uniform rate of profit has a purely *formal* significance and a rather weak relation to reality. However, there is an unfortunate tendency on Farjoun's part to *identify* the Sraffian (and neoclassical) conception of the uniform rate of profit with *Marx's* 'general' or 'average' rate of profit. Whereas Shaikh has sought to *differentiate* the Sraffian and Marxist understandings of the concept, while illuminating the methodological reasons for doing so, such theorists as Farjoun and Machover, together with Robert Langston, have sought to render such an exercise superfluous by insisting that the concept – however it is understood – lacks scientific verisimilitude.

While it is neither possible nor necessary to enter into a detailed evaluation of the Farjoun-Machover-Langston thesis here, the *consequence* of excising the concept of the general rate of profit from the body of Marx's theory of value, and of substituting for it the concept of a 'probabilistic profit rate perceived as a random variable,' should be well noted: it is to render somewhat *indeterminate* a crucial phase of the transformation of the value-form, namely the phase associated with the macroeconomic results of competition, capital mobility, and surplus-value redistribution. Moreover, while it is easy to sympathize with Farjoun's argument that 'Sraffian models are critically dependent on a very rigid notion of uniformity,' one should cautiously approach his associated implication that this 'rigid' notion of uniformity is really *equivalent* to Marx's own understanding of profit-rate uniformity as a *tendential* phenomenon, that is, a phenomenon reflecting just *one* of the social production relations of capitalism – the *competitive* relation between individual capitals in the market.

6   An Assessment of the Value
       Controversy

The controversy surrounding Marx's theory of labour-value may be assessed
at three relatively distinct levels: the philosophical-methodological, the sub-
stantive-theoretical, and the political-programmatic. This chapter is mainly
concerned with the philosophical-methodological dimension of the value
controversy. However, brief assessments of the theoretical and political
dimensions of the controversy are also elaborated in anticipation of the explo-
rations to be undertaken in chapters 7 to 11.

Philosophical and Methodological Considerations

Reference to the distinctive methodological aspects of Marx's value theory
is de rigueur for its proponents. Dialectics are counterposed to formal logic;
Marx's holism or methodological collectivism is invoked against the methodological individualism (and logical atomism) of the positivist tradition;
abstraction and contradiction are located in 'the real' instead of being viewed
as exclusively 'mental' constructs. Yet, during both of the major phases of
the value controversy, discussion of the scientific method that guided Marx's
elaboration of his theory of value has been inadequate and the salience of the
above-mentioned methodological principles to the value controversy has
remained obscure. This has led many of Marx's critics – and even some of
his more positivistically oriented defenders – to dismiss them as either
'obscurantist' or 'metaphysical.' Yet such characterizations could not be
further from the truth. Far from being obscurantist, the perspectives on scientific method that Marx brought to bear on the theory of value are vital
sources of illumination as to the content of that theory; and far from being
metaphysical, Marx's concept of science is formulated and applied in a
consciously *antimetaphysical* spirit. These points are well established in

Patrick Murray's important study of *Marx's Theory of Scientific Knowledge* (1988), which, despite some important weaknesses and lacunae, will serve as a useful point of departure for a consideration of the methodological and philosophical dimensions of Marx's theory of value.

Patrick Murray on Marx as Scientist

An overarching theme of Murray's study is that Marx's concept of scientific knowledge stands outside that of the positivist tradition, reflecting not only the enduring influence of Hegel's dialectics on his thought but also the results of his youthful critique of Hegel's absolute idealism. Marx's antipositivism, however, is not at all of a piece with any neo-Kantian insistence upon an epistemological gulf between the natural and the sociocultural sciences, and it therefore has little in common with the antipositivism of twentieth-century 'critical theory' (Adorno and Horkheimer 1972, Habermas 1971), despite the latter's Marxist overtones. As Murray points out, 'Marx disavows any radical separation of natural science from human, social or cultural science' (1988: 75). Rather, what distinguishes his theory of scientific knowledge from all positivist versions is its 'attention to the practical, historical root-edness of the concepts of science, as well as the values which guide it' (ibid.: xx). In this, as in so much else, Marx owes a considerable intellectual debt to Hegel: 'Marx accepts Hegel's demand for a unity of form and content in scientific knowledge. Method ought not to be some abstract, formalized procedure hovering over the specific content of a science. Rather, method needs to take its shape from the specific objects under scrutiny ... Marx views science as a matter of getting at the logic of things in themselves. Since this logic is not ascertainable *a priori*, purely formal methodologies have no place in Marx's conception of scientific knowledge' (ibid.: 110).

Murray neglects the point, but it is as well to register it, that an aversion to methodological formalism is one of the hallmarks of contemporary 'realist' theories of science (Benton 1985, Bhaskar 1979, Keat and Urry 1982). Among the scientific realists, Ted Benton in particular has argued that the methodological diversity of the sciences establishes no epistemological fault-lines either within or between the natural and the social sciences. To establish any formal methodological principle as inviolable – as Karl Popper did with 'methodological individualism,' for example – betrays not an appetite for scientific rigour but an authentically metaphysical and dogmatic inclination of the sort that positivists routinely condemn. In this sense, Marx's aversion to formal methodological precepts attests to a highly 'up-to-date' regard for the methodological pluralism celebrated by scientific realism.

For Marx, it is precisely the methodological open-endedness of the materialist dialectic that makes it a powerful tool of scientific analysis and a necessary antidote to both naïve impressionism and speculative metaphysics. On this view, the methods of scientific analysis are, of necessity, internally related to the real objects of analysis, objects involving 'abstractions that take shape according to the specificity of that object itself' (Murray 1988: 113). Murray refers to this methodological strategy as Marx's 'logically well-bred empiricism' or, alternatively, his 'empiricism in second intension.' And it is not to be confused either with the dogmatism associated with some versions of dialectical materialism (Stalin 1972a) or with the eclecticism and subjectivism of purely 'social-constructionist' accounts of the scientific enterprise (Kuhn 1970, Feyerabend 1988).

Key to an appreciation of the scientific principles underlying Marx's theory of value are his distinction between general and determinate abstractions as well as his understanding of the 'logic of essence.' Both derive from a critical encounter with Hegel's philosophy and with classical political economy, that is, with bodies of thought that Marx linked to the 'deep structures' of capitalist society.

Marx's methodological injunction concerning the need to ascend from the abstract to the concrete is well known and is properly regarded as fundamental to his analytical strategy. Frequently, however, the hurried invocation of this formula has served as a substitute for a careful recovery and specification of Marx's understanding of such notions as 'abstraction,' 'abstract,' and 'concrete.' In the first place, says Murray, 'Hegel's logic educates Marx to realize that abstraction is the medium of thought, and that the medium has a message which needs to be thoroughly heeded' (ibid.: 113). In science, abstract categories of thought cannot simply be dispensed with in favour of 'empirical facts'; yet science does demand that those abstractions that are 'prefabricated and subjectively applied to a particular object of scientific inquiry' should be replaced with abstractions that emerge from the specificity of the object itself. Thus, the movement from the abstract to the concrete does not refer to a movement from cognitive abstractions to a description of the empirically concrete; rather, the terms 'abstract' and 'concrete' are applicable to abstractions, as categories of thought, *themselves*. The movement from the abstract to the concrete corresponds to the development of ever-more concrete abstractions – of concepts that the labour of thought endows with increasingly complex determinations. As Murray puts it: 'On the one hand, Marx uses "concrete" to distinguish the actual from the conceptual [real versus ideal abstractions – MS], while on the other, he uses "concrete" and "abstract" within the sphere of the conceptual to distinguish concepts that are more or less synthetic' (115). (This also points directly to a key aspect of Marx's rupture with Hegel: 'Marx faults absolute idealism for failing to keep these two senses separate; Hegel superimposes onto reality the movement of thought from the abstract to the concrete' [ibid.]. Such a superimposition is precisely what Marx's *materialist* dialectic enjoins us to avoid.)

All of this contrasts in the starkest way with the procedures of positivism, that is, with what Hegel referred to as 'scientific empiricism.' 'The logical training that Marx gleaned from Hegel, in particular from the *Science of Logic*, taught him to demand a clear ordering of scientific categories in terms of their conceptual concreteness, and to respect the differences among them' (ibid.: 116). It was precisely the failure of the political economists to respect these 'differences of form' and to avoid positing concrete categories in the scientific elaboration of more abstract categories that moved Marx to reproach them for putting 'the science before the science.'

Marx is most emphatic on these themes in the introduction to the *Grundrisse*, where he highlights the methodological salience of the distinction between general and determinate abstractions. General abstractions consist of those abstract concepts (abstract abstractions) that are 'short on' determinations and relatively unladen with 'forms.' Typically, they are concepts that refer to phenomena abstracted from definite historical or social settings; for example, use-values (objects of utility), division of labour, social organization, population, means of production, and so on. These notions have *general* applicability to the description of a wide variety of historically constituted forms of human social existence. Yet it is impossible to find very much of scientific value to say about any one of them without considering the (determinate) forms in which they are necessarily manifested. Hence, while it may be true that a 'division of labour' is a general presupposition of human society, an expression of an imperative on the part of human beings to mediate their collective relation to nature through definite social arrangements governing the allocation and distribution of social labour, it is also the case that the division of labour assumes different forms (communal, trade-based, planned, and so on) and that no division of labour exists apart from such forms.

As soon as real, historically variant forms are taken into account in analysis, general abstractions are transformed into *determinate* abstractions, albeit of varying degrees of concreteness. The general abstraction 'product of labour' divides into the determinate abstractions 'potlatch,' 'tribute,' 'rent-in-kind,' 'tithe,' 'commodity' – each a definite socio-historical form of 'human products of labour.' The matter does not end here, however, since, from another point of view, at least some of these 'determinate abstractions' may require further analytical concretization. The form taken by commodities as means of production, for example, needs to be distinguished from the form assumed by commodities as 'wage-goods' or 'luxury-goods'; and all of these need to be distinguished from the 'money-commodity.' From a certain point of view, then, 'commodity' is one socio-historical form of the 'product of labour,' but from another standpoint, 'commodity' subsumes a variety of specific social forms, finding expression through one or more of them.

'The most demanding point of all,' says Murray (ibid.: 128), 'is that Marx's concept of scientific knowledge requires us to ascertain which are the determinate abstractions appropriate for a particular object of study and how to order them properly among themselves, moving from the abstract to the concrete.' In order to do this, the scientist must uncover the object's *logic of essence* – that is, the ways in which '*essence* must appear as *something other than itself*' (xvii). According to Murray, Marx regards the logic of essence as 'a logic of division, of alienation' under conditions in which essence is concealed by misleading appearances. In fact, scientific method is only needed where appearances serve to obscure or distort reality, and this is as true in political economy (where the law of labour-value appears vitiated by the multiple determinants of individual commodity price) as in natural science (where individual manifestations of gravitational law may seem 'distorted' by atmospheric events). Thus, for Murray, Marx's 'mature theory of value shows that the logic of value is the logic of necessarily appearing in something other' (161).

Value *must appear* and *find expression* in the money prices attaching to individual commodities. At the same time, this necessarily diverts attention from the structure of social relations outside of which value could have no existence whatever. Hence, 'Hegel's emphasis on the *immanence* of the law of appearance to the appearances themselves carries over into Marx's theory of price' (ibid.: 165). This understanding of the essence-appearance relation is fundamental to Marx's critique of the fetishism of commodities and to his *antimetaphysical* theory of value. As Murray observes:

Complaints such as Joan Robinson's about the metaphysical character of Marx's theory of value rest on a serious misunderstanding of Marx's model of essence and appearance. Is not the burden of Marx's critique of the 'fetishism' of commodities precisely to attack the metaphysical understanding of value on the model of a natural, sensuous object or quality? Marx's theory of value is not nonmetaphysical, it is *antimetaphysical*. In criticizing value, he criticizes the functioning of capitalist society according to a logic of 'appearing in an other'. Marx stresses that his theory of value is not intended to uncover some abstract essence existing behind the veil of appearances, but rather to characterize the relations of capitalist society as determined by the dualistic, third party logic of 'appearing in an other'. (231)

In his zeal to rid Marx's theory of value of all 'metaphysical' tropes, Murray eventually falters in his analysis by insisting that Marx does not 'ontologize' value. For Murray, 'value does not exist as an actual tangible thing, but as the reflection of actual things' (165). But this formula erroneously suggests that something can exist *only* as a 'tangible thing' *or* as a reflection of such things. Moreover, Murray is inconsistent to insist that value should not be 'ontologized' while also asserting that it *exists* as a reflection of things – for to say that value has a *real existence*, in any sense, is to pose the question of its precise ontological status, and thereby to 'ontologize' it.

The Ontology of Abstract Labour and Value

In chapter 4, we considered Boehm-Bawerk's argument that Marx has no justification for positing labour – even 'labour in general' – as the sole common property of commodity values. Boehm-Bawerk insisted against Marx that one can just as easily, and perhaps more reasonably, adduce 'utility' as such a common property. We then considered Geoffrey Kay's counter-argument according to which the category of abstract labour differs from utility in that the former is not a 'particular,' while the latter can only exist in particular forms. Kay maintained that because 'abstract labour' can achieve a form of existence independent of particular concrete expressions of labour, it is not a mere *mental generalization* of the sort that the category of 'abstract utility' can only be. Abstract labour is something more than a mental generalization because it has a real *existence grounded* in the labour process and expressed in money. Thus, for Kay, 'in searching for the form of existence of abstract labour we are merely looking for the value-form.'

The philosopher Norman Fischer has attempted to extend and complete Kay's argument, beginning with an observation concerning an important deficiency in Kay's position: '[Kay] argues that abstract labor (labor in general) *does exist* both in the commodity, and in money. But cannot Boehm-Bawerk make the same claim with respect to utility? Kay's analysis is incomplete insofar as he does not make it clear whether or not the existence of abstract labor in the form of the commodity or as money is the existence of a particular' (1982: 29). Fischer insists that to complete the argument against Boehm-Bawerk on this basis it is necessary to render explicit a significant difference between Boehm-Bawerk's empiricism and Marx's realism, a difference concerning whether or not 'universals' or 'generalities' can be said to have a *real existence*, and, further, whether these universals can be regarded as having ontological priority over individual particulars. Fischer (ibid.: 30) also suggests that this question should be considered in conjunction with Diane Elson's (1979) thesis that abstract labour and value are *internally related* to one another. The question posed by Fischer, then, is quite simply this: Is the category of 'abstract labour' an abstract universal or an abstract particular?

Fischer's answer is that Marx regarded abstract labour as an abstract universal, as the kind of 'general social structure' that suggests an ontology of 'social, non-particular entities.' Whereas empiricist or positivist conceptions of science are *two-tiered* (admitting only general laws and particular entities, and defining 'laws pertaining to particulars' as the primary objects of science), Marx's ontological position involves a *three-tiered* approach in which *real structures* mediate the relationship between general laws and particular entities (Murray's 'tangible things'). On this view, for science to *explain* the operation of laws as part of understanding reality, it must disclose the existence and explain the nature of these intangible yet actually existing structural entities. Abstract labour, value's 'substance,' is precisely one such structure – yet the question remains: *How* can it be said to exist as more than a mental generalization or ideal abstraction?

Fischer notes that 'what characterizes Marx's philosophy within those that are three-tiered is its holistic interpretation of the entities mediating laws and particulars' (1982: 30). Within Marx's theoretical construction there are several social-structural entities that enjoy holistic-ontological status, among them abstract labour, value, and 'the world of commodities.' In the initial reconstruction of Marx's theory of value in chapter 4, the holistic inflections of Marx's analysis in the first chapter of *Capital I* were deliberately stressed, particularly in the discussion of the distinction between 'value' and 'exchange-value,' where Marx implicitly establishes value as a 'general' or 'universal' concept corresponding to a real social process. But it is unnecessary to 'read between the lines' of Marx's texts in order to discover his commitment to a 'holistic' ontology; we need only consider the rather explicit holism of the following passage from Marx's appendix to the first edition of *Capital I*:

Within the value relationship ... the abstract universal is not considered to be a property of the concrete sensuously real, but on the contrary, the sensuously concrete is considered to be the form of appearance of the abstract universal. The labor of the tailor which, for example, is contained in the equivalent coat does not possess the universal property of being human labor. Rather, the opposite is the case. It is its essence to be human labor. To be the work of the tailor is only its apparent form ... This quid pro quo is unavoidable because the labor which is represented in the product is only the creator of value insofar as it is undifferentiated labor. Thus, the labor which is objectified in one product is completely undifferentiated from the labor which is objectified in the value of a different sort of product. This reversal, whereby the sensuously concrete is considered as only the form of appearance of the abstract universal, as opposed to the case where the abstract universal is a property of the concrete, characterizes the value expression. At the same time it makes its understanding difficult. (1953: 271; translated by Fischer 1982: 31)

Marx's observations here would seem to support the notion that abstract labour – a real structure – finds expression *through* the concrete particulars of the products of labour. Thus, to conceive of abstract labour as a 'universal structure' (or, more dynamically, as a 'universal process') is *not* to deny that it finds particular expressions or concrete forms (in which, indeed, it is apprehended as a 'property of the concrete'); it is to insist that it has an existence that is independent of these concrete particulars *as well*. The quantitative dimensionality of abstract labour is, therefore, not confined to concrete particulars (the money-form), but exerts itself *also* at the level of its social-structural existence (as socially necessary labour-time). On this conceptualization, Marx's theory of value constitutes the unity of a *qualitative* treatment of the value-form (exchange-value/money-price) and a *quantitative* concern with the 'substance of value.' Moreover, the conceptual nexus of the theory is revealed to be 'abstract labour' – a category that bridges the divide between value's 'particular' and 'universal' aspects. Key to this interpretation, as the above passage from Marx suggests, is an extension of the *ontological reversals* described by Marx in his discussion of the value-form (use-value/value, concrete-labour/abstract-labour, private-labour/social-labour) to include the relation between commodities as sensuously concrete particulars and abstract labour as a real universal structure (whose necessary form of appearance is money). As Marx makes clear in his discussion of the fetishism of commodities, these 'reversals' are not 'illusory,' but have a real basis in the social relations of commodity economy. The holistic social structures 'abstract labour' and 'value' are 'real,' not because they are empirically 'tangible,' but because they are the necessary projections of determinate social relations of production and reproduction.

This points to a key error in Patrick Murray's application of Marx's theory of scientific knowledge to his theory of value. Murray correctly notes that, for Marx, 'method needs to take its shape from the specific objects under scrutiny.' But if the specific objects that Marx scutinized possess a social-structural dimension distinguishable from, yet internally related to, their particular manifestation as 'tangible things,' then Murray is quite wrong to insist that Marx's 'theory of value is not intended to uncover some abstract essence existing behind the veil of appearances' (1988: 231). If the social structure of abstract labour is the 'abstract essence' in question, then *of course* Marx wanted to 'uncover' and expose it to the light of day by tearing away its veil of appearances. Moreover, in doing so, Marx wanted not only to 'characterize the relations of capitalist society as determined by the dualistic, third party logic of ''appearing in an other,'' ' but to show that this 'third party logic' has a real and persistent basis in the determinate social relations of production of capitalism. Only by overturning these social relations could the *reality* of economic regulation by the law of labour-value be dissolved.

The root of Murray's error here is his failure to consistently resist a 'formal methodology' – that of methodological individualism. Indeed, implicit in his treatment of Marx's theory of value is an unacknowledged ontological privileging of individual particulars and a general failure to acknowledge any holistic aspects in Marx's analysis. Small wonder then that in defining the differences between Marx's and positivist approaches to scientific inquiry he neglected to mention positivism's dogmatic insistence upon ontological *nominalism* – that is, the doctrine that only particulars exist. No wonder, too, that he labelled Marx's theory of scientific knowledge as 'empiricist in second intension' rather than as 'realist.' For one of the most important differences between scientific realism and all versions of positivism/empiricism is precisely the former's commitment to the kind of 'three-tiered' and holistic approach defined by Fischer.

Fischer's clarification of the ontological status of abstract labour and its relation to value has several important implications for the debate between the neo-orthodox and fundamentalist value theorists. Within the neo-orthodox camp there exists a strong tendency to either reduce abstract labour to a particular 'aspect' of social labour, an aspect finding expression only at the level of particular commodities (as an 'immanent measure' of value) and/or in particular money prices (as an 'external measure' of value); or to regard abstract labour as a structure that finds expression or 'embodiment' only in money. The first tendency, typified by Elson, results, as Fischer has noted, from an apparent unwillingness to 'pursue the issue of whether or not ... abstract labor is actual,' or to probe 'the ontological division between empiricist and non-empiricist approaches' (1982: 31). The second tendency, typified by Himmelweit and Mohun and carried to its furthest extreme by Eldred, is to deny that abstract labour finds any kind of embodiment or expression at the level of the individual commodity and that it can only be meaningfully measured at the level of individual money-price. The proponents of this position *also* skirt the issue of the ontological status of abstract labour; indeed, it is noteworthy that, like Murray, their thinking appears to be influenced by a residual empiricism expressed in a tacit adherence to a nominalist ontology. The practical result of both of these neo-orthodox tendencies is to evacuate Marx's problematic and to approach positions remarkably reminiscent of the neoclassical tradition.

Although Fischer argues that the holistic conceptualization of abstract labour lends itself to an improved version of Elson's 'value theory of labour,' in my view such a conceptualization is already the *implicit* ontological basis of the fundamentalist account of value theory, as represented by Shaikh in particular. As we have seen, the fundamentalist account stresses the importance of *both* the 'magnitude of value' and the 'form of value.' The magnitude-of-value problematic directs attention to the macro-level and to the measurement of value in terms of socially necessary labour-time. The form-of-value problematic directs attention to the micro-level issue of the quantitative relation between particular commodities as expressed through the money-form.

The *dissociation* of these problematics can only lead to a *dualism* of universal and particular, that is, to a denial of their dialectical unity. In practical terms such a dualism must eventuate in that methodological privileging of 'the particular' that is characteristic of all 'theories of value' that focus on the 'individual commodity' at the expense of an understanding of 'the world of commodities.' Such an approach is characteristic of Ricardo's theory (despite his concern with the macroeconomic issue of the distribution of income between classes); of Mill's 'cost of production' theory; and of neoclassical marginal-utility theory. 'Orthodox' (Ricardian-) Marxist value theory is characterized by an uneasy, and ultimately untenable, compromise between a dualistic and a dialectical (monistic) handling of the universal/particular relation, while neo-Ricardianism represents a bold reassertion of a dualistic position, but one that accords an analytical privilege to 'macro-level' economic phenomena (abstracted from any theory of value). Neo-orthodox Marxian value theory, in this context, can be interpreted as a reassertion of the 'microeconomic side' of Marx's value theory (the function of which is to 'remind' us that the product of labour is valorized only by virtue of the existence of determinate social relations) within a theoretical space that basically accepts both a dualistic framework and a macroeconomic analysis that eschews any 'value-magnitude' theory.

What needs to be stressed by the Marxist fundamentalists in relation to the neo-orthodox school is that *money* (that favourite neo-orthodox 'measure of value') becomes the form of value in its role as the *universal equivalent.* To cite Marx: 'Since all other commodities are merely particular equivalents for money, the latter being their universal equivalent, they relate to money as particular commodities relate to the universal commodity' (1977: 184). Money, as the 'universal commodity,' is the expression of undifferentiated abstract labour. Significantly, Marx goes on to say that 'the money-form is merely the reflection thrown upon a single commodity by the relations between all other commodities' (ibid.). This can be expressed otherwise as follows: money is the form of appearance or 'reflection' of a structure of abstract labour that mediates the relations existing between commodities. Yet to understand this structure and its mediative role, one must look to the problem of the 'magnitude of value.' Hence, *abstract labour needs to be conceived as a structure (of relations) grounded in production but reflected by individual commodities in the sphere of circulation* – and this is precisely the general position implied by the fundamentalist school of value theory. It seems to me that it is solely on this basis that the fundamental postulates of Marx's value theory, as these were defined earlier, can be sustained: that living labour and living labour alone is the source of all newly produced value (including surplus-value) and that value exists as a definite quantitative magnitude at the level of the capitalist economy as a whole. In other words, what is most *operationally significant* in Marx's theory of value can be defended only on a fundamentalist and not a neo-orthodox basis.

We are now in a strong position to specify a key difference between the neoclassical (marginalist) and Marxist accounts of 'economic value.' When the marginal-utility theorist Boehm-Bawerk argues that abstract utility can as easily serve as the 'common factor' shared by all commodities as abstract labour, he begs the question of the *ontological status* of 'utility.' As Kay observes, 'abstract utility' is merely a mental generalization, an *ideal* abstraction rather than a 'real structure' of relations. Furthermore, utility is a property of commodities, which, as Marx insists, must be 'abstracted from' in the exchange process. The use-value of a commodity is *always* a 'particular' use-value. This does not make it irrelevant to the price it can fetch, but it does make it irrelevant to a specification of the larger social processes in which 'value' is enmeshed and which set *limits* on 'purchasing power,' profits, and the realizability of set prices.

The methodological difference between Marx and Boehm-Bawerk, so often commented upon but inadequately defined by the 'orthodox' tradition of Marxian political economy, turns then on different conceptions of the ontology of social life: Boehm-Bawerk's positivism reflecting a narrowly nominalist outlook, Marx's dialectical method a realist one that allows for the existence of *both* individual and holistic entities. The necessary upshot of this difference is that the marginalist account of value expresses an indefinite and quantitatively indeterminate relation between two incommensurable spheres: an ideal sphere of human predelictions, norms, and 'rational calculations' and a material sphere of scarce 'economic resources.' Marx rejects such a psychologistic-naturalistic reduction of the concept of value, insisting that the value relation is irreducibly a *social relation among people* – a relation that forms part of a singular, monistic reality in which the material, the social, and the ideal (as well as the concrete and the abstract, and the universal and the particular) are 'internally related' aspects of an ontologically unified totality.

The foregoing considerations are equally germane to a response to the logico-analytical argument that G.A. Cohen (1981) has deployed to bolster the neo-Ricardian and 'Analytical Marxist' critiques of Marx's theory of value. The following passage is the core of Cohen's critique: '[Marx's] theory entails that past labour is irrelevant to how much value a commodity now has. But past labour would not be irrelevant if it created the value of the commodity. It follows that labour does not create value, if the *labour theory of value is true*' (209–10).

As we have seen, however, Marx's position is not that 'labour creates value' in some direct and *unmediated* sense, but that *abstract labour creates value*. Let us therefore consider Cohen's criticism as it would need to be amended to address Marx's actual position (that is, the position of *fundamentalist* value theory): 'The theory entails that past *abstract* labour is irrelevant to how much value a commodity now has. But past *abstract* labour would not be irrelevant if it created the value of the commodity. It follows that *abstract* labour does not create value, if the labour theory of value is true.'

Cohen's legerdemain can now be more easily exposed. It is of course quite true that *past* abstract labour does not create the value that a commodity currently represents. But it does not follow from this that 'abstract labour does not create value,' *provided that* abstract labour is understood to be a real structure of relations determining the value of that commodity on the basis of the social production norms *currently* required for its (re)production. Cohen's critique is therefore revealed to be based on a serious misunderstanding of Marx's theory of value as well as a refusal to appreciate the distinctive methodology informing it.

Alienation and Value Theory

No discussion of the philosophical dimension of Marx's theory of value can be complete without some attempt to articulate the latter with Marx's essentially humanist philosophy of praxis and his critique of alienation. Marx's humanism is grounded on an insight enunciated in *The German Ideology*: 'The premises from which we begin are ... the real individuals, their activity and the material conditions of their life, both those which they find existing and those produced by their activity' (Marx 1989: 22). In the course of 'making their own history,' human beings must, before all else, secure the material conditions of their existence. 'The first historical act is thus the production of the means to satisfy these needs, the production of material life itself' (ibid.: 23). This in turn leads to new needs, since the satisfaction of such elementary requirements as food and clothing (the means of subsistence) necessitates the development of means of production, forms of cooperation, and determinate, yet changeable, social relations of production.

By *objectifying* their labour, says Marx in his Paris manuscripts of 1844, human beings embark on a project of transforming nature through *praxis* (that is, purposive, self-directing activity), thereby affirming their 'species being.' Accordingly, Marx rejects Hegel's view that the *material* objectification of human capacities (labour) is the basis of human alienation. He proposes instead that this objectification entails the alienation of 'the worker' (that is, the direct producer) only under well-defined *social* conditions. The alienation of labour arises where labour is 'external' to the worker in the sense that it 'belongs to another,' is 'coerced' or 'forced' labour, and is performed only as a *means* 'to satisfy needs external to it' (1964: 111); where the worker experiences the product of labour 'as an alien object exercising power over him' and the objects of nature as 'an alien world inimically opposed to him' (ibid.); where the worker also experiences the labour process as an 'activity which is turned against him, independent of him and not belonging to him' (ibid.: 111–22); and where human beings are estranged from their 'species life' and from one another because of a compulsion to transform their capabilities into *means* to 'individual existence' (ibid.: 114). In short, for the young Marx, the alienation of labour is not an eternal anthropological condition, but is bound up with the presence of *class-antagonistic* social relations of production, in particular those associated with capitalism.

What needs to be demonstrated in response to the many 'Marxological' commentaries that have insisted upon a basic disjunction between the 'young' and the 'mature' Marx is that the methodological and philosophical precepts informing Marx's youthful writings on alienation and human history (most of them written before his espousal of a 'labour theory of value') are substantially the *same* as those that inform his later critique of political economy.[1]

In *The German Ideology* Marx and Engels write: 'The production of life, both of one's own in labour and of fresh life in procreation ... appears as a twofold relation: on the one hand as a natural, on the other as a social relation – social in the sense that it denotes the co-operation of several individuals, no matter under what conditions, in what manner and to what end' (Marx 1989: 23). This twofold relation involved in the 'production of life' (the 'first premiss' of human existence) is here defined as embracing both a natural aspect and a social aspect (involving different forms of human cooperation). With this statement Marx and Engels announce that the study of concrete forms of human existence (modes of life) must take as its starting-point a focus on the internal dialectical relation between *the natural and the social.*

Such an approach fundamentally distinguishes Marx's analytical project from the great majority of social theories that begin with a focus on a presumed external opposition between 'the material' and 'the ideal' (or, relatedly, 'the objective' and 'the subjective'), as we have already noted in chapter 2. Marx's dialectical social ontology stands irreconcilably opposed to the ontological dualisms sponsored by this material-ideal opposition: dualisms that posit discrete 'levels of reality' or even 'different worlds' as they problematicize the relationship between facts and values, subjects and objects, structure and agency, noumena and phenomena, what is and what ought to be, science and philosophy, and so on. It was precisely in light of such a dialectical social ontology that Marx berated Proudhon in 1847 for 'a *dualism* between life and ideas, between soul and body – a dualism which recurs in many forms' (1989: 12).

Of course, Marx does not deny that *dualities* are a persistent feature of human existence. But he does insist upon approaching these dualities (use-value/exchange-value; intellectual-labour/manual-labour; and so on) with due regard to their singular (monistic) foundation: the 'materialist connection of men with one another, which is determined by their needs and their mode of production, and which is as old as men themselves' (ibid.: 24). This 'materialist connection' holds pride of place in Marx's social ontology because it, and not 'consciousness' or 'ideas' springing from a realm considered 'independent' of the material world, is the real basis upon which the nature-society relation is mediated: 'This connection is ever taking on new forms, and thus presents a ''history'' irrespective of the existence of any political or religious nonsense which would especially hold men together' (ibid.).

This concept of an internal, dialectical relation between 'the natural' and 'the social' is the real starting-point of Marx's critique of political economy, a point he makes abundantly clear in *Notes on Adolph Wagner*. As we saw in chapter 4, Marx asserts here that his analysis does not begin with 'the concept of value' but with 'the simplest social form in which the labour-product is presented in contemporary society ... the commodity,' something which is revealed to have both a 'natural form' (a use-value) and a 'form of appearance' (an exchange-value) that is the 'autonomous mode of appearance of the *value* contained in the commodity' (ibid.: 41–2). Thus, thirty-four years after *The German Ideology*, Marx explicitly restates the methodological principle that had consistently guided him in his critique of political economy: that the objectifications of human praxis simultaneously express a relation to nature (a natural form) and a relation to society (a social form). If the inner anatomy of capitalism is to be understood, then the elementary form in which human praxis (labour) is manifested in a capitalist society, the commodity, must be seen for what it is: a contradictory unity of natural and social aspects, an expression of the concrete (mental and manual) labour that fashions its natural form and an individual manifestation of the larger social processes that define its value (its status in relation to all other products of labour) and its price (its power to command remuneration in exchange).

The Marx of *Capital* no less than the Marx of 1844 understood well the immanent tendency of capitalist production to subordinate the 'subjective' aspects of the process to the 'objective.' But if there is a shift in Marx's thinking it surely concerns the fact that the Marx of 1844 is far more pre-occupied with the 'subjective experience' of the individual worker than is the Marx of *Capital*. In *Capital* the human subjectivity requisite to *use-value* production (the material labour process) is now assigned to the 'collective worker' (that is, to a workforce increasingly characterized by segmentation and a divorce between what Carchedi [1991] calls 'mental and material' functions). At the same time, however, the 'subjectivity' requisite to securing surplus-value production (the valorization process) is assigned to the agents of capital – if only tenuously; 'tenuously' because these agents are far from controlling the Invisible Leviathan, that is, the structure of value relations and processes governing the magnitude and rate of surplus-value production and capital accumulation within the economy as a whole. Thus, the mutual powerlessness of worker and capitalist alike in the face of despotic market forces is the necessary point of departure of any attempt to articulate adequately Marx's theories of alienation and value on the basis of his philosophy of praxis.

On this view, the 'decentring' of the human subject in *Capital* is not at all a repudiation of 'humanism' or of 'praxis,' that is, of the idea that human beings are purposive, reflexive agents with the capacity to consciously transform their circumstances. Rather it is a theoretical expression of the consequences of an 'alienation' of human beings from a condition of mastery over the social division of labour – of a fragmented and necessarily *partial* praxis. Indeed, the whole of *Capital* can be read as an extended analysis of a phenomenon of 'objective alienation' more profound and more encompassing than those phenomena identified by Marx in 1844. The alienation of the producer from the (appropriated) product, from other human beings, from nature and from 'species life' (praxis) constitute the dimensions of an alienated condition *apprehended from the point of view of the producer as a 'real living individual.'* But in the *Grundrisse* and in *Capital* Marx shows that these are but aspects of a larger alienation – what might be called the 'collective alienation of the species' from an authentic human praxis.

'Abstract labour,' the 'substance' of value, is precisely 'alienated labour,' as Colletti (1972: 84) long ago pointed out; it is 'labour separated or estranged with respect to man himself' (ibid.). But abstract labour is also a concept that bridges the subjective-particularistic aspect of alienation and the objective-universalistic aspect. The young Marx's theory of alienation remained incomplete to the extent that it failed to identify the dialectical unity of these aspects, a task conforming to the methodological imperative to overcome any dualism of the general and the particular. The *implicit* theory of value of the Marx of 1844 was an obstacle to this task: not because he rejected *Ricardo's* labour theory of value (for this theory too posits a dissociation of the particular and the general) but because any 'value theory' other than that fashioned by Marx on the basis of his later *transformation* of Ricardo's theory must focus on the value of the 'individual comodity' in abstraction from 'the world of commodities' and must therefore tend toward a simple conflation of 'price' and 'value' rather than encourage an exploration of their complex, dialectical interrelationship. In coming to 'adopt' a 'labour theory of value,' then, Marx did not repudiate his youthful philosophy; on the contrary, he radically transformed the content of the Ricardian theory of labour-value in light of the results of his critique and critical appropriation of the philosophies of Hegel and Feuerbach.

Marx's analysis of the fetishism of commodities, of the value-form, and of the alienated social power of money (the universal equivalent) are replete with observations strongly reminiscent of the alienation critique of 1844. This suggests not only the obvious fact of 'continuity'; it also establishes that *Capital* represents the completion of this critique. Moreover, by more fully detailing the historically specific character of the pillars of human alienation, the Marx of *Capital* points the way to a historical resolution of the problem and to a future in which the field of praxis will be *generalized* – for collective humanity no less than for the individual.

Theoretical Considerations

There is, of course, no a priori basis upon which one can judge the 'truth' of Marx's social ontology in relation to the nominalism and dualism that pervade not only non-Marxist thought but much ostensibly Marxist thought as well. As Marx remarks in his (eminently humanist) second thesis on Feuerbach: 'Man must prove the truth, i.e. the reality and power, the this-worldliness of his thinking in practice' (1989: 8). If the fundamental postulates of Marx's theory of value can be sustained only on the basis of a realist-holistic ontology, this in itself does not establish the probity of that theory. Rather, it is that ontology which acquires credence to the extent that the theory and methodology that it informs demonstrate their power to *explain* social reality.

What then are the substantive theoretical implications of the postulates that 'living labour is the sole source of new value' and that 'value exists as a definite quantitative magnitude at the macroeconomic level'? Clearly, they are immense, bearing on virtually every aspect of life in a capitalist society. To begin with, they provide a powerful basis upon which to analyse the origins and nature of *social conflict* under capitalism; and, as such, they serve to radically distinguish the Marxist from the Weberian strands within the so-called conflict-power paradigm. An explicit confrontation between Marx's value-theoretical analysis and Weber's marginalist-informed account of 'power' can only result in a much-deserved implosion of this artfully contrived but hopelessly eclectic 'paradigm.'

But apart from such theoreticist considerations, the real power of these postulates derives from the fact that they breathe life into Marx's account of the *historical limits* of capitalism. Together they constitute the basis of Marx's famous 'law of the falling tendency of the rate of profit' – a law that Marx regarded as central both to his theory of cyclical crisis and to his account of the historical-structural crisis of capitalism. In a nutshell, this law states that the tendency of the social capital to increase its organic composition (that is, to replace 'living labour' by the 'dead labour' embodied in an increasingly sophisticated productive apparatus) must exert a downward pressure on the rate of profit, the decisive regulator of capitalist accumulation.

To be sure, Marx's law of value is merely a 'necessary presupposition' of the law of the falling tendency of the rate of profit, not a *sufficient* one. Yet, there is a sense in which the latter stands as a corollary to the former, even if not a theoretically ineluctable one. For capitalism is the one mode of production in which the object of production is only incidentally the production of particular things to satisfy particular human wants, but in which this object is directly and overwhelmingly the production of *value*, that 'social substance' which is the flesh and blood of Adam Smith's all-too-fallible 'invisible hand' – of our 'Invisible Leviathan.'

In the end, Marx's theory of value is concerned with the historical promise and fateful implications of a labour process that has assumed the social form of a 'valorization' process. Marx's theory serves to remind us that the imperative to 'produce value' is a *social* imperative, an imperative of *capitalist social relations*, not a technical or natural necessity inherent in the metabolic relation between humanity and nature. Only a society burdened by the need to 'produce value' could give birth to so absurd, and monstrous, a phenomenon as a 'crisis of overproduction.' And only such a society can transform the potential benefits flowing from labour-saving technological innovation into declining living standards, unemployment, bitter trade rivalries, depression, and war. Marx's theory of value, in sum, provides a compelling basis for the conclusion that capitalism is, at bottom, an 'irrational' and historically limited system, one that digs its own grave by seeking to assert its 'independence' from living labour while remaining decisively dependent upon this labour for the production of its own life-blood: the surplus-value that is the social substance of private profit.

Programmatic Considerations

Neither Marx's theory of value nor the controversy surrounding it are divorced from practical 'programmatic' considerations. Theoretical positions on Marx's analysis not only *generate* programmatic perspectives, but tend to reflect them as well.

First, it should be noted that the 'neo-Ricardian Marxists' constitute the left wing of a neo-Ricardian school that has sought to find a microeconomic foundation for Keynesian macroeconomic theory. Following the example of Bukharin's analysis of marginalism, Lebowitz has unearthed the 'social roots' of neo-Ricardian theory, locating them in the requirement of the managerial functionaries of capital for an *objective* understanding of price and profit formation: 'Neo-Ricardian theory in general is an attempt to analyze *all* of the concrete forms that appear on the surface of society. It does so from the perspective of the technostructure, and in this sense may be described as a new "vulgar economy"' (1973–4: 400–1).

'Marxist' neo-Ricardianism has essentially the same analytical agenda, but it claims to pursue its analysis in the interests of strengthening labour's position vis-à-vis capital. Characteristically, left neo-Ricardians place great emphasis on the role of the *class struggle* not only in altering the political relation of forces between labour and capital (as all Marxists presumably would), but also in *engendering* the crisis tendencies of the capitalist economy in a quite 'direct' sense. Since the division of the (Sraffian) 'surplus' between wages and profits supposedly reflects the balance of forces in the class struggle, and since this division 'determines' the prospects for capitalist accumulation, neo-Ricardians tend to echo the arguments of conservative and liberal economists according to which capitalist economic crises are typically the result of a 'wage-push/profit-squeeze' and/or declining labour productivity resulting from labour strength or recalcitrance at the point of production. However, whereas mainstream economists deplore the 'irresponsible and unrealistic demands' of labour, left neo-Ricardians tend to celebrate them as harbingers of consciously anticapitalist struggle.

Marxist fundamentalists take a very different view, even while arguing that capitalist economic crises both create opportunities for and necessitate anticapitalist action by the working class. In their view, capitalist economic crises are not directly attributable to economistic class struggles, but are produced by an ensemble of structural contradictions endemic to capitalism, as summarized in Marx's pithy observation that 'the barrier to capitalist production is capital itself.' But 'capital itself' encompasses a whole *set* of social production relations that increasingly ensnares the capitalist economy in a 'contradictory' logic and movement. To understand either conjunctural economic crises or the historical-structural crisis of the capitalist mode of production requires a scientific analysis of this contradictory movement that is endemic to capitalism.

Fundamentalists do not deny that the class struggle, even as this manifests itself in tepid 'business unionism,' plays some role in articulating the crisis tendencies of the capitalist economy. But they emphatically reject the neo-Ricardian/post-Keynesian notion that capitalism could enjoy a (relatively) crisis-free evolution if the class struggle could somehow be 'rationally' contained or managed. For the fundamentalists such a notion is a pure fantasy, in the first place because no economic, political, or managerial policy can 'eliminate' the class struggle under capitalism, and in the second because it involves a fundamentally false understanding of the etiology of capitalist economic crisis.

Neo-Ricardians have frequently reproached fundamentalists for having a 'fatalist' outlook – for underestimating the role of human agency and unjustifiably pinning their hopes for a 'general crisis' (or even a final, irremediable breakdown) of capitalism on deterministically understood 'laws of motion'

– that is, laws that unfold inexorably toward an anticapitalist 'negation of the negation' (see, for example, Hodgson 1975). Contemporary fundamentalists for the most part deny this charge. But they nevertheless insist upon the need to tailor political practice, education, and program in light of the results of Marx's scientific analysis of capitalism's laws of motion. On this view, any socialist political program or anticapitalist strategic perspective that ignores Marx's analysis must tend toward an accommodation with *bourgeois reformism* – that is, with the view that continuing real progress remains possible within the framework of capitalism.

The programmatic perspectives of the neo-orthodox value theorists are more difficult to pin down. Some appear close to the neo-Ricardian view, others to the fundamentalist. To some extent this reflects the theoretical heterogeneity of the neo-orthodox school; in part, a characteristically non-determinist understanding of Marx's economic laws of motion. Even such neo-orthodox theorists as Ben Fine, Laurence Harris, and John Weeks – all of whom lay great emphasis on the role of the law of the falling tendency of the rate of profit in the etiology of capitalist economic crises – tend to place this law on a *co-equal* footing with tendencies that counteract the fall in the rate of profit (Fine and Harris 1979; Weeks 1981). By doing so, however, they effectively deny the *inevitability* of capitalist economic crisis and suggest the possibility that the social capital (pre-eminently through state intervention in the economy) can contain or manage crises through the adroit mobilization of the requisite 'counteracting tendencies.'

There is another area that should be considered as a programmatic touchstone in the value controversy, namely how the transition to socialism as well as the specific content of the future socialist society should be envisioned. It can scarcely be stressed too strongly that the actual experience of 'socialist construction' in the twentieth century has weighed heavily on how Marxists have interpreted the theory of value and differed, often fundamentally, as to its meaning.

Several allusions have already been made to the fact that mid-twentieth-century 'orthodox' value theory was strongly tinged by a Ricardian approach. As we have seen, Ricardo regarded the law of value as 'eternal,' as a 'natural' constraint on all conceivable human economies. Against this, Marx believed that the socialist society of the future could and should dispense with the law of value and substitute for it a method of allocating social labour based on conscious planning and the satisfaction of human need. What, then, were academic Marxist economists (like Dobb, Meek, and Sweezy), who were either sympathizers or members of pro-Moscow Communist parties, to think when Stalin proclaimed in the Soviet constitution of 1936 that socialism had been realized in the Soviet Union? Moreover, what were Marxist economists to make of Stalin's opinion in the early 1950s when he wrote: 'It is sometimes asked whether the law of value exists and operates in our country, under the socialist system. Yes, it does exist and operate. Whenever commodities and commodity production exist, there the law of value must also exist' (Stalin 1972b: 458–9).

To those inclined to accept Stalin's view that a 'socialist system' was already in place in the Soviet Union, the 'admission' that commodity production occurs and that the law of value operates under 'socialism' could only open the way to a Ricardian embodied-labour theory of value – for the Soviet Union obviously did not evince the social production relations requisite for the social-structural existence of 'abstract labour.' For many fundamentalist theorists, however, Stalin was simply wrong to have characterized the Soviet Union as a 'socialist system,' and the fact that commodity production occurred and the law of value operated, albeit in an attenuated fashion, in the Soviet economy, only *proves* that the Soviet Union was never socialist. Ernest Mandel (1967), for example, argues that the Soviet economy was an economy transitional between capitalism and socialism, and that in all post-capitalist transitional economies, the law of value must continue to operate at some level until such time as planning becomes the exclusive principle of labour and resource allocation, dispensing with market allocation.

The neo-orthodox theorist John Weeks has also commented on Stalin's argument. For Weeks, 'the confusions and internal contradictions in [Stalin's] *Economic Problems* derive from considering the law of value as the "law of embodied (concrete) labor" ' (1981: 94). Yet, while this argument has merit, it fails to identify Stalin's contention that the Soviet Union is a 'socialist system' as the *most important* faulty premiss of Stalin's argument. By failing to do this, Weeks opens the door, perhaps unwittingly, to the notion that the kind of market phenomena that Stalin subsumes under a socialist law of value are, in fact, *compatible* with the operations of an authentically socialist economic system. The result is that his argument lends itself to political support for the 'market socialism' idea now in vogue as an alternative to the bureaucratically centralized planning of bankrupt Stalinism. But 'market socialism,' no less than Stalinist bureaucratic-commandism, constitutes an *obstacle* to the realization of a socialism that truly transcends the law of value, as I shall argue in chapter 10.

7   Value, Economy, and Crisis

The law of value, relative to the general abstraction 'economy-of-time' (Marx 1973: 173), is a determinate abstraction which dictates that the distribution of labour-time among economic branches will be regulated through processes of the social equalization of labour. In other words, where the law of value operates at all, at least some economic reproduction is governed by the exchange of commodities representing socially equalized labour. But where socially equalized labour assumes the still-more determinate (complexly determined) form of *abstract labour*, the law of value is further concretized as the *capitalist law of value*.

Historically, what distinguishes the capitalist law of value from the law of value operating under conditions of simple commodity production is that the latter stimulates progress in productive technique and exacerbates the internal contradictions of precapitalist societies, while the former, constituting the dominant principle of labour and resource allocation and having subsumed under itself the dominant mode of surplus appropriation (class exploitation), is subject to a historical limitation stemming from its own achievements. The logic of the law of value (its systematic promotion of technical rationality and labour productivity) becomes increasingly incompatible with the appropriative imperatives of the capital-labour relation.

In chapter 2 I argued that Marx regarded the drive to increase the productivity of labour as deeply rooted in the humanity-nature relation and that history could be said to possess a developmental pattern to the degree that this drive manifested itself in real and enduring developments in general human capacities. In this connection I also pointed to commodity-value relations as the social relations that have hitherto most consistently promoted a logic of technical rationalization conducive to advances in labour productivity. This is so for at least two reasons, both of which are logically and historically prior to the capital-labour relation. First, production for exchange (at first 'accidentally' and later with increasing deliberation and forethought) encourages the phenomena associated with what Sohn-Rethel calls the 'exchange abstraction'; that is to say, it encourages the emergence of cognitive faculties and forms of thought conducive to scientific breakthroughs and technical innovation. Second, production for exchange involves production for society rather than production for personal consumption, and, as such, it stimulates a competitive dynamic between commodity producers – a dynamic that promotes/facilitates product diversification, cost-cutting production innovations, and numerous technical departures that serve to enhance the productivity of labour. It is true that such competition is severely circumscribed in precapitalist formations by, for example, the presence of guild monopolies and other forms of social regulation of the activities of petty commodity producers. But this does not do away with competition entirely, and, with the extension of markets and the emergence of a *world market*, the competitive dynamic immanent in simple commodity production becomes altogether uncontainable.

What is distinctive about the capitalist law of value is that it operates through the *generalization* of commodity production and the value-form, and as the overwhelmingly dominant principle of labour and resource allocation. Because it also operates in a largely unconstrained way (that is, no longer in contradiction or tendential opposition to 'competing' but more dominant social forms), it is able to give much freer expression to its underlying drives and imperatives – perhaps most importantly, from the historical standpoint, to the drive to enhance labour productivity.

Much of the first volume of *Capital* is devoted to answering the question, What is the *source* of the formidable historical dynamism of the capitalist mode of production? The burden of the third volume of *Capital* is to answer a different question: What are the *limits* of capitalism's historically progressive mission? The elements of Marx's answer to the first question can be briefly stated. The historical dynamism of the capitalist mode of production stems from the insatiable drive of individual capitals to continuously *accumulate*. This drive is not a function of personal avarice, nor is it a function of any subjective proclivity to 'save' or to postpone personal consumption to the future. Such personal, subjective traits may play a more or less important role in the behaviour of different individual capitalists. But what compels *all* capitalists to be 'accumulators' is their *objective* role and position within the capitalist production process. All capitalists must contend with two ineliminable conditions of their activity: an antagonistic relation with their workers (resulting in a tendency to displace living labour from production in favour of labour-saving machinery), and a competitive relation with other capitalists (resulting in a tendency to seek a larger 'market share' through cost-cutting and price-slashing). Both of these relations push the individual capitalist (or the individual capitalist firm) in the direction of seeking out methods to enhance labour productivity. At the same time, each of these relations 'complements' the other in promoting the use of such methods. Thus, it is only because an individual capitalist firm can realize (that is, 'capture') the surplus-value produced by workers employed in other firms (through the process of surplus-value redistribution) that the displacement of living labour from production is a viable (micro-level) tactic for capitalists seeking greater 'independence' from recalcitrant workforces and attempting to cut production costs per unit of output. At the same time, the pressure of inter-capitalist competition is a most important factor in pushing individual firms to secure their positions in relation to the vicissitudes of the class struggle. By being less dependent on living labour, individual capitalists are better positioned to cut costs, expand markets, and meet the many challenges of competition.

The upshot is this: the fundamental social production relations that define capital push inexorably toward an enhancement of labour productivity *at the level of the individual capitalist firm.* At the level of the 'social capital,' however, things are not so straightforward. Indeed, a value-theoretical specification of the 'law of increasing productivity' under the capitalist mode of production permits a 'holistic' analysis of the contradictory developmental tendencies of capitalism – both its progressive role in developing the forces of production during its ascendant stages and its regressive role in restraining such development during the stage(s) of its historical decline.

Capitalist Development and Its Cyclical Crises

Capitalist production is production for *profit*, and profit is a money-form of surplus-value, realized through exchange in the sphere of circulation. At the macro-level, therefore, surplus-value must be produced if profits are to be realized. But the production of surplus-value is not the self-conscious aim of individual capitalists in the micro-level production processes occurring under their direction. Rather, the capitalist's aim is to produce the greatest amount of product that the market can bear at the lowest cost. By reducing the costs of production, the individual capitalist is positioned more favourably to compete successfully in the market and to realize the largest possible magnitude of profit. In the subjective calculations of the individual capitalist what is uppermost is not whether the rate of return on invested capital is equal to the average rate of profit, for this rate is never precisely known by capitalists.

What is uppermost is that the firm's rate of profit be on a par with that of its competitors, that the *mass* of profits be as large as possible, and that 'market-share' not be sacrificed on the altar of profitability (or vice versa). *All* of these considerations are taken into account when capitalist firms deliberate about the techniques they should employ in the production of their commodities. In general, the choice of technique will tend to favour increases in labour productivity – that is to say, new investment in capital stock (building structures, machinery, and so on) will be directed toward reducing the costs per unit of output (and thereby increasing the 'profit margin') through *labour-saving* innovation. The advantages of labour-saving innovation over so-called capital-saving innovation is that it allows the individual capitalist firm *simultaneously* to reduce unit costs and reduce its dependency on what Marx called the 'limited basis' of capitalist expansion: the working population.

The subjective microeconomic decisions of individual capitalists seeking to navigate the perilous waters of the capitalist market have major implications for what is transpiring at the level of commodity values. Labour-saving innovation has the objective effect of changing the form of surplus-value production. For the logic of inter-capitalist competition and of the antagonistic relation between capital and labour promotes a continuous 'revolution' in the capitalist process of producing surplus-value.

The historical presupposition and structural prerequisite for the production of surplus-value is what Marx termed the 'formal subsumption of labour by capital.' This involves the *separation* of the direct producer from ownership of the means of production, the 'commodification' of labour-power, and the intervention of the capitalist into the production process as its 'director' or 'manager.' According to Marx, for formal subsumption to occur, 'it is enough ... that handicraftsmen who previously worked on their own account, or as apprentices of a master, should become wage-labourers under the direct control of a capitalist' (1977: 1019).

In contrast to the process of formal subsumption, Marx defines the process of *real* subsumption of labour by capital as an on-going feature of what he terms the 'developed form' of the capitalist mode of production. This process involves not only a change in the situation of the agents of production but also a *revolution* in the 'actual mode of labour and the real nature of the labour process as a whole.' This revolution is necessarily *on-going* because of the capitalist imperative to continuously bring the labour process into a satisfactory relation with the valorization (value-creating) process. This has a very precise meaning, which is important to grasp: the labour process tends to lag behind the 'requirements' of the valorization process. With every improvement in labour productivity comes a change in the parameters of

socially necessary labour-time and, therefore, in the social-structural properties of abstract labour and value. To keep pace with these changes – which
may very well produce a 'competitive' challenge to the individual capitalist
firm and a diminishing *relative* magnitude of surplus labour-time for the
social capital as a whole – capitalists must be prepared to repeatedly 'revo-
lutionize' the labour processes under their direction.

Marx's theory has been substantially borne out by the actual history of
capitalist development. Fixed-capital stocks tend to become technologically
obsolescent *before* they become physically 'worn out.' Moreover, as Ernest
Mandel (1975) has shown, an actual 'acceleration of technological innovation' has occurred over the course of the history of capitalism.

Marx's distinction between the formal and the real subsumption of labour
by capital is closely related to the distinction he draws between the production
of *absolute* and *relative* surplus-value. The former corresponds to a form of
capitalist exploitation that relies on the prolongation of the working day in
order to reduce the proportion of necessary labour-time required for the social
reproduction of the labourer in relation to the surplus labour-time expended.
Accordingly, absolute surplus-value may be conceived as an *extensive* magnitude, an expansion of which depends upon increasing the *total quantity* of
labour-time performed. Relative surplus-value, by contrast, is an *intensive*
magnitude, which arises from 'the curtailment of the necessary labour-time,
and from the corresponding alteration in the respective lengths of the two
components of the working day' (Marx 1977: 432).

Since the working day cannot be indefinitely prolonged, absolute surplus-
value as an extensive magnitude faces a precise limit in the length of the
working day. Relative surplus-value, however, faces only those limits defined
by the level of development of labour-saving technology. Consequently,
relative surplus-value-creating techniques have become an increasingly
important method of raising the rate of surplus-value over the course of
capitalist history. Yet there is a certain paradox in this. Precisely because
such techniques allow individual capitalists to produce more output with less
labour, there is a tendency for all capitalists to seek productivity improve-
ments through an increase in what Marx called the 'technical composition of
capital.' The 'problem,' argues Marx, is that such an increase will find a
value expression in the diminishing relative role of living labour in the overall process of production. Living labour will be displaced by labour-saving
machinery representing a proportionally expanding magnitude of invested
constant capital values, signifying a relative diminution in the role of living
labour in the process of production. At the level of the social capital as a
whole, this displacement must entail a fall in the average rate of profit (the

fundamental regulator of capitalist accumulation), since what is involved in this increased 'value' or 'organic' composition of capital is an *overaccumulation* of constant capital in relation to the volume of surplus-value being produced by living labour. Thus, Marx's argument is squarely based on what is the key postulate of his theory of value: that *living labour and living labour alone generates the new value from which surplus-value arises.*

The upshot of all this is that capital 'moves in contradiction' – compelled by the imperatives of the accumulation process to adopt relative-surplus-value techniques, even though these techniques tend to produce a decline in the average rate of profit and, therewith, crises of accumulation. The crisis tendencies associated with declining profitability can have both a short-term (cyclical) expression and long-term (secular) influences upon regimes of accumulation. Yet the key to understanding both short-term and long-term expressions of capitalist crisis is to grasp the 'law of the falling tendency of the rate of profit,' a law that stands as something of a corollary to the capitalist law of value. This law and its relation to capitalism's crisis tendencies will be considered in greater detail in the next section. For now, it will suffice to consider its intimate relation to the *law of increasing productivity* under capitalism. Concerning this Marx states:

The barriers to the capitalist mode of production show themselves as follows: 1) in the way that the development of *labour productivity* involves a law, in the form of the falling rate of profit, that at a certain point confronts this development itself in a most hostile way and has constantly to be overcome *by way of crises*; 2) in the way that it is the appropriation of unpaid labour in general ... that determines the expansion and contraction of production, instead of the proportion between production and social needs, the needs of socially developed human beings. (1981b:367)

Marx presents the law of the falling rate of profit in this passage in a way that suggests that this law is a precipitant of conjunctural interruptions of the accumulation process. In this connection, capitalist economic crises are conceived to be the mechanism whereby a rate of profit adequate to resumed accumulation can be *restored*. In a sense, then, Marx is arguing that a fall in the rate of profit, entailing a development of labour productivity, is the *cause* of capitalist crises; at the same time, however, he suggests that (cyclical) crises produce the conditions in which the rate of profit can experience an upswing and accumulation can proceed.

The above passage also establishes very clearly that, for Marx, the *capitalist* process of promoting the productivity of labour is 'internally related' to the tendency of the rate of profit to fall. The technical composition of capital, expressing the *material* relationship between accumulated and living labour in production, is an index of labour productivity, while the *value* expression of this composition, Marx's 'organic composition of capital,' is an index of profitability. Capital promotes increased labour productivity and *in this way* undermines profitability.

When profitability suffers, a crisis occurs characterized by economic contraction, low capacity utilization, unemployment, and other well-known phenomena that, at the level of the social capital as a whole, signifies a massive decline in aggregate productivity. But the ultimate function of such cyclical crises is to bring about a *restructuring* of the regime of accumulation through a 'slaughterting of the values of capitals.' As capital *values* fall, reflecting the inability of capital stocks to sustain an adequate level of valorization, the organic composition of capital falls and the average rate of profit begins to rise. The recovery is based substantially upon a devalorized stock of capital operating at a higher rate of return. As employment and capacity utilization are restored to pre-crisis levels, the *technical* composition of capital, together with labour productivity, may remain as high as ever. But the composition of capital will also have a *value* expression that is not immediately inimical to 'production for profit.'

While Marx is often concerned to establish how the 'overaccumulation of capital' associated with a falling rate of profit is a (mere) 'barrier' to capitalist production, a barrier surmountable through 'temporary' short-term crises, it is quite clear that Marx also saw the law of the falling rate of profit as the expression peculiar to capitalism of a historical-structural crisis reflecting the growing *incompatibility* of the social relations and material forces of production. Indeed, 'the Law' may be regarded from this standpoint as a basic *limit*, as well as a conjunctural *barrier*, to capitalist development. Marx's own analysis of the law of the falling rate of profit and of its counteracting tendencies provides the necessary basis for addressing this question; but, for reasons that will be explained shortly, this analysis needs to be extended somewhat if it is to adequately account for and explain the concrete manifestations of contemporary capitalism's 'historical-structural crisis.'

The Falling Rate of Profit and the Dimensions of Capitalist Crisis

As conceived by Marx, the law of the falling rate of profit is an ineluctable concomitant of the capitalist process of accumulation. Capital's drive to augment the physical means of production (especially the fixed constant capital represented by increasingly sophisticated labour-saving machinery) *without* a corresponding augmentation of the 'living' labour-force that sets them in motion can only signify a relative diminution of the role of living labour in the overall process of accumulation. Such a pattern of accumulation *must* precipitate a fall in the average rate of profit since it entails an increase in the total capital advanced for production without a corresponding increase in the magnitude of surplus-value produced.

Contrary to the interpretations of some of his critics (notably Robinson 1942), Marx's law of the falling rate of profit is not predicated on a 'constant rate of surplus-value.' On the contrary, Marx explicitly states that the 'law of the falling rate of profit, as expressing the same or even a rising rate of surplus value, means ... an ever greater portion of [average social capital] is represented by means of labour and an ever lesser portion by living labour' (1981b: 322). The same point is made in his following succinct formulation of 'the law':

The progressive tendency for the general rate of profit to fall is thus simply the expression peculiar to the capitalist mode of production of the progressive development of the social productivity of labour. This does not mean that the rate of profit may not fall temporarily for other reasons as well, but it does prove that it is a self-evident necessity, deriving from the nature of the capitalist mode of production itself, that as it advances the general rate of surplus-value must be expressed in a falling general rate of profit. Since the mass of living labour applied continuously declines in relation to the mass of objectified labour that it sets in motion, i.e. the productively consumed means of production, the part of this living labour that is unpaid and objectified in surplus-value must also stand in an ever-decreasing ratio to the value of the total capital applied. But this ratio between the mass of surplus-value and the total capital applied in fact constitutes the rate of profit, which must therefore steadily fall. (1981b: 319)

Marx's contention that an increasing rate of surplus-value finds expression in a falling general rate of profit merits underscoring here because of the enormous confusion that has attended the interpretation of the rate of surplus-value (s/v) and the organic composition of capital (C/v or $C/s + v$) as *co-determinants* of the average rate of profit. Both Robinson (1942) and Sweezy (1968), in company with many others, have detected a telling indeterminacy in Marx's theorization of the falling rate of profit – an indeterminacy having to do with the supposed capacity of an increasing rate of surplus-value to *negate* the depressing effect of a rising organic composition of capital on the average rate of profit. What needs to be shown is that such indeterminacy is suggested *only* when the organic composition of capital is given an inadequate definition. Before this question can be approached more closely, however, a few preliminary observations are in order.

The discerning reader will have noted that in the preceding paragraph the upper-case 'C' was used to denote the constant capital in the formula(s) for the composition of capital. Up to this point, I have specified the quantitative relationships of Marx's theoretical system (the rate of surplus-value, the rate of profit, and the composition of capital) in the fashion that Marx himself did for purposes of simplified arithmetical illustration – that is to say, only as relationships between *flow* variables. However, although it is theoretically appropriate to treat variable capital and surplus-value *exclusively as flows*, compelling grounds exist for distinguishing between stock and flow expressions of constant capital. This mainly has to do with the fact that, in both theoretical and empirical investigations of the organic composition of capital and the movements of the rate of profit, it is necessary to treat constant capital as a *stock* subject to long-term depreciation as well as short-term consumption.

Marx's theory of the falling rate of profit involves as a crucial element the *fixed* constant capital embodied in technologically sophisticated machinery, the value of which is not completely consumed in a single production period. The upper-case 'C' in the formulas C/v and C/s + v refers, then, to the total value of the constant capital stock: the capital 'advanced' for purposes of capitalist production, to use Marx's own terminology. For mathematical as well as theoretical reasons this conceptualization of constant capital also enjoins us to redefine Marx's expression for the rate of profit in a particular way: instead of s/c + v, we now have s/C, where the capital 'advanced' or 'invested' in production is simply the value of the total constant capital stock (machinery, building structures, fuel, as well as raw material stocks). This procedure may seem odd in light of the crucial role played by variable capital in the accumulation process, but its advantages more than outweigh any disadvantages, particularly in the *empirical* analysis of trends in the rate of profit.[1]

With this matter clarified, we are better able to address the question of how determinate the relationship between a rising organic composition of capital (OCC) and a falling rate of profit really is. If the social OCC rises, *must* the average rate of profit fall? Sweezy, having defined the OCC as c/v (where the lower-case 'c' refers to capital used up) and the rate of profit as s/c + v, presents the following formula to express the 'co-determining' influences of the rate of surplus-value and the OCC on the rate of profit:

$$r = \frac{s/v}{1 - c/v} .$$

On the basis of this formula he concludes that 'there is no general presumption that changes in the organic composition of capital will be relatively so much greater than changes in the rate of surplus-value that the former will dominate movements in the rate of profit' (1968: 102–3). But this is correct *only* if Sweezy's formula for the rate of profit *fully* reflects Marx's understanding of the relationships between the quantitative ratios in question. This may be doubted for two reasons. First, Sweezy operates entirely within the conceptual ambit of flow variables and in this way elides the important role of fixed capital in the law of the falling rate of profit. Second, his conceptualization of the OCC as the ratio of constant to variable capital is questionable. Indeed, an excellent case can be made for conceptualizing the *organic* composition of capital as the ratio of the constant capital stock to the total value newly created by living labour in production, that is, as $C/s + v$.

The revised formulas for the rate of profit and the OCC provide the basis for a different specification of the relationships between Marx's three fundamental ratios, one that renders the relationship between the OCC and the rate of profit far more determinate than does Sweezy's formula. This specification, originally proposed by Shane Mage (1963: vii), proceeds as follows. The rate of surplus-value is the ratio of two *flows* of living labour (L), which together constitute the 'net value' of the commodity product: surplus-value and variable capital. Hence, $s' = s/v$. It follows from this that $s = L - v = L - (s/s') = L/(1+1/s') = L(s'/1 + s')$. Now, if the OCC is Q and this equals $C/s+v$, then $Q = C/L$, and the capital stock C equals $L \times Q$ ($C = LQ$). If the rate of profit is the ratio of surplus-value to the capital stock (s/C), then through substitution we arrive at

$$r = L(s'/1 + s')/LQ = s'/Q(1 + s').$$

In this formula, changes in the rate of surplus-value will impact on *both* the rate of profit and the OCC, so that *if* the OCC increases, this *must* mean a fall in the rate of profit. An increase in the rate of surplus-value contributes to maintaining or increasing the rate of profit only if it occurs without an increase in the OCC defined as $C/s + v$.

There are several good theoretical reasons for specifying the OCC as $C/s+v$ rather than as c/v or C/v. Perhaps the most important one is that, by positing a far more determinate relationship between the OCC and the average rate of profit, this formula allows us to see more clearly the relationship between the law of the falling rate of profit and the tendencies counteracting that law. For it is in the *interaction* between the 'law as such' and these counteracting tendencies that we can locate many of the law's 'internal contradictions.' An appreciation of these contradictions allows in turn for a clearer perspective on the 'real history of the capitalist mode of production' as this is determined by the capitalist law of value.

By employing C/s + v in preference to C/v we are able to allow for a *non-constant* rate of surplus-value while retaining the element of *determinacy* in the relationship between the OCC and the rate of profit that is so vital to Marx's theoretical exposition of the law of the falling rate of profit. Moreover, C/s + v is probably a more faithful and adequate representation of the burden of Marx's own conceptualization of the impact of a rising OCC on the profit rate.

In both *Capital I* and *Capital III* Marx distinguishes between 'technical,' 'value,' and 'organic' expressions of the composition of capital as follows:

The composition of capital is to be understood in a two-fold sense. As value, it is determined by the proportion in which it is divided into constant capital, or the value of the means of production, and variable capital, or the value of labour-power, the sum total of wages. As material, as it functions in the process of production, all capital is divided into means of production and living labour-power. The latter composition is determined by the relation between the mass of production employed on the one hand, and the mass of labour necessary for their employment on the other. I call the former the value composition, the latter the technical composition of capital. There is a close correlation between the two. To express this, I call the value-composition of capital, *in so far as it is determined by its technical composition and mirrors changes in the latter*, the organic composition of capital. (1977: 763; emphasis added)

This passage leaves little room for doubting that Marx saw the *value-composition* of capital as 'determined' by the proportion in which it is divided between constant and variable capital, that is, as c/v or C/v. But as capital actually functions within production, it has a technical composition (in 'material' terms) in which it is necessary to distinguish between 'means of production and living labour-power,' or between 'the mass of means of production employed on the one hand, and the mass of labour necessary for their employment on the other.' But the 'mass of labour necessary for their employment' must be specified in relation to what the means of production are being employed to do: the production of value and surplus-value. For the *organic composition* to be an expression of the value composition that 'mirrors' changes in the technical composition of capital, it must be understood as a value expression of the constant and variable capital relationships *as these appear in production*, where variable capital is no longer 'the sum of total wages' but the living labour-force engaged in creating new value (Marx 1978a 3:382).

In summary, the OCC is most adequately conceptualized and measured as the ratio of dead to living labour in production understood in value terms, that is, C/s + v. If and when this ratio rises, the rate of profit s/C *can only fall*.

Tendencies Counteracting the Fall in the Rate of Profit

In evaluating the factors cited by Marx as possible counteracting tendencies to the falling rate of profit, it is useful to distinguish between those factors that can have only a short-term (conjunctural) impact and those that can have a long-term (secular) positive influence on the average rate of profit. It is also necessary to distinguish between those factors that may contribute to an increase in the rate of surplus-value and those that pertain directly to the OCC. Under the former we should list (1) 'increases in the intensity of exploitation,' (2) 'reduction of wages below their value,' and (3) 'relative over-population,' while under the latter we should list (1) 'the cheapening of the elements of constant capital' and (2) 'foreign trade.' (See Marx 1981b: chapter 14.)

By 'increasing the intensity of exploitation' Marx understands two quite different modes of raising the level of exploitation. On the one hand, there are 'many aspects to the intensification of labour that involve a growth in the constant capital as against the variable capital, i.e. a fall in the rate of profit, such as when a single worker has to supervise a larger amount of machinery' (1981b: 339). Obviously this is *not* the sort of 'labour intensity' that Marx considers 'counteracting.' An increase in the intensity of exploitation can only counteract the tendency of the rate of profit to fall if it does not entail an increase in the OCC. Thus, Marx looks to those methods typically employed by capitalists to increase labour productivity (and therewith the rate of exploitation) without investment in labour-saving or productivity-enhancing technology conducive to an increase in the OCC. Among these methods are speed-up (which has definite physiological limits and tends to push up the wage-rate); prolongation of the working day serving to increase absolute surplus-value (which likewise faces physiological limits as well as eventual worker resistance); and productivity-enhancing technical innova-tions as these are applied by individual capitalists 'before they are universally applied' and, presumably, before they have an impact upon the economy-wide OCC.

Like the tactics employed to increase the intensity of labour exploitation, 'the reduction of wages below their value' is an episodic or ephemeral factor in countering the fall in the rate of profit; for to speak of a 'permanent reduction' of wages below their value is really to speak of a change in the value of the commodity labour-power, albeit one imposed through far more draconian methods (for instance, union-busting) than are 'normally' employed.

'Relative overpopulation' can also contribute to an increase in the rate of exploitation by forcing down wages. But this faces a limit in the limited size of the working population. Only where capitalism is in the process of uprooting precapitalist modes of production and constantly replenishing a massive 'reserve army' of the unemployed can this factor have anything more than a short-term influence as a tendency counteracting the fall in the rate of profit.

On a purely conjunctural basis, all three of the above factors can play a more-or-less important role in increasing the rate of surplus-value without inducing an increase in the OCC. Yet Marx's apparent expectation that the rate of surplus-value would display a *secular* tendency to rise was inseparable from the expectation that it would rise as a result of an increasing technical composition of capital (TCC); and such an increase, Marx assumed, would find a value expression in a falling rate of profit. Only to the extent that a rising TCC is possible *without* a concomitant increase in the OCC could this result in increasing productivity and exploitation without a fall in the rate of profit. It is precisely in this connection that 'the cheapening of the elements of constant capital' derives its great importance as a counteracting factor: '[The] same development that raises the mass of constant capital in comparison with variable reduces the value of its elements, as a result of a higher productivity of labour, and hence prevents the value of the constant capital, even though this grows steadily, from growing in the same degree as its material volume, i.e. the material volume of the means of production that are set in motion by the same amount of labour-power' (1981b: 343).

This suggests that the OCC will not rise as impetuously as the TCC, but it does not suggest that a rise in the OCC will be *prevented* simply 'as a result of a higher productivity of labour.' For a rise in the OCC to be prevented, the elements of constant capital must 'increase [in mass] while their total value remains the same or even falls' (ibid.). Marx is clearly alluding here to a range of possible 'capital-saving' innovations and techniques: for example, fixed capital of greater durability, increased efficiency in fuel and energy consumption, or the discovery and application of inexpensive substitutes for fuels or raw materials currently in use. As Marx suggests, however, such capital-saving is only possible in 'certain cases.'

The limitation of 'constant capital saving' as a factor inhibiting the fall in the profit rate is not well specified by Marx, but it can be assumed that he regarded labour-saving innovation as a *greater priority* for individual capitalists for reasons rooted in the *totality* of social production relations in which individual capitalists are enmeshed – relations that impel capitalists not only to cut costs per unit of output but to cut them in a way that simultaneously strengthens their hand in relation to labour.

Marx's fifth factor is 'foreign trade and investment,' a matter that is considered in some detail in chapter 9. Suffice it to say at this point that this factor can play a role in elevating the rate of profit only to the degree that either the terms of trade *continue* to improve and/or the rate of return on capital invested abroad *continues* to rise from the standpoint of a given 'national' social capital. Foreign trade and investment must be considered a two-edged sword, capable of depressing as well as raising the rate of profit.

This survey of the tendencies counteracting the law of the falling rate of profit shows, above all, that 'the law as such' and the counteracting tendencies to the law do not enjoy a *co-equal* status as 'tendential laws,' as has been suggested by such neo-orthodox theorists as Weeks (1981). All of the counteracting tendencies cited by Marx, with the possible exception of the cheapening of the elements of constant capital, have clearly defined *limits* as means to checking the tendency of the rate of profit to fall as a result of a rising OCC. The law itself, however, has no such limits (which does not mean, of course, that the rate of profit is inexorably headed downward). It is capitalist *crisis*, frequently involving the counteracting tendencies, that alone creates the conditions for conjunctural recoveries of the rate of profit and resumed accumulation. Importantly, however, it is also the recurrence of capitalist crises that induces the capitalist class to deploy historically ever-changing 'tactics' to shore up the rate of profit, to ensure the conditions of accumulation, and to mitigate the destabilizing influences of severe economic dislocations on capitalist society's 'class equilibrium.'

Theoretical Arguments Surrounding the Law of the Falling Rate of Profit

Apart from Sweezy's and Robinson's 'indeterminacy' argument discussed above, three basic arguments have been associated with the attempt to refute Marx's theory of a rising OCC / falling rate of profit. These are (a) the 'neutral technological progress' argument; (b) the 'rising technical composition / stable organic composition' argument; and (c) the 'choice of technique' argument (aspects of which were discussed in chapter 6). These arguments have received a good deal of attention in recent years and I will seek here merely to summarize their broad contours without entering into the 'algebra' of the controversies. In each case, I believe it can be demonstrated that Marx's theory stands its ground against the theoretical challenges that have been mounted. The question of the *empirical* actuality of a long-term fall in the rate of profit correlated with a rise in the OCC will be considered in chapter 8.

A. The Neutral Technological Progress Argument
Marx's theory of the falling rate of profit is predicated on the notion that

technological progress under capitalism has an inevitably *labour-saving bias*. Against this, his critics argue that, *given a constant real wage*, 'there are no good reasons ... why [capitalists] should economize on labor more than on constant capital' (van Parijs 1980: 3). Neo-Ricardians like van Parijs typically lay great emphasis upon the assumption of a given real wage precisely because they conceive of fluctuations in the rate of profit as deriving primarily, if not exclusively, from movements in the wage rate. Accordingly, in their opinion, a rising OCC / falling rate of profit scenario can be theoretically sustained only if a changing wage-rate is abstracted from in the analysis. The problem, however, is that it is precisely the 'threat' of variations in real wages (that is, wage increases that outstrip the growth of net productivity) that is one of the most powerful arguments in favour of Marx's thesis that technological progress will exhibit a labour-saving bias.

Reference was made earlier to some of the theoretical considerations that mitigate against the notion that 'capital-saving' innovation is as common as 'labour-saving' innovation in the attempts of capitalists to reduce their costs of production. What should be emphasized here is that the labour-saving bias of capitalist technical innovation has its most fundamental basis in the 'real subsumption of labour by capital,' involving the relegation of living labourers to mere detail functions of the production process, the de-skilling of the labour-force to the greatest extent possible (since skilled labour represents a barrier to the harmonious development of the labour and valorization processes), and the denial of the primacy of living labour to capitalist production (as a process of producing use-values). More insidiously, the real subsumption of labour by capital also 'mystifies' the capital-labour relation by further obscuring the fact that living labour is the sole source of new value; and it does so by transforming the subjective living agents of production into mere adjuncts of the machines that they set in motion. In this way, capital's claim to 'independent' productive power (as a distinct 'factor of production') is strengthened, and the claims of labour to be the source of all 'wealth' are progressively eroded. Thus, labour-saving technical innovation (the utility of which is to increase relative surplus-value) strengthens the hand of capital as against labour by making capital as independent as possible of living labour in general and skilled labour in particular. This might be referred to as the first 'functional' benefit to capital stemming from a rising technical composition of capital: the real subsumption of labour by capital is advanced and the mystification inherent in capital-labour relations is intensified.

The second functional benefit of labour-saving (and TCC-increasing) innovation is more straightforward, and has been alluded to earlier. Since the limited size of the working population is an obvious barrier to the accumulation process, capitalists must find ways of increasing their output in the face of a limited supply of labour. Labour-saving and labour-displacing machinery represent the most viable solution to this problem – for if the TCC remains constant, the capital stock cannot grow *faster* than the labour-force, and this is precisely what is required if accumulation is to proceed independently of its limited basis, the working population. If, however, technical change were to exhibit a neutral tendency or a constant capital-saving bias, capital's dependence on the available working population would become ever greater, threatening the very existence of a reserve army of labour. As Mage observes, ' ''neutral'' technological progress creates a full-employment situation in which there are irresistible pressures for a rapid increase in wages' (1963: 156).

A clear-cut and easily answerable *empirical* question flows from the 'neutral technological progress argument': Has the technical composition of capital, defined as the ratio of physical means of production to living labour employed, exhibited a tendency to rise or to remain constant? This question does not lend itself to immediate empirical operationalization, since the question of how both the numerator and the denominator are to be measured necessarily enters into it, and Marx was never explicit as to how the TCC should be measured. There are, however, compelling grounds for agreeing with Mage that by the TCC Marx meant to signify 'what modern economists call ''capital intensity'', the quantity of capital goods in ''real'' terms co-operating with each worker at some ''normal'' level of full employment' (1963: 72). If this is correct, then the TCC can be simply designated as the ratio of means of production expressed in 'constant dollars' to the number of production workers, or, better still, as constant-dollar value of capital stock employed per man-hour worked.

Wassily Leontieff, the distinguished economist who introduced input-output theory into the neoclassical system, has furnished data on the long-term trend of this very ratio for the U.S. economy from 1949 to 1977 (see figure 4 on next page, taken from Leontieff 1982: 190). The data show that the TCC ratio increased by a function of 1.9; that is, it almost doubled in the twenty-eight-year period examined. All theoretical speculation aside, the empirical evidence shows that in the United States (the leading capitalist country, if not always the leader in labour-saving innovation) technological change showed a labour-saving rather than a neutral tendency, and that this tendency involved a marked increase in the TCC.

B. The Rising TCC / Stable OCC Argument
The most frequently encountered theoretical objection to the law of the falling

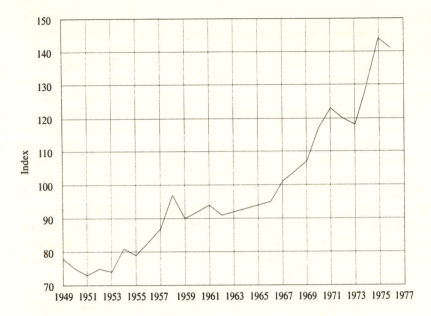

Figure 4 Value of capital stock employed per man-hour in manufacturing industries in the United States, 1949–77, plotted on a constant 1967-dollar index (SOURCE: Wassily Leontieff, 'The Distribution of Work and Income.' Copyright © 1982 by *Scientific American*, Inc. All rights reserved)

rate of profit concerns Marx's expectation that a rise in the TCC (a ratio of use-value magnitudes) will be accompanied by a rise in the OCC (a ratio of value magnitudes). This may be referred to as the rising TCC / constant OCC argument, and variants of the argument have been elaborated by Hodgson (1974), Lebowitz (1976), and van Parijs (1980), among many others. Marx himself acknowledged that the rise in the OCC would not be as pronounced as the rise in the TCC owing to the productivity increases associated with the latter. His critics add that productivity increases in industries producing means of production in particular would have the effect of reducing their value, in this way deflating the magnitude of value in the numerator of the OCC. There are, however, substantial reasons to believe that these productivity increases cannot *completely* negate the tendency of the OCC to rise along with the TCC.

As we have seen, the rise in the TCC itself is attributable to a labour-saving bias in capitalist technical innovation – a notion rooted in Marx's explicit recognition of the capital-labour relation as *antagonistic*. This notion is not present in neoclassical theories of technical progress, and so it is difficult to see from a neoclassical perspective that the use-value (or the 'marginal utility') of a 'capital good' is a function not only of its 'capacity increasing effect' but of its 'labour-saving effect' as well (Mage: 159). However, once this *dual* function of means of production is recognized, it becomes clear that the TCC could not be synonymous or co-extensive with labour productivity. Labour productivity is measured as the ratio of the mass of use-values produced (capacity) to the number of productive workers (or hours worked). The TCC, by contrast, refers to the ratio of the use-value of the means of production to the number of productive workers (hours worked). If technical innovation does display a labour-saving bias, for all the reasons pointed to by Marx, then the numerator of the TCC should increase at a faster rate than the numerator of labour productivity (since all changes in the latter will be reflected in the former, but not all changes in the former will find expression in the latter). The logical implication is that the TCC should rise at a faster rate than labour productivity. Since the OCC is the 'value expression' of the TCC, it follows that the OCC's rise will be restrained by increased labour productivity, but not blocked. (For a detailed development of this argument, see Smith 1984: 144–8.)

C. The Choice of Technique Argument

If a rising OCC is compatible with a stable or rising rate of profit for *individual capitals*, it becomes necessary to establish the precise criteria by which individual capitalist firms will evaluate different techniques of production. Okishio's (1961) theorem sought to demonstrate that the criteria actually employed by capitalists would rule out the possibility of a fall in the *average* rate of profit resulting from technical innovation, and that these criteria are shaped by the exigencies of capitalist competition. Van Parijs summarizes the argument as follows: 'Under competitive capitalism, a profit-maximizing individual capitalist will only adopt a new technique of production ... if it reduces the production cost per unit or increases profits per unit at going prices. A technical innovation which satisfies this requirement ... enables the capitalist to get (temporarily) a transitional rate of profit higher than the initial general rate in the economy' (1980: 10).

In keeping with the neo-Ricardian shibboleth of an absolute tendency toward profit-rate uniformity, the Okishio theorem assumes that 'the new average rate will be higher than the old average, due solely to the introduction of a cheaper technique (real wages being given)' (Shaikh 1978: 242).

In his response to the choice-of-technique argument Shaikh shows that what Okishio has proved with his elaborate theorem is what Marx himself asserted, namely, that 'the battle of competition is fought by the cheapening of commodities' (*Capital I*) and that 'the cheapest method of production will win out in the wars among capitals' (ibid.: 245). Shaikh also makes the crucial point that there is a *difference* between the 'cheapest method of production' *per unit of output* and the 'cheapest method' from the standpoint of *capital invested*. In order to grasp this distinction, we must return to the one made earlier between *stocks* and *flows*. The cheapening of commodities is predicated on the lowering of unit cost-price, that is, a reduction of the *flow* of capital used up in the production of each unit. Marx argues that this is usually accomplished through an *increase* in the fixed-capital *stock*. The price paid by capitalists for the 'increase in the productive powers [of labourers]' (Marx 1973: 776–7), which brings about the lowering of unit costs, is an increased 'roundaboutness' of production. Shaikh elaborates upon Marx's argument as follows:

[A] lower production cost per unit of output is achieved by means of a greater investment cost per unit of output. Once the difference between production costs and investment costs is grasped, it immediately follows that there in fact exist two *different* measures of profitability; profits in relation to capital used up in production (i.e. in relation to cost price), which I shall call *profit-margin on costs* and profits in relation to capital advanced, or the profit rate. The former is a ratio of two flows, the latter a ratio of flow to stock ... it becomes apparent that what Okishio has in fact demonstrated is that such a choice will raise the average *profit-margin* which corresponds to a given real wage. (1978: 242–3)

Since the rate of profit is a ratio of the surplus-value flow to the constant-capital *stock*, the increased fixed capital needed to cheapen commodities 'will lower not only the maximum but also the actual rate of profit – precisely because this cheapening "necessitates a costly and expensive apparatus" [Marx]' (ibid.: 244).

The argument does not end here, however; it merely shifts its ground from the realm of 'rigorous mathematical proofs' to the realm of theory. Why, the neo-Ricardians might ask, would innovating capitalists opt for a technique that would lower their transitional rate of profit, even if it increased profit margins? After all, even Marx asserts that no capitalist 'ever *voluntarily* introduces a new method of production ... so long as it reduces the rate of profit' (Marx 1978b: 264). The answer is that the (individual innovating capitalist's) transitional rate of profit will *not* be lowered, *unless* he seeks to turn his technical advantage against his competitors immediately: 'Every such new method of production cheapens the commodities. Hence, the capitalist sells them originally above their prices of production, or, perhaps, above their value. He pockets the difference between their costs of production and the market prices of the same commodities produced at higher costs of production' (ibid.).

If the innovating capitalist sells the cheapened commodities at prevailing market prices, then a surplus profit can be reaped and the transitional rate of profit on the capital investment will rise. If they are sold at a market price reflecting their lowered cost-price, a decent rate of profit can still be realized, competitors can be undercut in the market, and increased market-share may produce a larger *mass* of profits. Faced with all this, the innovating capitalist's competitors are no longer confronted with a voluntary choice as to whether or not to adopt the new technique of production; they are *compelled* to do so on pain of competitive ruin. Once the new technique becomes generalized, however, the result must be a lower average rate of profit.

Dimensions of Capitalist Crisis

While the law of the falling average rate of profit obviously occupies a central place in Marx's own theory of capitalist crisis, it has not enjoyed a comparable status in the crisis theories elaborated and defended by most twentieth-century Marxists. To be sure, in recent years the 'wage-push/profit-squeeze' hypothesis has been rather prominent in Marxist economic literature. Unquestionably, however, Marxist underconsumptionism has been and likely remains the dominant paradigm within Marxist crisis theory. Of course, the underconsumptionists do not deny that crises are caused by a decline in profit rates; but they differ decisively from Marx in pointing to *insufficient effective demand* as the precipitant of profitability crises. In other words, underconsumptionists view capitalist crises centrally as *crises of realization*.

Some elements of an underconsumptionist position can certainly be found in Marx. However, these elements do not stand in contradiction to his theory of the overaccumulation of capital; on the contrary, they are part and parcel of this same theory. It is, in fact, the Marxist underconsumptionists who *counterpose* Marx's observations in this vein to the law of a rising OCC and falling average profit rate. And in so doing, they distort the real meaning of these 'underconsumption' observations.

Let us consider what is perhaps the most frequently cited of these observations: 'The ultimate reason for all real crises always remains the poverty and restricted consumption of the masses, in the face of the drive of capitalist production to develop the productive forces as if only the absolute consumption capacity of society set a limit to them' (Marx 1981b: 615). What Marx is *not* saying here is that consumption necessarily lags behind production because of the poverty and exploitation of the working masses under capitalism. Rather, he is saying that the 'restricted consumption of the masses' is an *immanent* barrier to capitalist production – a kind of 'structural constant' the dimensions of which might *exacerbate* capitalist crises while not necessarily causing them. Regardless of the concrete events that may trigger a particular crisis (and these are many and varied), there is no doubt that its manifestations can be contained and its consequences mitigated through an expansion of effective demand, making possible the sale of commodities at prices that might otherwise not be realized. As Marx suggests, the 'overproduction' of commodities associated with capitalist crises can be mitigated to the extent that their sale is not wholly dependent on the 'narrow basis on which the relations of consumption rest' (ibid.: 353). In this connection, Marx points to the central importance of an expanding world market: '*The internal contradiction seeks resolution by extending the external field of production*' (ibid.).

This implies that the penetration of the world market and the investment of capital in foreign countries become increasingly important strategies for the curbing of crisis tendencies *within national capitalist contexts*. The same thesis is suggested in Marx's discussion of foreign trade and investment as influences that can counteract the falling rate of profit. Yet, as already noted, all of this is very much a two-edged sword. *Every* capitalist country seeks to use such strategies to curb its 'locally manifested' crisis tendencies, even though it is only too obvious that not all of them (or even most of them) can succeed in any given conjuncture. The *condition* for 'resolving the internal contradiction' through an extension of the external field of production (and realization) for the social capital of one country is that the social capitals of other countries fail in this same strategy of 'exporting,' as it were, their crisis tendencies. Furthermore, as all capitalist countries become increasingly *interdependent*, as the weakest of them reach the limits of their capacity to absorb the global effects of these tendencies, and as capital exerts itself more and more as an *international power*, unhampered by national loyalties or nation-state regulation, such strategies become less effective, even to the point of becoming counter-productive.

Because capitalist crises take the surface form of crises of realization ('inadequate effective demand'), even though they have their most fundamental roots in an over-accumulation of capital in relation to the prevailing rate of profit, all capitals are concerned with securing their ability to *sell* their products at prices reflecting the expected profit margin, and therefore the anticipated rate of return on invested capital. Accordingly, both individual capitalist firms and the capitalist state tend to pursue what might be called 'circulationist' strategies for mitigating capitalist crisis tendencies. It is generally only when the limits of these strategies have been met that the social capital will resort to political-economic policies of a more draconian and openly antilabour nature (such as, monetarism, capital flight, union-busting, wage-slashing) aimed directly at shoring up the average rate of profit through cuts in working-class living standards.

Because circulationist strategies are generally the *preferred* modus operandi for sustaining profitability (for political and ideological reasons), it is not surprising that the *costs* of cirulation have increased dramatically as the fundamental contradictions of capitalism have intensified. A value-theoretical conceptualization of these costs, as well as related increases in the costs of maintaining an interventionist and ever-expanding state apparatus, is therefore of great importance to specifying, on the basis of the theory of labour-value, the concrete contours of contemporary capitalism's crisis tendencies. This issue is pursued in chapter 8.

The Historical-Structural Crisis of Capitalism

Contrary to the opinion of some Marxist commentators (Fine and Harris 1979, Weeks 1981), a substantial basis exists in Marx's work for understanding the law of the falling rate of profit as not only a precipitant of cyclical and/or conjunctural interruptions of the capitalist accumulation process, but also as an expression peculiar to the capitalist mode of production of a growing and irresolvable contradiction between the social relations and forces of production, that is, of a 'historical-structural crisis' of capitalism. This idea is clearly expressed in the following passages from Marx's *Grundrisse*:

[The declining profit rate] is in every respect the most important law of modern political economy, and the most essential for understanding the most difficult relations. It is the most important from the *historical* standpoint ... Beyond a certain point, the development of the powers of production become a barrier for capital; hence the capital relation a barrier for the development of the productive powers of labour. When it has reached this point, capital, i.e. wage-labour, enters into the same relation towards the development of the social wealth and of the forces of production as the guild system, serfdom, slavery, and is necessarily stripped off as a fetter. The last form of servitude assumed by human activity, that of wage-labour on one side, capital on the other, is thereby cast off like a skin, and this casting-off itself is the *result* of the mode of production corresponding to capital; the material and mental conditions of the negation of wage-labour and of capital, themselves already the negation of earlier forms of unfree social production, are themselves results of its production process. The *growing incompatibility* between the productive development of society and its hitherto existing relations of production expresses itself in bitter contradictions, crises, spasms. The *violent destruction* of capital not by relations external to it, but rather as a condition of its self-preservation, is the most striking form in which advice is given it to be gone and to give room to a higher state of social production. (1973: 748–9; emphasis added)

Several points in these passages should be especially noted. First, Marx refers to the 'development of the powers of production' as a *barrier* to capital, and to the 'capital relation' as a 'barrier for the development of the productive powers of labour.' This suggests a dialectical interaction between the material forces and the social relations of production in which, increasingly, each stands as a barrier to the other. If the material forces of production undermine the social relations of production, the social relations of production *also* undermine the material forces of production. As long as capitalism survives, this destructive interaction must persist. The material forces of production can 'prevail' over the social relations of production only in a 'higher state of social production.'

Second, Marx refers to the 'growing incompatibility between the productive development of society and its hitherto existing relations of production.' This point is crucial to the *historical* significance of the law of the falling rate of profit. A falling rate of profit resulting from an over-accumulation of capital is a feature of *both* the period of capitalist ascent and the period of capitalist decline. But if this law is also the *harbinger* of capitalist decline – the expression of an irremediable contradiction fatal to capital's continuing ability to systematically promote the development of labour productivity and with it human culture – then it must have a somewhat *different* significance and expression during the era of capitalist decline than it had when capital was still playing a historically progressive role. This seems to be the burden of Marx's reference to a 'growing incompatibility' – and yet the expression of this growing incompatibility is left unspecified by Marx, except for a reference to 'bitter contradictions, crises, spasms' – that is, to phenomena that have been recurrent features of capitalism since its birth.

This brings us to a third point. Marx also implies that this 'growing incompatibility' between the forces and relations of production will find expression in the 'violent destruction of capital not by relations external to it, but rather as a condition of its self-preservation.' Here Marx proved to be remarkably prescient – for it has been the quite literal physical destruction of capital in

world wars (themselves interpretable as *products* of the 'growing incompatibility') that has led many twentieth-century Marxists to conclude that capitalism has indeed entered into historical-structural crisis. In Lenin's terms,
capitalism has reached its 'highest stage' with the advent of *imperialism*, a
phenomenon that expresses, above all, the attempt of the most developed
capitalist countries to resolve their 'internal' contradictions at the expense of
each other as well as at the expense of their less-developed colonies and neocolonies in the Third World.

But if imperialism and its associated conflicts have demonstrated how
'destructive' the capital relation can be to existing stocks of physical capital
(not to mention human beings), the growth of 'unproductive' sectors within
the most-developed capitalist countries *also* signifies that the capital relation
is destructive to the productive and emancipatory *potential* of the technology
that has developed under its wing. Indeed, in an era when nuclear weapons
have made a resolution of the internal contradictions of capitalist production
through a *military extension* of the external field of production highly perilous, this *thwarting* of the great potential of science and technology, together
with the 'wasteful' reallocation of social labour to unproductive tasks that
are 'socially necessary' only from the standpoint of capital, may be 'the most
striking form in which advice is given [capital] to be gone and to give room
to a higher stage of social production.' It would nevertheless be foolish to
ignore the very real tendencies toward inter-imperialist war that world capitalism continues to breed and that have only been strengthened by the change
in geo-political dynamics ushered in by the collapse of the Soviet bloc.

8 Respecifying Marx's Value Categories: An Empirical Study of the Law of the Falling Rate of Profit

Since the 1960s Marxist economists have produced a large and impressive body of empirical research pertaining to the historical trends of the rate of surplus-value and the organic composition of capital as well as unique measures of the more familiar economic phenomena of profitability, productivity, and real wages. Yet what is most striking about the findings that have been reported to date is not their unitary distinctiveness in relation to non-Marxian accounts of contemporary economic trends, but rather their markedly different approaches to operationalizing Marx's concepts as empirical variables. Consequently, different analyses have arrived at widely divergent conclusions concerning both the meaning of observable economic trends and the acuity of Marx's analysis of the 'laws of motion' of capitalism.

The root of the problem is in the alternative ways in which Marx's concepts – his 'value categories' in particular – have been theoretically specified for purposes of 'empirical Marxian research.' For, clearly, without a theoretical consensus regarding the empirical content of these concepts, there can be no meeting of minds concerning what 'the facts' reveal. The problem is compounded by the fact that the relative underdevelopment of Marxist economics has made it susceptible to 'alien' influences. Empirical Marxian economics has, after all, been the preserve largely of Marxists trained in the ideas of the neoclassical synthesis, a tradition permeated with what Marx would have considered vulgar and fetishistic notions. It is therefore quite reasonable to assume that many of the differences of opinion existing between Marxian empirical studies may stem from a kind of uneven cognitive break from conventional (neoclassical or Keynesian) influences.

A further problem is that most Marxian economists subscribe to theories of capitalist crisis that are *not* dependent on Marx's value theory and that often share much in common with Keynesian and/or neoclassical perspectives. This consideration points to the *political* import of the debate between those who adhere to a Marxian underconsumptionist theory, those who subscribe to a 'profit squeeze' account of capitalist crisis, and those who insist, with Marx, that such phenomena as 'deficient effective demand' and 'rising labour strength' need to be theoretically articulated with the tendency of the social capital to increase its organic composition, in this way undercutting its prospects for valorization, i.e. its profitability (Smith 1984: chap. 2). Marxian underconsumptionism often lends itself to a traditional *reformist* perspective to the extent that it sees the class struggle as centring on the disposition of an ever-expanding 'economic surplus' that the system must find some way of 'absorbing.' The affinities to Keynesian theory and policy are striking and have been frequently noted.[1] Alternatively, proponents of the 'profit squeeze' theory essentially share the view of conservative economists that the troubles of the capitalist economy are attributable to an overpaid and recalcitrant workforce.

Although Marx's theory of a falling rate of profit stemming from a rise in the organic composition of capital has been adduced, mistakenly, to support the notion of an inevitable and irrevocable collapse or 'breakdown' of the capitalist system, its contemporary proponents tend to view it simply as the theoretical heart of a programmatic perspective that denies that the contradictions of capitalism can be significantly attenuated through 'reform' or that capitalism can any longer play a 'progressive historical role.'[2] This perspective must *inform* the program and strategic perspective of the labour movement if it is to avoid the illusions of reformism and effectively rebut the anti-labour hysterics of the crisis theorists of the right.

But can Marx's theory be reasonably adduced to explain the recent troubles of the North American and world economies? In considering this question, my concern in this chapter will be with the manner in which Marx's 'value categories' should be specified to test empirically the leading propositions of his theory of capitalist accumulation. This is by no means a question of making the theoretical categories fit the empirical evidence, but of specifying them in a fashion that is as faithful as possible to Marx's theory of value taken as a whole. In attempting such a specification (which is also a 'respecification' when compared to traditional Marxian approaches), I have been influenced principally by the work of Shane Mage (1963).[3]

Contradictory Testimony of Empirical Marxian Research

The distinctiveness of empirical Marxian research in relation to non-Marxian economic analysis is rooted in its attempt to find empirical counterparts to a set of economic categories and relationships unique to Marxist theory. These are Marx's 'value categories' of constant capital, variable capital, and surplus-value, and the ratios defining the rates of surplus-value and profit as well as the composition of capital.

In the process of its production, the commodity product receives value from both 'living' and 'dead' sources: from wage labour, on the one hand, and from various elements of the means of production, on the other. In furnishing these sources of value, capital appears in two forms: as constant capital and as variable capital. *Within production*, constant capital takes the material form of means of production (machinery, raw materials, fuel, and so on), which can impart to the new commodity product no more value than they represent. In other words, the elements of constant capital transfer 'previously existing' value to the newly produced commodity.

Marx attributes the role of creating *new* value to the variable capital 'invested' in the acquisition of labour-power. Labour-power is the sole commodity-input to production that releases *living labour*, the unique source of new value. The value newly created by living labour in production is considered by Marx to account for both the value embodied in the wages received by productive workers and the surplus-value created by these workers during the 'unpaid' portion of their working day.

The total value of the commodity product may therefore be defined as $P = c + v + s$, where c represents the value objectified in those embodiments of 'congealed labour' that contribute indirectly to the value-expansion process (that is, through a transfer of value effected by living labour), v represents the value embodied in the wage bill of productive workers, and s represents the surplus-value created by the surplus labour of productive workers.

It is upon the secular trend of the organic composition of capital that the theoretical probity of Marx's law of the falling rate of profit depends. As we saw in chapter 7, this law asserts that the productivity-enhancing imperative of the capitalist mode of production must impart to the process of accumulation a *labour-saving* bias, the result of which will be a diminution in the role of living labour relative to 'accumulated labour.' The law further asserts that this diminution will find a *value* expression such that the OCC (the ratio $C/s + v$) will exhibit a tendency to rise and the rate of profit (s/C) a tendency to fall.

Mathematically, the association of such a rising organic composition of capital with a falling average rate of profit is indeed unassailable, even if the inevitability of a rise in $C/s + v$ is not entirely obvious (see chapter 7). Accordingly, if a clear empirical tendency for $C/s + v$ to rise can be established and this can be correlated with a decline in s/C, this would provide strong support for what Marx termed the 'most important' law of modern political economy. The problem is that the empirical evidence on this point appears to be highly contradictory.

In very general terms it is possible to distinguish between three groups of empirical studies with some claim to having assessed Marx's 'hypotheses.'

The first group highlights a rising rate of exploitation as the most salient feature of modern capitalist development. Frequently, the studies associated with this approach are only tenuously based on Marx's own (value-theoretical) categories of analysis. This is particularly true of the empirical work associated with the 'monopoly capitalism' school initiated by Baran and Sweezy, for whom the tendency of the 'economic surplus' to rise has displaced the tendency of the rate of profit to fall as the key problem of modern capitalism.[4] However, it should be noted that this school's notion of the economic surplus is based in some measure on an acceptance of Marx's distinction between productive and unproductive labour, and to this extent it represents a continuation of Sweezy's (1968/1942: 283) 'expanded' specification of surplus-value. The upshot is that the underconsumptionist method of specifying the value categories (by radically expanding the estimates of surplus-value) results in an analysis that minimizes the decline in the average rate of profit, emphasizes a rise in the rate of surplus-value, and undermines the notion of a rise in the organic composition of capital.

Studies belonging to the second and third groups agree that there was a long-term decline in the rate of profit extending from at least the early sixties to the early eighties in most of the major capitalist countries. This trend is illustrated for the United States by Shaikh's graph, shown in figure 5 (page 168).[5] The second and third groups, however, are divided concerning the *cause* of this long-term decline in the average rate of profit. The second group of studies, by far the most numerous in recent years, attributes the observed crisis of profitability to a decline in the rate of surplus value, a wage-push/ profit-squeeze, or related phenomena resulting from a slowdown in productivity growth. At the same time, most of these studies report a falling or relatively stable organic composition of capital. Studies by Weisskopf and Wolff are representative of these results.[6]

In contrast, the third group of studies provide results that support Marx's expectations concerning the dynamics and trends of capitalist accumulation. Studies by Shaikh (1987), Fred Moseley (1987), and myself (Smith 1984) follow Mage's (1963) pioneering study in establishing a strong correlation between a decline in the rate of profit and a rise in the organic composition of capital. And for the postwar period at least, they are in agreement concerning the upward trend of the rate of surplus-value. Figures 6 and 7 provide

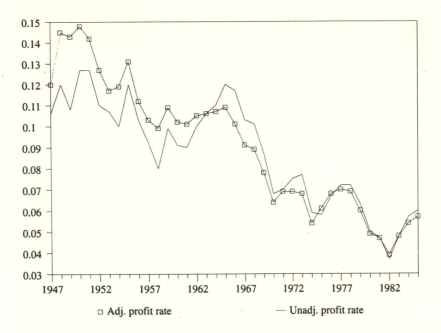

□ Adj. profit rate   — Unadj. profit rate

Figure 5 Profit rates, U.S.A.

a graphical comparison of Moseley's results (1987) with those of Weisskopf and Wolff concerning the trends of the rate of surplus-value and the composition of capital in the U.S. economy.

The single most important factor accounting for the discrepancy between the results of the second and third groups of studies concerns the manner in which variable capital should be empirically specified. While important theoretical differences exist between the Group 3 studies, they are united in rejecting as a proper measure of variable capital an all-inclusive wage-labour bill in which the remuneration to unproductive labour (for instance, retail clerks) is indiscriminately added to the income of *productive* workers (those involved directly in the production, rather than the realization, of surplus-value).

The exclusion of the values flowing to the unproductive sectors of the workforce from the measurement of the category variable capital is, in my view, the first, elementary step to a specification of Marx's value categories adequate to the task of empirically evaluating his theory on its own terms. Indeed, the difference that this step makes empirically is so great that it is

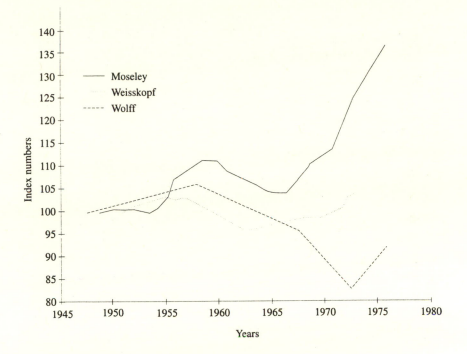

Figure 6 The composition of capital, U.S.A. (three estimates)

mystifying how any researcher, least of all a Marxist one, could 'empirically test' Marx's theory without confronting this problem directly.

It is true that Marx in volume three of *Capital* rather confusingly refers to commercial capitalists exchanging 'variable capital' for the labour of their employees, implying thereby that circulation workers are productive of surplus-value. But Marx's discussion makes clear that he is speaking here of a variable capital sui generis; that the remuneration to such unproductive workers in the sphere of circulation is 'variable capital' solely from the standpoint of commercial (or financial) capital; and that the signficance of the activity of such workers from the standpoint of the social capital as a whole is that it effects a *transfer* of values (including surplus-value) from productive (primarily industrial) capital to unproductive capital in the sphere of circulation. Marx is unequivocally clear in *Capital* as elsewhere that the variable capital sui generis exchanged with circulation labour contributes *nothing* to the self-expansion of the social capital as a whole.[7] But if the remuneration to such

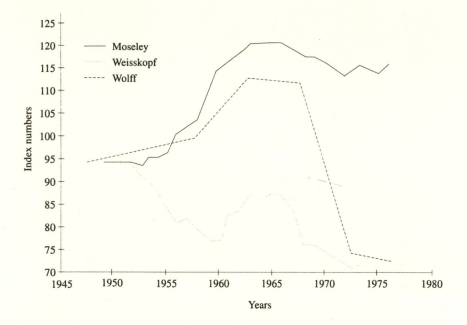

Figure 7 The rate of surplus-value, U.S.A. (three estimates)

labour is not 'really' variable capital, how is it to be conceptualized in value-theoretical terms? And if the first step to entertaining and empirically evaluating Marx's theory 'on its own terms' entails a recognition of the delimited character of variable capital as a value category, how are we to take the second step of treating that which has been excluded?

A Theoretical Respecification of the Value Categories

The problem of unproductive labour in Marxist theory is a multifaceted and much-debated one, with many aspects that cannot be addressed here.[8] My concern here is strictly with the remuneration to unproductive labour considered as a component of the costs of circulation and of maintaining the capitalist state. The 'value-theoretical' treatment of these costs that has been followed by most Marxists has been to define the value of these costs as *deductions* from the surplus-value created by productive capital and transferred to commercial capital, financial capital, or the state. In other words, the procedure has been to treat these costs as non-profit elements of 'social surplus-value.'[9]

In challenging this procedure, it will be helpful to reflect again upon Marx's account of the circuit of capital:

$$M - C \ (LP \ and \ MP) \ ... \ P \ ... \ C' - M',$$

where LP denotes labour-power (the value-producing input commodity), MP the means of production, P the production process that transforms input commodities C into output commodities representing greater value C', and M and M' money capital as before. The key point in this formula is that, through the purchase of commodities constituting inputs to production, money capital is transformed into productive capital capable of yielding the commodity capital C'. The realization of the value represented by C' involves their *sale*. Hence, the circuit of capital embraces two overlapping phases of activity: the circuit of money and commodity capital, and the process of production, which transforms inputs into new outputs while imparting to these outputs a quantity of new value derived from living labour.

Again, the circuit of capital is completed only when the commodity capital produced has been transformed into money-capital; but it is only *successfully* completed when the magnitude of this realized money capital exceeds the capital invested in *both* the production and the circulation of commodity capital. For just this reason Marx regards the sphere of circulation as both a necessity and a barrier to the valorization of capital.[10]

In the second volume of *Capital*, Marx suggests that an increase in the 'annual rate of surplus-value' (referring essentially to a reduction in the turnover period of capital) will result in an increased volume of surplus-value relative to the capital advanced. However, such a reduction in circulation time is by no means easily accomplished. Not only is circulation time governed by market accessibility and the 'effective demand' existing for the commodities in question; the attempt to address these problems carries with it significant material and labour costs above and beyond those associated with the direct production of commodities. These costs are subject to rationalization through a historically evolving functional division of labour between industrial, commercial, and financial capital, as well as through state interventions of various sorts; however, it would also seem that they have had a tendency to rise as the contradictions of capitalism have intensified and as individual capitals have pursued 'circulationist' strategies to shore up profit margins.[11]

In a very important sense, then, commercial and financial capital, through their investments in the sphere of circulation and their employment of 'circulation labour,' participate with industrial capital in bearing the aggregate costs of production and reproduction. Moreover, they are rewarded for this by participating in the division and redistribution of social surplus-value (as this emerges from the sphere of production) on the same basis as the various industrial capitalists, that is, on the basis of the 'average rate of profit' calculated on invested capital. It should be noted that to the extent that the 'costs of circulation' rise faster than the costs of production this can only signify that the social capital as a whole is investing proportionately more in the *realization* of commodity values than in the production of surplus-value. It is therefore quite possible that circulationist strategies for sustaining the profitability of individual capitals can end up reducing the average profit rate of the social capital as a whole.

Much controversy has surrounded the conceptualization of 'unproductive labour' in general and 'circulation labour' in particular. What needs to be stressed here is that Marx recognized the existence of two very distinct *forms* of unproductive labour. In many of his writings on the subject, particularly those intersecting the debates of the classical economists on labour outside the capital-labour relation, Marx was concerned with a form of unproductive labour that presents itself as a kind of 'luxury' item consumed by the wealthy (for example, the labour of domestic servants). For Marx, this form of unproductive labour receives as its reward a portion of capitalist revenue, a kind of absolute 'deduction' from surplus-value.

But Marx also recognizes the existence of a form of unproductive labour that Mage (1963: 65) has described as 'socially necessary' to the reproduction process of capital. This form of unproductive labour is not 'exchanged with revenue' but with capital, as Marx makes abundantly clear in the third volume of *Capital*. Specifically, this unproductive labour is exchanged with capital values 'invested' by commercial and financial capitalists (the 'variable capital sui generis' already mentioned), although industrial capitals will also employ a certain number of such 'socially necessary' but unproductive workers.

What these two forms of unproductive labour have in common is that neither are productive of surplus-value. Where they differ – and differ decisively – is in their respective roles in capitalist reproduction. Socially necessary unproductive labour contributes 'indirectly' to the valorization of capital by helping to realize commodity values and by increasing the 'velocity' of commodities as they move through circulation. The other form of unproductive labour performs 'personal' services that are no part of the value-expansion process of capital, but represent a simple deduction from the circuit of revenue.

The problem is, once it is accepted that 'circulation labour' is a 'socially necessary' form of unproductive labour, one that is exchanged with capital rather than revenue, how do we then conceptualize the capital with which it is exchanged? Marx's theory of value enjoins us to regard this capital in only one of two possible ways: either the income of these unproductive workers constitutes a portion of the aggregate constant capital or it constitutes a portion of the aggregate variable capital. But since variable capital is capital invested in the acquisition of productive labour, it follows that we are left with only one possibility: to subsume the income of 'socially necessary unproductive labour' under an 'expanded' definition of constant capital. While Marx himself did not explicitly do this, there is considerable support for such a conceptualization in *Capital*. More important than 'exegetical' support, however, is the fact that this conceptualization conforms to a methodological imperative to free the category of constant capital from the *fetishistic* notion that it can only find phenomenal expression as 'physical means of production.'

Before attempting a 'non-fetishized' definition of constant capital, it will be helpful to consider Moseley's ostensibly 'value-theoretical' definition – for his is a particularly clear statement of a fetishism common among even the most sophisticated Marxist economists. For Moseley (1987: 106), 'Marx's concepts of constant capital and variable capital include only the capital invested in *production activities*, where "production" is defined fairly broadly to include such activities as transportation and storage' but does *not* include 'circulation' or 'supervision' activities. Moseley seeks to sustain this position by appealing to Marx's theory of value, arguing that 'the (past and current) labour required to perform the non-production functions of circulation and supervision, although entirely necessary within the capitalist mode of production, nonetheless does not add to the value of the commodities produced.' Moseley subsumes such labour under 'unproductive capital' and then asserts that 'since this unproductive capital produces no value, it cannot be recovered out of value which it produces' (107). But this begs the obvious question of how constant capital in production 'recovers value' even though *it too* produces no value.

In my view this problem is not solved by amalgamating constant capital with variable capital under the notion of 'productive capital'; indeed, such a procedure merely attenuates Marx's key insight that variable capital is solely responsible for the production of all new value, and readmits, through the back door, the capital-fetishistic notion that machinery can be a source of new value.[12] The problem is only satisfactorily resolved by recognizing that there is a fundamental difference between 'adding' (old) value to the new commodity product and 'producing' the (new) value that attaches to it. Once this distinction is grasped, it no longer follows that the 'unproductive capital' values 'consumed' in the process of reproduction should be seen as 'recovered ... out of the surplus value produced by productive labor employed in capitalist production' (ibid.).

Contrary to Moseley, constant capital is not merely a value expression of its material elements in the direct process of production. Rather, it is a particular expression of the social relations of production constituting capital and is therefore properly understood in relation to its 'complementary' if 'opposite' expression, variable capital. If the *differentia specifica* of variable capital is that it is transformed into the living labour *directly* productive of surplus-value, the distinguishing characteristic of constant capital is that it is transformed into all the elements of the capitalist process of production and reproduction *indirectly* implicated in the total process of value creation and surplus-value production. As such, it can take the 'material form' of socially necessary unproductive labour just as easily as it can take the form of a punch-press, a building structure, a ton of sheet metal, or a cash register.

The conclusion is this: the costs of circulation, including the costs of circulation labour, are legitimately treated as a component of the *constant capital* expended in the total process of capitalist production and reproduction (Mage 1963: 66). Value is *added* to the commodity product by these costs in the same way that it is added by the elements of constant capital in the immediate process of production: through an addition of *previously existing* values. To cite Marx: 'The additional value that [the merchant] adds to commodities by his expenses is reducible to the addition of previously-existing value' (1981b: 293).

The relationship of circulation capital to the commodity product can be compared to that of a machine. Within the production process a machine can only transfer its own previously existing value to the new product; to this extent it is 'indirectly' productive – a mere 'means' through which living labour produces surplus-value. The analogy is strikingly supported by Marx's own imagery: 'The capital advance [required to meet the labour costs of circulation] creates neither products nor value. It proportionately reduces the scale on which the capital advanced functions productively. It is the same as if part of the product was transformed into a *machine* that bought and sold the remaining part of the product' (1981a: 211; emphasis added).

In principle there is no reason to regard the costs of maintaining the capitalist state any differently. Like commercial and financial capital, the state carries out a range of tasks indispensable to maintaining the institutional framework of the valorization process; like them, the state appears both as a 'socially-necessary' apparatus and as a 'barrier' to capitalist accumulation;

and like them, the state's role in the production of surplus-value is an 'indirect' one (except, of course, where the state is itself involved in commodity production).

Unlike commercial and financial capital, however, the capitalist state is not a 'private accumulator.' Most of its revenues are obtained through taxation rather than through participation in surplus-value redistribution on the basis of the general rate of profit. Rather than compete with capitals for a share of social surplus-value, the capitalist state is principally concerned with obtaining adequate value (revenue) to allow it to continuously acquit its historically developed tasks. This is not to say that the state *never* captures a portion of currently produced surplus-value in order to *expand* its activities; on the contrary, the state has exhibited a strong historical tendency to do precisely this.[13] Yet, while the state regularly appropriates a certain share of newly created surplus-value as a means of further entrenching its role in social reproduction, it would be wrong to regard *all* of its tax revenues as a 'deduction from surplus-value,' just as it would be wrong to treat the tax on labour income as a deduction from variable capital.[14]

From the standpoint of the social capital, the state is a machine of social reproduction.[15] Like any other machine, it requires maintenance, amortization, new parts, and a continuous supply of fuel and energy. Accordingly, the social capital – in whose historical interests the capitalist state functions – must set aside a considerable portion of the value it realizes (with the assistance of the state) in order to continuously finance state activity (just as it must 'set aside' some of the same 'realized value' to replenish raw material stocks, depreciated fixed capital, and expended fuel supplies in the mines, mills, and factories that are the principal sites of surplus-value production).

Constant capital represents and *re*-presents value. The form that it assumes in the circulation and state spheres is unquestionably different from the form it takes in the sphere of immediate use-value production. But, again, it is a *fetishistic* error to assume that constant capital must be directly implicated in use-value production to be indirectly implicated in the production of *value*. What all forms of constant capital have in common is that they constitute elements of the *total* process of capitalist production and reproduction that owe their existence to the *past* transformation of surplus-value into capital. Upon some reflection, then, it is not difficult to see that what Marx said about the means of production can apply just as well to the means of circulation, realization, and reproduction: 'As regards the means of production, what is really consumed is their use-value, and the consumption of this use-value by labour results in the product. There is in fact no consumption of their value and it would therefore be inaccurate to say that it is reproduced. It is rather preserved ... Hence the value of the means of production reappears in the value of the product, but it is not strictly reproduced in that value. What is produced is a new use-value in which the old exchange-value re-appears' (Marx 1977: 315–16).

The use-value of socially necessary unproductive labour consists, in the broadest sense, of maintaining the social conditions requisite to commodity production and exchange. Its value, however, is not 'consumed'; rather, it *reappears* in the product, 'adding' to the value of the commodity.

These considerations provide a new angle from which to assess Moseley's fetishized account of Marx's distinction between 'productive capital' and 'unproductive capital.' It is only in its role as a direct instrument of use-value production that constant capital in the sphere of production should be subsumed under the notion of 'productive capital.' Insofar as the *value-expansion* process is concerned, this form of constant capital is qualitatively indistinguishable from the constant capital unproductively invested in 'reproduction.' In my view, this is the unmistakable burden of the following passage from Marx's *Grundrisse*: 'To the extent that the instrument of production is itself a value, objectified labour, it does not contribute as a productive force ... If capital could obtain the instrument of production at no cost, for o, what would be the consequence? The same as if the cost of circulation = o' (1973: 265).

The argument may be summarized as follows. Means of production exist in all modes of production, but they take the social form of constant capital only under capitalism. In all modes of production their function is to produce or facilitate the production of use-values. Capital (defined as value-seeking-an-increment) transforms them into means of producing *commodities* embracing *value*. However, the production of commodity values requires an ensemble of social conditions and relations that impose a particular social form on the immediate process of use-value production. It requires a free and egalitarian market-place (the sphere of commodity circulation and exchange) and a state apparatus that can facilitate the smooth-running operation of the whole system. Simply expressed, the production of value requires the existence of special 'social machinery' (including unproductive living labour) specific to capitalism. This social machinery not only assists in the realization of value and surplus-value; it also sustains the 'institutional means' for the production of value. Understood in this way, the costs of circulation and of state activity are *indirectly* productive of value in the same way as an industrial robot. They are simply *means* of presenting living productive labour as new value.

To conclude, it should be noted that the 'constant capital' to be found in the sphere of circulation is subject to the same distinction that was made earlier – that is to say, the distinction between capital stocks and flows. The wage-bill of circulation workers is appropriately treated as a component of the constant capital *flow*, but it should not be regarded as a component of the constant capital *stock*. Like the wages paid to productive workers, the variable capital, this wage bill of unproductive workers is an investment sui generis of the capitalist class, one qualitatively different from an investment in fixed capital of any sort.

Reassessing the Empirical Trends

In the above sections I have argued for a specification of Marx's value categories that (a) limits the category of variable capital to the income of productive workers and (b) treats the income of socially necessary unproductive workers as a component of the constant-capital flow. By thus limiting the category of variable capital and broadening the category of constant capital, we are better placed to specify the phenomenal content of aggregate surplus-value. Following Marx, surplus-value is defined as the sum of profit of enterprise, ground rent, and interest (together with *some* government revenues).

To the best of my knowledge, Mage's study of the U.S. economy and my own study of the Canadian economy are the only empirical attempts that have been made to assess the long-term trends of the fundamental Marxian ratios on the basis of the value specifications defended above. (See the appendix to this chapter for a discussion of the data sources and methods used in carrying out my study.) The full implications of this specification are dramatically revealed by a comparison of these studies with other studies covering comparable periods.[16] However, the simplest way to assess the importance of this 'respecification' is to compare the results obtained on this basis with those obtained using 'conventional' definitions.

In my own study, two principal methods of calculating 'aggregate surplus-value' were employed. The first method involved a definition of surplus-value as 'surplus-value privately appropriated' (inclusive of after-tax profits) plus 'surplus-value transferred to the state as a result of a real increase in the tax flow' (Smith 1984: 261). This sum was referred to as the 'S_4' measure of aggregate surplus-value. The second method involved a definition of surplus-value as inclusive of all taxes, the after-tax wage-bill of unproductive labour in the private sector, as well as the non-tax components of S_4; this measure of aggregate surplus-value was designated as 'S_5' (ibid.: 263–4).

Comparisons of the S_4 and S_5 ratios reveal very different trends for the rate of surplus-value, rate of profit, and organic composition of capital over

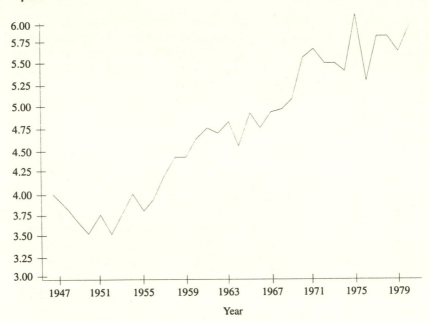

Figure 8 Organic composition of capital: C/V + S4 (Canada)

the period 1947 to 1980 in Canada. Figures 8 and 9 allow a comparison of S4 and S5 trends in the organic composition of capital. Clearly, the S4 organic composition of capital displays a significant upward trajectory, while its S5 counterpart has no discernible trend, fluctuating within a quite narrow range.[17]

Both the S4 and S5 data series disclose a tendency for the rate of surplus-value to rise; but this is far more pronounced in the case of the S5 ratio than for the S4.[18]

Finally, figures 10 and 11 (pages 180–1) present markedly different trends for the average rate of profit in Canada from 1947 to 1980, with figure 10 representing the S4 rate of profit and figure 11 the S5 rate.

Overall, the S4 data series provides strong support for Marx's fundamental prognostications regarding capitalist accumulation, revealing a long-term fall in the average rate of profit that is significantly correlated with a secular rise in the organic composition of capital.[19] While these results are complementary to those obtained by Moseley and Shaikh for the U.S. economy, it should be noted that they are not dependent on drawing a distinction between a 'conventional rate of profit' and a 'Marxian rate of profit' after the fashion

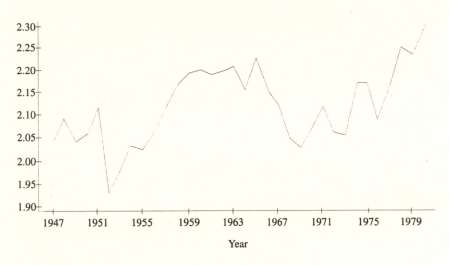

Figure 9 Organic composition of capital: C/V + S5 (Canada)

of Moseley (1987: 110–11) and, implicitly, Shaikh (1987: 125). In my
view, it is utterly erroneous to regard the income of unproductive workers
and most tax revenues as components of 'gross surplus-value' – whether or
not one then proceeds to measure the rate of profit in a way that excludes
these elements from its numerator.

This brief conspectus of the results of a respecification of Marx's value
categories suggests that empirical trends – the 'actual facts' of capitalist
development – may well provide sufficient warrant for a serious reconsideration of the theoretical fertility of Marx's law of the falling tendency of the
rate of profit. It also demonstrates that the empirical evidence that has been
marshalled against this law to date may well depend on a series of assumptions
that are contrary to Marx's theory of value, upon which the law is indissolubly
predicated.

The 'Adulteration' of the Law of the Falling Rate of Profit

While agreement exists across a broad range of economic analyses, Marxist
and non-Marxist, concerning a long-term decline in the rate of profit in the
postwar period, arguments persist over the *cause* and *extent* of this decline,
as well as the prospects for a *long-term* reversal of the trend. Studies that fail
to distinguish between productive and unproductive labour income are liable
to cite a wage-push/profit-squeeze, declining productivity, or deteriorating

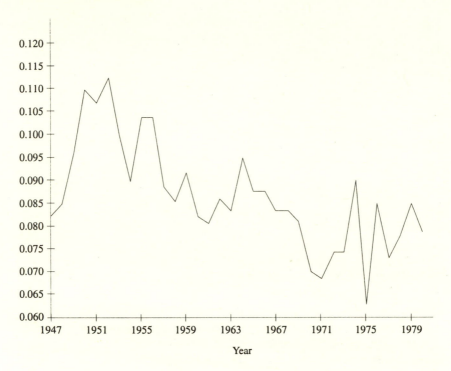

Figure 10 Rate of profit: S4/C (Canada)

terms of trade. On the other hand, studies that make this distinction generally conclude that the growth of real wages among production workers has not exceeded the growth of productivity and that the organic composition of capital has shown a marked tendency to rise.[20]

In light of the argument made in this chapter, the difference of opinion between the two sets of studies is a striking conceptual reflection of a certain 'adulteration' of Marx's law of the tendency of the rate of profit to fall. For if the growth of constant capital in relation to newly created value once signified a growth in the productivity of labour, it now *also* signifies a relative diminution of productive labour in relation to socially necessary unproductive labour. If Marx argued that the rate of profit would fall cyclically as well as secularly owing to progressive increases in the technical and organic compositions of capital, profitability now seems to be subject to a downward pressure stemming both from technical changes enforced by capitalist com-

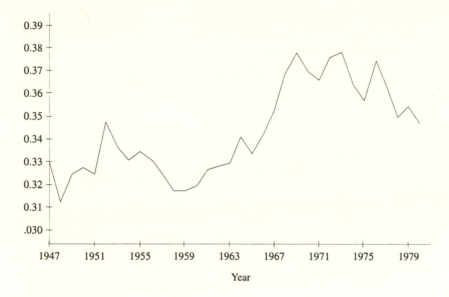

Figure 11 Rate of Profit: S5/C (Canada)

petition *and* from the circumstance that a diminishing percentage of the working class is involved in surplus-value production, as distinct from real- ization. If capitalism's tendency to promote the 'objective socialization' of labour and of production once reflected its historically-progressive role in developing the forces of production, it now *also* reflects a hypertrophy of the capitalist state and the sphere of circulation – a hypertrophy that impedes the advance of the productive forces by diverting enormous economic resources *away from* production.

The considerable expansion of the 'reproduction sector' and of 'unpro- ductive labour' in the twentieth century has substantially complicated the overall empirical picture that Marxists are called upon to analyse, while further mystifying the fundamental laws of motion of the capitalist economy. Our concern should not be with Marx's 'failure' to predict these develop- ments, but with whether or not the concrete course of historical development is explicable on the basis of his value-theoretical analysis of capitalism. In my view, this analysis is not only 'consistent with the facts'; it provides the most profound available means to elucidate and explain them.

And yet it would also seem that, *increasingly*, a proper Marxist assessment of capitalism's historical tendencies of development hinges on a correct conceptualization of productive labour as labour creative of surplus-value. The irony is that such a conceptualization can only remain irrelevant to those for whom Marx's law of value remains 'unproved.'

Appendix: Data Sources and Methods

1. **Constant Capital** (stock): The sum of fixed and circulating constant capital in both the sphere of production and the sphere of circulation (inclusive of commercial services, trading, and finance, insurance, and real estate) in the non-farm, incorporated business sector of the economy. Current-dollar figures on the fixed capital stock were obtained from the Statistics Canada bulletin *Fixed Capital Flows and Stocks, 1926–1978*, and from a more recent bulletin for 1974–80. Figures on the *net* capital stock (the measure used) include the value of four components of fixed-capital expenditure and investment: building construction, engineering construction, machinery and equipment, and capital items charged to operating expenses. The circulating constant capital stock for manufacturing was obtained from the Statistics Canada bulletin *General Review of the Manufacturing Industries of Canada, Vol. 1*, and calculated as the sum of 'cost of fuel and electricity' and 'cost of materials and supplies used.' Comparable data for the non-manufacturing sectors, unfortunately, could not be located. Detailed description in Smith 1984.

2. **Variable Capital** (annual flow): The after-tax income of all workers employed by 'productive capital' plus estimated employer and employee contributions to unemployment insurance and pension plans. Current-dollar figures for V were obtained from the Statistics Canada bulletins *National Income and Expenditure Accounts, Vol. 1, 1926–1974* and *NIEA, 1967–1981*. Excluded from consideration as variable capital were wages and salaries paid out in agriculture, wholesale and retail trade, the FIRE sector, Public Administration and Defence, and community, business, and personal services. All figures from Statistics Canada concern before-tax income; consequently, a comprehensive tax-rate table had to be constructed to obtain after-tax estimates. Detailed discussion in Smith 1984.

3. **Surplus-Value** (annual flow): The sum of profits and other investment income (after tax), the estimated corporate officer share of 'wages, salaries and supplementary labor income' (from *NIEA*), and the estimated amount of surplus-value transferred to the state. As with variable capital, the after-tax measurement of surplus-value required the use of a comprehensive tax-rate table. The ratio of 'total

taxes' (received by all levels of government) to 'net national income at factor cost' (Table 1, National Income Accounts) was defined as the 'effective tax rate on income.' For detailed discussion, see Smith, 1984.

9 International and Inter-Regional Value Transfers

Up to this point, we have been considering the operations and effects of the capitalist law of value under conditions in which (a) the mobility of capital, as between branches of production and fields of investment, is relatively unobstructed and (b) the mobility of labour is sufficient to dictate that the main determinant of differentials in rates of surplus-value is the relative sophistication of the tools, equipment, and machinery with which workers in different industries are working, rather than variations in the 'intensity of labour.' These two conditions may be taken as 'given' in the relatively homogeneous capitalist economic environments associated with 'nation-states' – although even in such ethnically homogeneous and politically centralized countries as France and Japan, significant regional variations can mitigate these conditions to a degree. Looser federative or confederational states may circumscribe an economic environment in which regional variations will play a larger role, and in which fragmented political authority may significantly reduce the scope for unfettered capital and labour mobility. But it is above all in the *international* arena that the above-mentioned conditions are most compromised, and that serious questions are raised about the operation of the law of value.

The problem of the *internationalization* of the law of value has received the closest attention from theorists concerned with issues of imperialism and Third World underdevelopment. Hence, it is in this theoretical context that our discussion finds its natural starting-point.

Unequal Capitalist Development on a World Scale

It has become something of a commonplace to observe that Marx 'failed to anticipate' the formidable obstacles to economic development and social progress that capitalism has erected in many of the less developed (or 'under-developed') countries of Asia, Africa, and Latin America. In this connection, his 'optimistic' predictions concerning the impact of British colonialism in India and his prediction in the *Communist Manifesto* that European capitalism would create 'a world after its own image' have been frequently cited. Yet it is also quite clear that Marx significantly 'revised' the projections of the *Manifesto* by subsequently disclosing the laws of capitalist development and *decline*.

From a perspective informed by the law of the falling rate of profit, in particular, the 'development of underdevelopment' is an inexorable concomitant of capitalism's historical-structural crisis – a phenomenon portending increasingly formidable barriers to capital accumulation not only in the weaker capitalist nations and the semi-capitalist periphery, but in the citadels of world capitalism as well. Furthermore, an intensification of the contradictions of 'developed capitalism' could not fail to have the most profound implications for *world-wide* economic development and serve to exacerbate the already *uneven* tempo of indigenous capital accumulation as between the more developed and the less developed regions of the world capitalist economy. It is precisely in connection with these considerations that Marx's discussion of foreign trade and investment as 'counteracting tendencies' to the law of the falling rate of profit needs to be approached:

In so far as foreign trade cheapens on the one hand the elements of constant capital and on the other the necessary means of subsistence into which variable capital is converted, it acts to raise the rate of profit by raising the rate of surplus-value and reducing the value of constant capital ... Capital invested in foreign trade can yield a higher rate of profit, firstly, because it competes with commodities produced by other countries with less developed production facilities, so that the more advanced country sells its goods above their value, even though still more cheaply than its competitors ...

As far as capital invested in the colonies, etc. is concerned ..., the reason why this can yield higher profit rates is that the profit rate is generally higher there on account of the lower degree of development, and so too is the exploitation of labour, through the use of slaves and coolies, etc. (Marx 1981b: 344–5)

Marx's comments here are useful in identifying some key factors underlying the uneven and restricted development of capitalism in sectors of the world under the domination of foreign capital and exhibiting a degree of interpenetration of capitalist and precapitalist relations of production. Precisely because the 'internal contradiction' of developed capitalism 'seeks resolution by extending the external field of production' (ibid. 353), a pronounced tendency exists for capitalist *countries* to exploit every possible advantage in their efforts to mitigate their internal economic problems at the expense of other *countries* (whether weaker capitalist nation-states, or semi-capitalist colonies and neocolonies). This tendency is both complemented and *countered* by the tendency of individual capitals to seek opportunities for valorization without regard to the 'national interests' of the social capital to which they belong – i.e., by the contradiction between the internationalization of capital and the continued existence of the nation-state as the pre-eminent political unit in which the contradictions of the social capital are addressed.

From Lenin on, most Marxist theories of imperialism have emphasized the importance of the direct production and subsequent transfer of surplus profits from the underdeveloped to the imperialist countries. With few exceptions, however, these theories have not had a *value-theoretical* approach as their analytic basis, a circumstance reflecting the prevalence of underconsumption and 'disproportionality' theories of capitalist crisis within Marxism.

This situation began to change with the emergence of the 'unequal exchange' (UE) school in the 1960s and 1970s. Not only did Arghiri Emmanuel's (1972) theory of the 'imperialism of trade' point to *exchange* mechanisms on the world market as the most significant means of imperialist exploitation of the less developed capitalist (and semi-capitalist) countries; it sought to do so on the basis of an analysis of the operations of the law of value in an *international* context. Accordingly, the lessons of the debate that ensued around the theory of UE are important to understanding the dynamics of international value transfers as a phenomenon affecting international trade between the imperialist countries themselves and not just between the developed and the less developed countries.

Emmanuel's Theory of Unequal Exchange

The central question posed here is, To what degree can we speak of international value transfers occurring through exchange mechanisms on the world market? Our concern is not primarily with the appropriateness of Emmanuel's (1974) dismissal of the 'myth of investment imperialism,' but with the adequacy of his alternative theory of the 'imperialism of trade.' It should nevertheless be noted that Emmanuel seems to miss a rather important point when he asserts that the advanced capitalist countries are 'too rich' not to 'absorb' *all* of the new capital formed in them – an apparent reference to

Lenin's thesis that imperialism is characterized by the export of 'surplus capital' to sectors where a higher rate of profit can be obtained. In effect, Emmanuel implies that 'being rich' prevents capitalists from suffering the effects of a falling rate of profit! But it is precisely the *overaccumulation of capital* that creates the problem of surplus-capital disposal and impels the search for investment opportunities in external capital markets, whether in the less-developed capitalist formations or in other imperialist countries.

The foundation of Emmanuel's UE theory is that the operations of the capitalist world market are determined by a particular law of price formation distinct from that found within 'national' economies. This law involves centrally an 'unequal rewarding of factors,' particularly the labour factor, which is systematically 'under-valued.' It follows that poor countries exhibiting a relatively low level of labour productivity, and a high degree of labour intensity, will be disadvantaged in world trade. A commodity produced in a highly developed capitalist country can be exchanged for a commodity 'embodying greater value' that has been produced in a less-developed country owing simply to the 'unequal rewarding of factors.' And this is key, in Emmanuel's view, to explaining how value is transferred from the poor to the rich countries.

It should be noted that Emmanuel distinguishes this form of UE from the UE that occurs as a result of variations in the organic composition of capital and in productivity levels between firms, industries, and branches of production. Wage differentials are the basis of the UE that concerns him most. Thus, in typically neo-Ricardian fashion, Emmanuel views wages as the 'independent variable' in capitalist development.

Can international exchange ratios be explained on the basis of the law of value? Emmanuel argues that they can be, but to do so one must first contend with Ricardo's still-influential arguments against the notion.

Ricardo argued that in international trade the law of value breaks down as an adequate explanation of exchange ratios precisely because the tendency for the rate of profit to equalize *across* national lines is qualitatively attenuated by the phenomenon of international capital *immobility*. The immobility of capital on the world market means that there is no general rate of profit governing the formation of prices of production across national lines – which means that a different law of price formation is required to explain the exchange ratios of commodities in international markets. Ricardo's solution was 'the law of comparative costs,' a law which asserts that, through a process of specialization in the production of particular commodities, exchange inequalities between trading partners will be cancelled out. This notion was central to Ricardo's case for free trade, and, in part because it is detached from his labour theory of value, it has been prominently incorporated into neoclassical theories of world trade.

Emmanuel does not entirely reject the law of comparative costs; he simply amends it, arguing that since Ricardo's time there has been a fundamental change in the economic intercourse between nations. Not only do commodities flow between them, but so does capital. Increased international capital mobility has brought with it a tendency for profit rates to equalize on an international basis, and this has meant the formation of international prices of production. This phenomenon has not been accompanied, however, by a corresponding increase in the *mobility of labour*, and the persistent immobility of labour accounts for the huge differentials in wages, and rates of exploitation, that exist between the developed and the less developed countries in the capitalist-dominated world. Thus, it is the conjunction of international capital mobility and international labour immobility in a situation where the law of comparative costs continues to determine international patterns of specialization and trade that accounts for the phenomenon of the 'development of underdevelopment' in the Third World. The implications of Emmanuel's theses have been summarized by Shaikh, as a prelude to a critique, as follows: 'Since wages tend to be much lower in the underdeveloped regions, in the absence of capital mobility between regions, profit rates will tend to be higher in the underdeveloped regions than they will be in the developed regions. If profit rates are now equalized through international mobility of capital, the profit rate in the underdeveloped regions will be lowered and that in the developed regions raised. It follows from this that profits (surplus value) are transferred from the former to the latter' (1979: 298–9).

Critiques of Emmanuel

Criticisms of Emmanuel's theory have centred on his theory of wages and his account of the international equalization of profit rates. The close connection between the two is underlined by Emmanuel's statements that 'inequality of wages as such, all other things being equal, is alone the cause of the inequality of exchange' (1972: 61) and that 'relative wages determine relative prices' (100). Geoffrey Pilling (1974: 174) observes that Emmanuel's wage theory is predicated on a quantity theory of the means of subsistence necessary for the reproduction of labour-power, while a proper Marxist theory of wages must proceed from the idea that 'the *value* (and hence price) of labour power is determined not by the quantities of the means of subsistence which will enable the worker to mainatin himself and his family and represent himself on the market, but by their *value* (that is, the socially-necessary labour time required to produce these means of subsistence).'

Ernest Mandel's critique centres on Emmanuel's 'international equalization of profit rates' thesis:

The hypothesis of international equalization of the rates of profit ... presupposes *perfect* international mobility of capital – in effect, the equalization of all economic, social and political conditions propitious to the development of modern capitalism on a world scale. Such equalization, however, is completely contradicted by the law of uneven and combined development which dominates this development ... [T]he vast international differences in the value and the price of the commodity labour-power, which Arghiri Emmanuel rightly underscores, are not causes but results of the uneven development of the capitalist mode of production, and of labour productivity in the world. (1975: 352–3; emphasis added)

Mandel proposes an alternative theory of unequal exchange in international trade that is predicated on: (1) 'the fact that [by dint of its technology-enhanced productivity – MS] the labour of the industrialized countries counts as more intensive ... on the world market than that of the underdeveloped lands'; and (2) 'the fact that *no* equalization of the rates of profit occurs in the world market, where different national prices of production (average rates of profit) exist side by side and are articulated with one another' (1975: 351). According to Mandel, Emmanuel's theory is 'incapable of showing why countries with high wages undergo industrialization while underdeveloped nations possess relatively little industry' (ibid. 352) *if* indeed a situation of 'perfect' international capital mobility exists in the capitalist world economy.

Mandel's critique of Emmanuel scores some direct hits, but his alternative account of UE, predicated as it is upon completely unique 'national prices of production,' is unconvincing. To begin with, it is rather surprising to find Mandel, a devoted expositor of the dialectical law of uneven and combined development, resorting to such undialectical formulations as *'perfect* international capital mobility' and *'no* equalization of the rates of profit ... in the world market.' Since when has 'perfect' capital mobility been a condition for the formation of a general rate of profit in a nationally circumscribed capitalist economy? Capital mobility is *nowhere* 'perfect,' and, consequently, the formation of a general rate of profit can only be a *tendency*, as Mandel points out elsewhere. Once we grant that capital mobility *exists* between countries – however 'imperfectly' – then it immediately follows that a *tendency* must also exist for the equalization of the rates of profit on the world market. Emmanuel is certainly overstating the strength of this tendency (a common neo-Ricardian pitfall, as we have seen), but he is nevertheless right to recognize its importance.

Mandel thinks that he can refute the idea of 'perfect international capital mobility' (which he unfairly attributes to Emmanuel) by suggesting that it poses, but fails to resolve, the following riddle: 'How does it come about that the prospects for valorization of capital are not more advantageous where wages are lowest, and that for a hundred years capital has *not* decamped on a massive scale from countries with high wages to countries with low wages?' (1975: 353). But Mandel's *own* answer to this question is not, in principle, inconsistent with Emmanuel's theory of unequal exchange: 'Problems of the "domestic market", the alienation of capital accumulation, the transfer of surplus-value and the narrow limits imposed on "internal" capital accumulation by the existing social structure' (ibid.). Indeed, Emmanuel's theory goes one step further by positing a transfer of surplus-value from the under-developed to the developed countries that tends to equalize the rates of profit existing between them and, in so doing, undercuts the incentive for capital to relocate to low-wage regions. The mobility of capital is therefore *limited* on an international scale by the *same tendencies* that this mobility creates: the internationalization of profit rates and the consequent tendency toward an international redistribution of surplus-value through exchange.

A proper critique of Emmanuel's theory of UE must in fact recognize the disturbing *circularity* of this latter argument. If we return to Shaikh's summary of Emmanuel's conclusions, quoted above, we can isolate the following propositions as central to the argument: (1) *until* international capital mobility becomes significant, the *rate of profit* prevailing in the underdeveloped regions will be higher than in the developed owing to lower wages; (2) *once* international capital mobility becomes significant, the international equalization of profit rates will create comparable prospects for the valorization of capital in both regions (and will, logically enough, slow the flow of capital from the developed to the underdeveloped regions).

Taken together, these two propositions constitute something of a conundrum. In the first place, how can we speak of the existence of a 'rate of profit' or even of 'wages' *before* capital has penetrated the (formerly non-capitalist) 'underdeveloped' regions (a penetration that naturally presupposes significant international capital mobility)? Second, how can the tendency toward the international equalization of profit rates sustain itself if it produces conditions discouraging international capital mobility? Clearly, these questions can only be satisfactorily addressed by recognizing the centrality of *production* to the appropriation of surplus-value by capital. Emmanuel's exclusive focus on exchange – and his related neo-Ricardian habit of treating *capitalist* categories *ahistorically* – leads away from this insight and, not surprisingly, results in paradoxical conclusions. There can be no participation by the underdeveloped regions in the formation of a general international rate of profit unless capitalist production occurs there; there can be no capitalist production there unless favourable prospects for the valorization of capital exist; and, consequently, the direct *production* and subsequent transfer of surplus-value from the underdeveloped to the developed countries remains the foundation of imperialist exploitation. In other words, Emmanuel's 'imperialism of trade' must *presuppose* the 'imperialism of production' – something that Emmanuel clearly considers a secondary issue and which, in any case, he makes no effort to integrate into his over-all theory.

A second line of criticism concerns the fact that, while Emmanuel exaggerates the strength of the tendency toward a 'uniform' international profit rate, he overlooks the significance of *inter-sectoral* differentials in profit rates – differentials that *also* cut across national lines. He therefore misses the point that, *ceterus paribus*, capital will flow not to *countries* with higher-than-average profit rates but to *branches of production* promising higher rates of valorization, irrespective of where they are located.

As part of an ambitious attempt to develop a Marxist alternative to the Ricardian theory of comparative costs and international trade, Anwar Shaikh (1979–80) has developed a highly suggestive critique of Emmanuel's theory of UE. Shaikh begins by establishing that no *Marxist* theory of international trade can incorporate the Ricardian theory of comparative costs, however 'amended.' Not only is this 'law' a transparent ideological justification for 'free trade' policies that can only serve the interests of the more developed traders; it is also intimately bound up with Ricardo's theories of value and money – both of which were strongly and effectively criticized by Marx. More precisely, Shaikh argues that it is '*absolute a*dvantage, not comparative, which rules trade' (1979: 301). Thus, the net inflow of gold into a country resulting from a trade surplus will *not* lead, as Ricardo maintained, to a general increase in prices undercutting the 'comparative advantage' of this country in international trade. Nor will the gold outflow from the weaker trading partner necessarily result in a lowering of its prices, such that its comparative position will be enhanced. Instead, the *absolute* disadvantage of the weaker trading partner will be 'manifested in a chronic trade deficit, balanced by a persistent outflow of gold,' while the greater efficiency of the stronger trading partner will 'manifest itself in a chronic trade surplus, balanced by a persistent accumulation of gold' (1980: 38). Given such a situation, the weaker trader must seek to specialize in branches of production where it possesses some natural absolute advantage, while the stronger trader must seek out avenues for profitable investment of its money capital (for example, the export sector of the weaker trading partner).

In general, the underdeveloped countries must concentrate their production for export on commodities that they can produce most efficiently (that is, at a lower value) and/or those commodities that are *peculiar* to them (for instance, specific raw materials). Both of these types of export commodities will reflect a specific *local advantage* that will tend to compensate for the *generally* lower level of productive efficiency in these countries (advantages like a favourable climate, a wealth of relatively unique natural resources, and favourable geographical location). These natural absolute advantages of the export sectors of underdeveloped countries will likely attract foreign capital in search of favourable investment opportunities; consequently, the export sectors will become the main focus of foreign capital penetration. The combined result is this: first, trade with the more developed countries will bring about the ruination of traditional industries unable to compete with cheap imports, and second, it will create the conditions for such an extreme form of specialization that the economic development of the underdeveloped country will be highly distorted, in part, by foreign capital domination of the most viable export sectors: 'Foreign investment appears as the agency of modernization from the outside. This helps create the dual character of UCR [underdeveloped capitalist region] exports: large-scale modern industries in which foreign capital predominates, side by side with backward industries in which local capital predominates. It thus expands and strengthens the export sector, and, taken by itself, it tends to improve the balance of trade' (Shaikh 1980: 46). At the same time, however, 'Direct investment accelerates the devastation of local (capitalist and non-capitalist) production which free trade brings about, while the introduction of modern techniques requires increased imports of machinery and materials from the [developed capitalist region]' (ibid.).

Other possible effects of this direct foreign investment include: the displacement of more workers from native industries than can be absorbed by the relatively capital-intensive (high OCC) modernization sector; the repatriation of profits produced by foreign capital to its 'mother country,' starving the underdeveloped regions of investment; increased productive efficiency of the export sector, resulting in the lowering of export prices and in a deterioration of the commodity terms of trade of the underdeveloped country; and a deterioration in the balance of payments associated both with falling export prices and the repatriation of profits, and tending to offset the initially positive effect of direct investment on the balance of payments of the underdeveloped country.

Importantly, Shaikh points out that the formation of a general rate of profit involves a transfer of surplus-value from industries with lower OCC to those with higher ones, and that this occurs both *between* and *within* industries. Moreover, both intra-industry transfers, 'which depend on differences between individual and average producers within the same industry,' and inter-industry transfers, 'which depend on differences in the organic compositions of the average producers in the different industries,' occur *across national lines*: 'For any individual set of capitals, defined for instance by their location, nationality, or degree of development, the net transfer of surplus-value will be the sum of these two effects' (ibid. 49).

Shaikh's conclusion regarding the implications of this for international transfers of surplus-value *resulting from commodity exchange alone* is sufficient to call into question the whole thesis of the 'imperialism of trade': 'It is perfectly possible for all the structural patterns of international uneven development ... to exist while at the same time there is a *zero or even positive transfer of value* for the UCR export sector as a whole ... It is of course possible that even if the above were true for export sectors as a whole, the underdeveloped region might still lose value through its purchase of imports ... When this is coupled with the possibility of a gain in value on the side of exports, it becomes clear that the net effect can easily be zero.' (ibid.: 50).

According to Shaikh, Emmanuel's unwarranted assumption that all high-OCC industries exist in the developed capitalist countries while all low-OCC industries are to be found in the underdeveloped ones allows him to ignore *intra-industry* transfers altogether (for instance, transfers within the auto industry as between Hyundai Motors of South Korea and General Motors in the United States). By doing this, and by assuming that interregional wage disparities exacerbate these transfers (a point denied by Shaikh on the grounds that they merely increase the magnitude of two opposing flows of surplus-value between high- and low-OCC sectors), Emmanuel leaps to the erroneous conclusion that the equalization of profit rates internationally must involve a continuous drain of surplus-value away from the Third World.

Shaikh also rejects Mandel's theory of unequal exchange. By arguing that there is *no* tendency for the rates of profit to equalize on an international scale, Mandel ignores the effects of inter-industry transfers on international exchange, and illegitimately concludes that the only value transfer occurring through exchange is the one from low- to high-efficiency producers. While Mandel's derivation of UE is thus the opposite of Emmanuel's, it leads to similarly incorrect conclusions.

Shaikh summarizes the results of his analysis as follows: 'Since uneven development on a world scale is a direct consequence of free trade itself, these transfers of value and the theories of unequal exchange which rely on them emerge as secondary phenomena, not primary causes, of underdevelopment. In fact, a critical examination of the theories of unequal exchange shows that even the net dirction of value transfers cannot be simply established' (1980: 57).

This conclusion is important for establishing one of the limitations of Marx's counteracting tendencies to the law of the falling rate of profit as well, reinforcing the point made in chapter 7 that foreign trade and investment should be regarded as a 'two-edged sword.' It should nevertheless be reaffirmed that even if imperialist exploitation of the underdeveloped capitalist regions does not *primarily* take the form of the 'imperialism of trade,' unequal exchange may well play a secondary role in the 'development of underdevelopment.' Moreover, in trade relations between the developed, imperialist countries themselves, unequal exchange may well play a role of signal importance in determining the relative economic fortunes of nations.

The methodological upshot of Shaikh's critique is that value transfers through processes of international exchange and profit-rate equalization must be analysed at a far more *concrete* level of analysis than any UE theory yet advanced. Such an analysis would require a careful specification of the whole range of 'absolute advantages' and 'absolute disadvantages' that any two trading partners might evidence – including such 'institutional externalities' as the role of the capitalist nation-state in enhancing the competitive position of its national capitals on the world market and/or in protecting these same capitals from competition in the domestic market. Only by taking into account the full range of factors influencing patterns of trade can one determine the *direction* of value transfers effected through trade alone.

10   Beyond Value

Despite the practical-programmatic relevance of value theory to the socialist project that Marx intended all of his theoretical work to serve, most participants in the value controversy have been reluctant to explore the intimate link that it has always had with practical political concerns. In what follows, I will focus on two interrelated aspects of the interface between the theory of value and socialist politics: the first pertaining to the practical task of delineating a programmatic orientation for the workers' movement to end the rule of capital, and the second pertaining to issues of 'socialist construction.' Given the enormity and inherently contentious nature of the questions addressed, as well as the limited attention that can be given to them here, this chapter is highly selective in terms of the theoretical issues and political perspectives it highlights. The intention of the discussion is therefore essentially exploratory – of *suggesting* some of the ways in which Marxian value theory may be articulated with the class-struggle politics of Marxian socialism – and no pretence is made of exhausting the topic.

The Working Class, Value, and Anticapitalist Struggle

The questions we begin with are these: Can Marx's value-theoretical analysis contribute significantly to explaining historical changes in the physiognamy and social weight of the working class? And if it can, does a value-theoretical analysis of class help us to understand the uneven and discontinuous development of working-class consciousness and class struggle over the history of capitalism?

The answers to these two questions are of signal importance to Marxism understood as an 'integrated' theoretical-political project, for this project has always been predicated on the idea that the working class not only has a 'historical interest' in ending the rule of capital and in abolishing capitalist relations of production but is also 'strategically positioned' to undertake the reorganization of society along socialist lines. From the perspective of the 1990s, Marx's vision of 'workers' revolution' may seem quixotic to many – particularly if the 'working class' is defined, as it so often has been, to exclude the more skilled and better educated wage and salary earners. But once it is grasped that the working class, as Marx understood it, constitutes a majority of the population of the developed capitalist countries, and once it is stipulated that this majority may well be able to rally the support of at least some segments of the middle class in its more serious confrontations with the capitalist order, Marx's vision of workers' revolution begins to lose it aura of 'unrealism' – while the antithetical notion of capital's 'eternal rule' acquires the unmistakable aspect of a fantastic, albeit reactionary, utopia.

Marx's Proletarianization Thesis

Class theorists have frequently contrasted two of Marx's prognostications concerning the likely evolution of the capitalist class structure. In the *Communist Manifesto* and some of his other writings, Marx refers to the inevitability of a process of polarization as between the two fundamental social classes of capitalist society, the bourgeoisie and the proletariat, and a concomitant decline of all other classes. This may be referred to as Marx's 'proletarianization' thesis. In other places, however, Marx speaks of the growing weight of the 'middle class' as an inexorable consequence of capitalist development. In *Theories of Surplus Value*, for example, he states that '[Malthus's] supreme hope, which he himself describes as more or less utopian, is that the mass of the middle class should grow and that the proletariat (those who work) should constitute a constantly declining proportion (even though it increases absolutely) of the total population. This in fact is the *course* taken by bourgeois society' (1978 3: 63).

It is possible to read entirely too much into such an off-hand remark, scribbled down, as it was, as a simple note on the opinions of another thinker. Furthermore, it is well known that in the first volume of *Capital*, in the famous, climactic chapter on 'The General Law of Capitalist Accumulation,' Marx predicted the historical ruination of the middle class and its proletarianization consequent to the concentration and centralization of capital. This, together with the fact that Marx's notion of the 'middle class' is not at all coextensive with the notions of many contemporary class theorists, directs us to the conclusion that it is Marx's 'proletarianization thesis' that most faithfully reflects his real prognostication. But the question remains: Is the proletarianization thesis correct?

Before answering this, two preliminary observations are in order. The first is that Marx, unlike many Marxists, never disqualified 'unproductive' labourers from the ranks of the working class (understood, in Carchedi's [1977, 1991] sense, as the 'collective labourer'). The second is that Marx appeared to believe that unproductive labour was a phenomenon subject to historical decline with the further development of capitalism. In this, however, he was both correct and incorrect. Marx was certainly correct to expect that the traditional ranks of the unproductive labour-force – domestic servants and other hangers-on of the privileged classes – would manifest a proportional decline, especially with the disappearance/transformation of the landed aristocracy. But his prognostication was wrong to the extent that it failed to anticipate the momentous expansion of *new types* of unproductive labour – the socially necessary yet unproductive workers employed by the state and by commercial, financial, and industrial capital (clerks, bookkeepers, accountants, civil servants, and so forth). Arguably, Marx's failure in this respect may have been due to an overly 'optimistic' expectation that capitalism would not overstay its historical welcome. The growth of socially necessary unproductive labour has, after all, been attendant on a rather long and drawn-out 'historical-structural crisis' of the capitalist mode of production. Even so, the proliferation of such labour, as I indicated in chapter 8, is eminently explicable in terms of the unfolding of the capitalist law of value, and in particular the law of the falling rate of profit.

While Marx never disqualified all unproductive labourers from the ranks of the proletariat, the same cannot be said for a great many twentieth-century class theorists, Marxist and non-Marxist alike. It has been all too common for neo-Weberian and functionalist theorists to distinguish between 'white collar' and 'blue collar' workers and to rather impressionistically draw a class line between them. In a similar vein, Nicos Poulantzas (1978) has argued, from an ostensibly Marxist standpoint, that wage-labourers who are not directly productive of 'material' commodities, and/or who are engaged in mental labour or supervisory functions, are properly classified as non-proletarian constituents of a 'new petty-bourgeoisie.'[1]

Other Marxist theorists have maintained that membership in the working class should be reserved to those wage-labourers who create surplus-value, whether in the course of producing material or service commodities. J.K. Lindsey (1980), a good representative of this approach, argues that the 'production working class' should be distinguished from the 'circulation working class' on the grounds that the former is *exploited* while the latter is merely 'oppressed.' Lindsey makes the unobjectionable point that the relation between production and circulation workers is not an antagonistic one; yet this sits uneasily with his thesis that circulation workers, along with the members of what he calls an 'ideological class,' live off the surplus-value appropriated by capitalists. Like many Marxists, Lindsey conflates the categories of unproductive labour and then asserts that all unproductive labour is 'exchanged with revenue.' In this way, socially necessary unproductive labourers are treated, in value-theoretical terms, as a kind of 'luxury good' of the social capital, employed at the sufferance of the bourgeoisie and supported out of the revenue component of social surplus-value. Even though *socially necessary* to the reproduction process of capitalist society, these workers are regarded no more as victims of capitalist exploitation than are the domestic servants with whom they are conceptually assimilated.

I have already given an extended argument for rejecting such an understanding of socially necessary unproductive labour in chapter 8, and I will not repeat the arguments made there. However, a further argument should be considered at this point that is directly relevant to Lindsey's mistaken notion that circulation workers are not exploited.

In his discussion of the costs of circulation in *Capital II*, Marx discusses the case of a 'buying and selling agent' who sells labour-power to a capitalist. 'Whatever his payment,' says Marx, 'as a wage-labourer he works for part of the day for nothing. He may receive every day the value product of eight hours' labour, and function for ten. The two hours' surplus-labour that he performs no more produce value than do his eight hours of necessary labour, although it is by means of the latter that a part of the social product is transferred to him' (1981a: 210). Two critical points are made in this passage. The first is that the working day of this unproductive wage-labourer is, like that of a productive labourer, divided into *two* components: a component during which 'necessary labour' is performed, and one during which 'surplus labour' is performed. The second point is that *none* of this labour is productive of value. Rather it is simply a means of effecting a *transfer* of a portion of the social product from the sphere of production to the sphere of circulation. The significance of the 'unpaid' portion of the unproductive labourer's work day is that it permits the labourer's (commercial) employer to appropriate a part of the product that has been transferred through the efforts of the 'buying and selling agent.'

These considerations enable us to understand Marx's otherwise mystifying reference in Capital III to the 'variable capital' that the commercial capitalist exchanges for the unproductive labour of commercial workers. Recall that commercial capital's role in reducing the costs of circulation within the division of labour between industrial, commercial, and financial capital is the basis for its participation in the formation of a general rate of profit and in the distribution of aggregate surplus-value among the various capitals according to 'capital advanced.' 'Productive capital' thereby *shares* a portion of the social surplus-value produced with commercial and financial capital. In the case of financial capital, productive (mainly industrial) capital must pay interest on loans and purchase other financial services. But in relation to commercial capital, the situation is more opaque:

Commercial capital makes a profit by not paying productive capital in full for the unpaid labour contained in the commodity ... and, as against this, itself receiving the additional portion which it has not paid for once the commodity has been sold. Commercial capital's relationship to surplus-value is different from that of industrial capital. The latter produces surplus-value by directly appropriating the unpaid labour of others. The former appropriates a portion of this surplus-value by getting it transferred from industrial capital to itself. (1981b: 407)

Even so, however, a condition for the transfer of surplus-value to commercial capital is the performance of unpaid labour (surplus labour) by commercial capital's (unproductive) employees: 'The very function by virtue of which the commercial capitalist's money is capital is performed in large measure by his employees, on his instructions. Their unpaid labour, even though it does not create surplus-value, does create his ability to appropriate surplus-value, which, as far as this capital is concerned, gives exactly the same result: i.e. it is its source of profit' (ibid. 407). Accordingly, the capital that the commercial capitalist exchanges for the labour-power of commercial workers is 'variable' *only from the standpoint of commercial capital.* From the standpoint of the social capital, it is simply an overhead cost of capitalist reproduction – a component of constant capital. None of this signifies that the circulation worker is 'not exploited' by capital; it simply signifies that circulation workers are subject to a different mode of exploitation.

The different locations of production and circulation workers within the overall process of capitalist reproduction should nevertheless be noted. Circulation workers, along with workers employed or maintained by the capitalist state, are rather 'directly' involved (whether consciously or unconsciously) in the reproduction of capitalist social relations, while production workers are directly involved in the reproduction of the 'material' elements of society. Theoretically, this circumstance may make circulation workers less likely to develop anticapitalist attitudes than workers involved in production. Even so, such a hypothetical difference in consciousness is an inadequate basis for contending that circulation workers are 'not exploited' or that they belong to a 'different class' than production workers. Moreover, it is questionable whether such a difference in consciousness can be convincingly established, much less linked to different structural locations in reproduction (see Wright [1985] and Carchedi [1987] for contrasting insights relevant to these issues).

Although a clarification of Marx's ideas regarding socially necessary unproductive labour is of great moment to a value-theoretical mapping of the contemporary class structure, it can hardly resolve all the pertinent questions under debate. For example, Wright (1978), following a cogent critique of Poulantzas's catch-all category of the 'new petty bourgeoisie,' fruitfully suggests that 'positions within the social division of labor can be objectively contradictory,' and, on the basis of this insight, identifies several 'contradictory class locations' existing in variegated relations to three principal social classes: the bourgeoisie, the proletariat, and the (traditional, self-employed) petty bourgeoisie. For Wright, contradictory class locations can exist between any pair of these classes, suggesting that the individuals occupying such locations share structural characteristics in common with more than one class (for instance, a foreman, who 'commands' the labour of others but who is also subject to exploitation).

Whether ambiguously positioned wage-labourers like foremen, engineers, and managers are most appropriately conceptualized as members of a contradictory class location, as constituents of a 'service class' (Abercombrie and Urry 1983), or as elements of a 'new middle class' (Carchedi 1977, 1987), the analysis of their proliferation under advanced capitalism can only benefit from a value-theoretical perspective which recognizes that the problems of value production and realization call forth an ever-more elaborate technical and social division of labour, and an increasingly heterogeneous occupational structure that tends to obscure the real contours of the class structure.

How then do these observations pertain to Marx's thesis concerning the progressive polarization of the capitalist class structure and the historical tendency toward the proletarianization of ever-larger segments of the population under contemporary capitalism? In my opinion, they substantially support it. The complexity of the contemporary class structure is most apparent within the working class itself, which has become increasingly differentiated with respect to its roles in social reproduction. At the same time, the increasing weight of the working class is also indirectly reflected in the fact that the 'contradictory class location' or 'new middle class stratum' that has experienced the greatest expansion in advanced capitalist societies over the course of this century is precisely that which straddles the bourgeoisie and the proletariat (Wright 1978; Carchedi 1977, 1991).

Value, Class Struggle, and Bureaucracy

The problem of how the productivity-increasing imperative of the capitalist law of value has been 'adulterated' over the course of capitalist development cannot be adequately specified without reference to the central role played by class conflict. Purely structuralist accounts of Marx's economic laws of motion tend to depict the class struggle as a mere epiphenomenon of the 'objective' contradictions of capitalist production/reproduction. The implication of such a view is that class practices, mediated by consciousness, can have little impact on the overall direction of capitalist development. Yet precisely because subjectively oriented practices do not belong to a realm autonomous from 'objective laws,' but, to the contrary, belong to the same order of social being, a value-theoretical account of capitalist development must specify the ways in which the class struggle impacts on the expression – that is, the concrete historical forms – of these laws.

To a certain degree, the role of the class struggle as a barrier to capitalist accumulation and as a stimulus to technical innovation has already been registered in our discussion in chapters 7 and 8. Precisely because capital encompasses an antagonistic relation between capitalists and workers, and not just a competitive relation between private commodity producers, a strong tendency exists for capitalists to reduce their costs of production through labour-saving and/or labour-displacing innovation. In this connection, capitalists derive two main functional benefits from the resulting increase in the 'technical composition of capital': (1) it promotes the real subsumption of labour by capital, and (2) it reproduces the industrial reserve army of labour required to maintain a downward pressure on wages. Both of these benefits to capital are substantial and even indispensable for 'subjective' as well as 'objective' reasons. The reproduction of unemployment, for example, is not only useful in keeping the labour movement 'off balance' and in mitigating wage-push/profit-squeeze phenomena; it is also vital to instilling a sense of *insecurity* in workers, rendering them less likely to undertake militant anti-capitalist action. Similarly, while the real subsumption of labour by capital involves an increased production of relative surplus-value, it also entails a continuous de-skilling of 'qualified labour,' a process that fosters the 'capital-fetishistic' illusion that labour is a mere appendage to the 'independent power of capital.' Accordingly, both unemployment and the real subsumption of labour by capital have *subjective* as well as objective consequences that are favourable to capital.

There is, however, another side to the coin. Not only do workers *resist* 'technological redundancies' and de-skilling technical change, they also *react* to the crisis tendencies bred by a rising organic composition of capital. Moreover, it is precisely because workers have an anticapitalist option open to them (namely, the struggle for a socialist transformation of society) that the capitalist class must tread carefully in its efforts to follow the 'objective dictates' of the capitalist law of value. While workers (consciously or unconsciously) can and do challenge the limits of the law of value, capitalists can seek only to *modify* the effects of the law of value in accordance with their class interests, including their interest in maintaining some 'reasonable' level of 'class peace.' What this suggests is that the laws of motion of capital create a framework within which a multitude of choices are made pertaining to class practices. Capitalists have no choice but to *limit* their class practices to this framework, and they bend every effort to get the working class to do the same. Yet the working class remains within this framework only to the degree that the *consciousness* of workers remains limited to it. Because there is no fundamental 'community of interests' between capitalists and workers, *bourgeois class interest* dictates that capitalists 'respect' and 'obey' the law of value, just as *proletarian class interest* demands that workers repudiate and seek to supersede it.

The historical tendency of the class struggle under capitalism has been to push toward an ever greater 'objective socialization' of the reproduction process. On the one hand, one aspect of the progressive historical mission of capitalism has been to promote 'the growth of technical coordination, interdependence and integration in production, by which capitalism increasingly generates the negation of the private labour and private production from which it was born – first inside single factories, then within a number of production units and branches of industry, and finally between countries' (Mandel 1975: 595). On the other hand, the pressure of the class struggle and of capitalism's sharpening objective contradictions has forced the capitalist class to also promote a 'bastardized socialization' in which the overhead costs of capitalist reproduction (the state, the administration of industry, the sphere of circulation, and so on) have grown enormously. Given the antagonistic and exploitative character of capitalist social relations of production, the predominant 'organizational' mode emerging from these socialization tendencies has been the *bureaucratic mode*.

The essence of all bureaucracy, and especially industrial bureaucracy, is a thorough-going division between mental and manual labour (Braverman 1974, Deutscher 1973, Sohn-Rethel 1978, Clawson 1980). Such a division is implicit in the real subsumption of labour by capital as this was conceived by Marx, and is rendered explicit in the principles of 'scientific management' elaborated by Frederick W. Taylor and others. Short of a complete elimination of living labour from production, what the capitalists seek to achieve is effective *control* over the labour process and a qualitative attenuation of the class struggle at the point of production on terms propitious to valorization. In general, this project is furthered by efforts to continuously 'transfer' the skills formerly wielded by living labourers to machinery, thereby eliminating all vestiges of *craft production* – a state of affairs in which (some) workers perform both mental and manual functions. The separation of 'conception' and 'execution,' together with the relegation of living manual labour to repetitive detail functions, is integral to a capitalist *class strategy* to enforce the domination of capital over the working class within production (Marx's 'despotism of the factory regime'). The essential content of this strategy is a 'cognitive appropriation' of the skills and technical knowledge of skilled craftspeople, their incorporation into machinery through scientific and technological innovation, and the development of a managerial-bureaucratic layer whose task is both to ensure the technical efficiency of the production process and, under the guise of 'maintaining labour discipline,' to undercut any tendencies toward worker control of the labour process.

It should be emphasized that the above features of the bureaucratization of industry are promoted by value relations *in general*, and not *only* by class struggle at the point of production. Moreover, it is important to note that the tendency toward the de-skilling and dequalification of labour is *partially* offset by a counter-tendency toward the creation of new types of skilled labour, a process that is itself an inexorable consequence of the drive of capitals to reduce production costs per unit of output in order to more effectively meet the challenges of competition.

The real subsumption of labour by capital attests to the on-going role of capital in enhancing the productivity of labour *at the level of the individual productive enterprise*. For Marx, this role is historically progressive and its results form the material presuppositions of socialism: '[To] the degree that large industry develops, the creation of real wealth comes to depend less on labour-time and on the amount of labour employed than on the power of the agencies set in motion during labour-time, whose powerful effectiveness is ... out of all proportion to the direct labour-time spent on their production, but depends rather on the general state of science and on the progress of technology, or the application of science to production' (1973: 705).

This passage suggests that Marx did not condemn capitalism for its tendency to free material production from the need for living labour of all types; rather, he indicted it because it could not realize the full potential of the technological revolutions that it sponsored under the whip of the law of value.

The tragedy, for Marx, was not that craft skill, a relic of the 'artisanal mode of production,' was giving way to automation; the tragedy was rather that capitalist relations of production, involving the measurement of social wealth in terms of labour-time, reserved all the benefits of automation for the capitalists, while condemning the working class to increasing alienation, economic insecurity, and cognitive degradation.

Technological revolutions are one thing, however, and bureaucratization something else again. The claim of most sociological apologists of industrial bureaucracy is that bureaucratic organization itself – the centralization of knowledge about production in the hands of a managerial stratum enjoying the confidence of the capitalist owners – is an 'essential ingredient' to optimal productivity and efficiency in industrial enterprises. But this is a claim that can be easily dismissed. For while the separation of conception and execution might be a necessary feature of labour-saving technological innovation, the 'division of head and hand' does not follow from this, especially as the role of the 'hand' continues to decline in importance with the automization/robotization of large-scale industrial production processes. There is really *no* reason why 'conception' cannot be the privilege of *all* of the associated producers, regardless of their specialized roles in the technical division of labour – no reason, *except* for the desire of capital to hoard an esoteric body of knowledge useful to fortifying its domination over the labour process.

In sum, it is vitally important from a value-theoretical standpoint to *distinguish* those aspects of the real subsumption of labour by capital that promote the productivity of labour and real progress in liberating human labour from drudgery from those aspects that involve a bureaucratic expropriation and centralization of knowledge and decision-making in the hands of capitalist management. The latter aspects pertain to the exploitative capitalist form of the law of value, while the former pertain to a perennial tendency of the law of value to promote technical rationality – a tendency that capital supports only up to a point. To pose the matter a little differently, the bureaucratic organization of the production process is not an inexorable concomitant of labour-saving technological innovation. To the contrary, the displacement of living labour from production and the spread of automation, robotics, and computers should *undermine* any purely 'technicist' rationale for bureaucratic relations of authority, while liberating the social time required to educate and involve the associated producers as a whole in the management of industry – and of society as a whole. Only because capitalist production is not merely a material process of producing use-values, but pre-eminently a social process of extracting surplus labour that assumes the form of surplus-value, the social form assumed by technical progress remains one that guarantees for capital a monopoly of effective control over the labour process and ensures that the creation of surplus-value must remain the sine qua non of production.

The Value of Labour-Power: Labour-Market Segmentation and Working-Class Fragmentation

As already pointed out, the tendency toward the de-skilling and homogenization of the working class is partially negated by a counter-tendency toward the creation of 'new' skills and qualifications. This counter-tendency is partly dictated by the exigencies of technological innovation in the on-going quest of capitals to reduce unit costs of production. However, differentials in wages are not solely the result of differences in levels of skill, and processes of de-skilling/re-skilling may be somewhat tangential to *other* factors that contribute significantly to labour-market segmentation and class fragmentation.

The value of individual labour-powers is not determined simply by an 'objective' calculus in which the cost of reproducing the ability to work is defined in terms of physiological subsistence expenditures plus the educational and other costs incurred by workers in acquiring, exercising, and maintaining a particular set of skills. In *Capital I*, Marx makes it quite clear that, in his view, the 'value of labour-power' has a 'historical' and 'moral' component as well (1977: 274–5). Marx is ambiguous on the point, but it seems appropriate to apply this consideration to the definition of both the value of 'simple' labour-power and the value of 'qualified' labour-power. From this perspective, the incorporation of a 'social-constructionist' view into a theory of labour-power 'valuation' becomes a rather simple matter (Thompson 1989).

Qualified labour is not simply 'skilled' labour, nor are skills entirely objective attributes of individual workers who have incurred determinate costs in acquiring them. To put the matter bluntly, a 'qualification' for a relatively privileged and well-paid position within the division of labour may simply be maleness, a white skin, or the 'right' social connections (whether with upper management or the boss of a union hiring hall). Similarly, the criteria for distinguishing between skilled, semiskilled, and unskilled work tasks may have less to do with formal education and training than with how these tasks are distributed in terms of gender, race, and status background. For example, a highly talented seamstress may be defined as 'semi-skilled' and a male truck driver as 'skilled' simply because the very notion of skill has traditionally been associated with male *craft organization*. More generally, the 'value of labour-power' is very much determined by prevailing social norms, lifestyle expectations, racial and gender inequalities, and other strictly 'non-economic' considerations. In the world of commodities, the social equality of commodity-producing labour is the rule, and the 'level playing field' the accepted norm. But commodities *share* the real world with human beings whose social relations and consciousness reflect the influence not only of commodity exchange but of an entire cultural continuum, not to mention cross-cultural antagonisms. Not surprisingly, it is precisely in the area of determining the value of individual labour-powers that these relatively autonomous cultural influences can be most profoundly felt – trampling underfoot all attempts to 'objectively' compare the 'value' of different work tasks.

In a provocative contribution to the development of a 'political economy of the working class,' Michael Lebowitz (1991) has suggested that

[The] value of labor-power has a tendency to adjust to its price – rather than the reverse! Accordingly, Marx was *wrong* to state that 'as with all other commodities, so with labour, its *market price* will, in the long run, adapt itself to its *value*' (Marx, [*Value, Price and Profit*]). Rather than a fixed magnitude, the set of necessities entering into the value of labor-power is inherently *variable*: 'This historical or social element, entering into the value of labour, may be expanded or contracted, or altogether extinguished, so that nothing remains but the *physical limit*' ([Marx, *Value, Price and Profit*], 1991: 144–5).

In my view the burden of Lebowitz's critique of the Marx of *Value, Price and Profit* is unobjectionable, and I share his regret that neither Marx nor his immediate successors elaborated the sort of 'political economy of the working class' that Marx had apparently envisaged for his planned volume on wage-labour. The struggle of the working class, with all its vicissitudes, has a major bearing on how the price and therefore the historically and morally determined value of labour-power is established in any given period.

The same point applies to 'qualified' as well as 'unqualified' labour-powers. But it should be borne in mind that the variability of the value of labour-power pertains principally to the 'historical,' 'social,' or 'moral' elements in its determination, and that the 'physical limit' does indeed provide a relatively enduring objective 'floor' below which the quality of even the simplest, most unskilled labour-power is seriously compromised. The value of the necessities entering into this physical floor may be said to determine the *subsistence* component of the price of labour-power, just as the total price of specific labour-powers, mediated by cultural factors, will determine the *historically constituted* value of labour-power.[2]

These considerations do not vitiate the fact that the value of total labour-power (that is, the magnitude of variable capital) is a given datum in a particular capitalist society at a particular time. But the substantially arbitrary way in which the value of labour-power may be determined beyond the physiological minimum necessary to the social reproduction of its simplest forms suggests the possibility that a 'redistribution' of value may occur among workers just as it occurs among capitals (even though, of course, for different reasons and through different mechanisms). Diverse levels of class organization (unionization, in particular), gender and racial discrimination, and culturally constructed definitions of skills and qualifications may enter into the distribution of the value available to wage and salary earners and may thereby contribute to acrimonious political divisions within the working class. Whether furthered by the capitalist ruling class or by workers themselves, such fragmentation can only contribute to the emergence of disparate, and quite contradictory, forms of working-class consciousness.

Class Consciousness: Regional and International Dimensions

International capital mobility and the dismantling of barriers to 'free trade' within the capitalist world market provide the basis for the formation of tendentially uniform prices of production on a world scale. This, in turn, allows for the possibility of significant transfers of surplus-value across national lines. The more prominent the tendency toward the equalization of profit rates on a world scale, the more scope there is for technologically-superior capitalist countries to offset crises of profitability at the expense of their weaker trading partners. The pool of social surplus-value available for distribution amongst individual capitals becomes internationalized, and the distribution of this surplus-value determines the relative fortunes of regions, countries, and even whole continents.

On a world scale, the distribution of internationalized social surplus-value comes close to resembling a zero-sum game, particularly under conditions of economic contraction and crisis within the capitalist world economy as a whole. The condition for prosperity, growth, and rising average living standards in one zone of capitalist economic activity becomes the failure of other zones to adequately compete and prevent a transfer of value to the more competitive zones.

Workers living in the more 'advanced' or 'developed' zones of the world capitalist economy enjoy the benefits of an economic environment that is not only wealthier but also less prone to the most severe manifestations of capitalist economic crisis. Indeed, through the various mechanisms of international value transfer, the developed capitalist zones may use the less-developed zones as a kind of shock absorber for the crisis tendencies originating in their own economies. The recent Third World 'debt crisis' is a prime example of this phenomenon (George 1988; Magdoff 1992). It goes without saying that individual developed countries or trading blocs will seek to 'export' their crisis tendencies to other developed regions as well. The possibility of resolving the 'domestic' manifestations of capitalist crisis at the expense of other regions, other countries, and other nations encourages a tendency on the part of working people to seek a solution to their economic problems in 'regional,' 'national,' or 'continental' (trade-bloc) terms. Such strategies almost invariably involve a perspective of collaboration with one's 'own' capitalist class in a cross-class project of 'winning the war for markets,' and frequently contain significant elements of racism and xenophobia. As such, they are profoundly at odds with the internationalist working-class perspective that alone can confront and challenge the logic of a law of value that refuses to recognize national boundaries or regional peculiarities, and that operates in such a way as to seduce the unwary into a class-collabora-tionist perspective of 'beggar-my-neighbour' competition.

The Social Psychology of the Exchange Abstraction

In chapter 2, I argued that Alfred Sohn-Rethel's (1978) thesis concerning the development of the 'real abstraction of exchange' offers a materialist explanation of the origin of the 'categories a priori' at the heart of Kant's philosophy. At the same time, however, he points to the division of mental and manual labour as critical to a materialist critique of Kant's epistemology: 'The presuppositions of Kant's epistemology are quite correct in so far as the exact sciences are indeed created by mental labour in total separation from and independence of the manual labour carried out in production. The division between head and hand, and particularly in relation to science and technology, has an importance for bourgeois class rule as vital as that of the private ownership of the means of production ... The class antagonism of capital and labour is linked intrinsically with the division of head and hand' (Sohn-Rethel 1978: 37).

Kant's antinomies and his epistemological account of the division of mental and manual labour reflect the profound impact of the exchange abstraction in engendering a *dualistic* consciousness and world-view. Indeed, Kant's very opposition of principles a posteriori and principles a priori (correspond-ing to the division between the contribution of the *senses* and the contribution of *reason* to human knowledge) could only have occurred to a philosopher living in an era in which the division of mental and manual labour had been powerfully ramified by the devlopment of a body of scientific knowledge and 'method' increasingly dissociated from 'practical' manual tasks. Kant accepted this epistemological dualism without inquiring into its socio-historical foundation; indeed, he based it upon a none-too-disguised ontological dualism (noumena-phenomena, *Müssen-Sollen*, and so forth). Other philosophers have suggested that cognitive dualism is rooted in 'human nature' and is consequently the 'natural' way of regarding the world. By contrast, Sohn-Rethel's analysis suggests that cognitive dualism appears natural only so long as its roots in the division of head and hand as well as in the elements of the exchange abstraction remain hidden.

The unfolding of the capitalist law of value has not only brought the division of mental and manual labour to its apotheosis; it has also, through the generalization of the exchange abstraction, encouraged a generalized dualistic consciousness. This consciousness is characteristic not only of the dominant forms of bourgeois philosophy and social theory, but of the world-views of broad sections of the population, including the working class.

The significance of this should not be missed. The dualist outlook is *profoundly* at odds with the conviction that 'the material' can be brought into correspondence with 'the ideal.' It therefore encourages a fundamentally conservative and 'anti-utopian' posture according to which 'what ought to be' (Kant's *Sollen*) must always be at odds with 'what is (or must be)' (Kant's *Müssen*). A dualistic perspective on the relation between social form and material content also perpetuates the ideologically potent notion that social forms are *externally* linked to persistent and unyielding 'material realities.' This notion too has conservative implications, for it opens the door wide to a veritable avalanche of commodity- and capital-fetishistic notions, and undermines the capacity of the human imagination to 'erect in thought' a social order that positively transcends the 'eternal verités' of capitalism and the market economy.

The exchange abstraction is a powerful element of that 'social being' that Marx says 'determines' human consciousness. Throughout history, it has influenced human consciousness in such a way as to encourage scientific rationality – but also to perpetuate deeply engrained ideological notions that are crucial to conferring legitimacy on the power and privileges of dominant classes. *Its generalization* under capitalism therefore constitutes a factor of some importance in determining the uneven and discontinuous development of class consciousness within the labour movement and the working class as a whole.

The Uneven and Discontinuous Growth of Class Consciousness

Our discussion up to this point has identified a plethora of factors that may affect the consciousness of working people as they wrestle with the persistent social and economic problems bred by capitalism. These factors range from the uneven impact of capitalist crisis tendencies on various segments of the international working class, to racial and gender inequalities countenanced by cultural traditions, to skill differentials, to the dull compulsion of fending for one's self and one's family in an insecure economic environment, to the insidious naturalization of capitalist relations engendered by the exchange abstraction. To these factors should be added, of course, the conscious efforts of the capitalist class to diffuse its values and world-view to the wider working population through the mass media, the churches, the educational system, and the family.

Despite the large number of factors that serve to obstruct the emergence of an anticapitalist, socialist consciousness on the part of the working class, such a consciousness has repeatedly and stubbornly asserted itself. Often it is confined to relatively small segments of the working class (as it clearly is today in the United States and Canada). But at other times, it has embraced the majority of the working class and seriously posed the question of working-class power and the socialist transformation of society (as it did, for example, in Russia in 1917, in Germany in 1918–19 and 1923–4, in Spain in 1936–7, in Italy in 1920, 1945–7, and 1969, in France in 1936 and 1968, in Chile in 1970–3, in Portugal in 1974–5, and in South Africa today). The fact that such a consciousness could emerge at all, given the strength of the factors arrayed against it, calls for some explanation. The explanation that Marx himself adduced remains the most compelling: the working class, despite its divisions and its relative dearth of resources, is united by powerful common interests that periodically assert themselves in the most unexpected of ways and that demand the formulation of a common working-class program based on socialist principles and goals.

The development of socialist consciousness within the working class is a powerful tendency apparent in the 'real history of the capitalist mode of production' – a tendency rooted in the social being and common historical interests of working people. But like every tendency, it is confronted by powerful counter-tendencies that determine a certain unevenness in its artic-ulation and spread, and that always threaten its reversal or 'roll-back' in specific times and places. This uneven and discontinuous quality of the development of socialist class consciousness poses serious programmatic and strategic problems for those who have achieved something more than a visceral dislike of capitalism and a vague attraction to the socialist idea. For those who have internalized Marx's critique of capitalist political economy and come to understand the necessity of socialism, the task becomes one of *informing* the strategic and programmatic perspectives of the workers movement with the results of Marx's scientific analysis, the better to heighten the political consciousness of the working class as a whole.

The Role of Value Theory in the Anticapitalist Struggle

Marx's theory of value, and his critique of capitalist political economy as a whole, is a theory of the historical limits of the capitalist mode of production and of the social forms that serve to conceal them. His scientific analysis is at once an explication of the laws of motion of the capitalist economy and an account of how false, or one-sided, ideas about that economy come to arise and flourish. *No other theory*, however critical of capitalism, has even come close to elucidating *both* of these problems, much less establishing their common foundation in value relations.

The programmatic upshot of Marx's value-theoretical analysis of capitalism is that the latter is not at all susceptible to socialist transformation through a process of gradual, incremental reform, and that neither is it constitutionally capable of a 'progressive,' 'crisis-free' evolution that would render the socialist project, in some sense, dispensable. Capitalism must be destroyed root and branch before there can be any hope of social reconstruction on fundamentally different foundations, and such a radical reconstruction is vitally necessary to ensure further human progress. The alternative facing humankind, as Rosa Luxemburg realistically posed it, is socialism or barbarism.

Despite the urgency of socialist transformation, none of the objective laws of motion of capitalism can bring about a final and irrevocable breakdown of the capitalist system. Capitalism may be 'digging its own grave,' but it will never carry out its own execution. Its burial awaits and requires the concerted action of a *class-conscious* working class. The central practical problem facing Marxian socialism is that under conditions of advanced capitalism (which alone can furnish the material presuppositions for a dynamic socialist transformation) the working class has so far failed to carry through its anticapitalist struggle to the end.

In part, this failure may be attributed to insufficient class consciousness, in part to strategic errors on the part of revolutionary workers' movements (for instance, Germany 1919–24), and in part to the betrayal of revolutions by the ostensible 'leaders' of the working class (for example, Spain 1936–7). By themselves these three sets of factors go quite far in explaining why, despite the experience of depressions and wars, social decay amidst material plenty, and so on, the working class in advanced capitalism has not yet risen to its historic task of overthrowing the regime of capital. The question is thus posed: What program can assist the proletariat in bridging the gap between its existing consciousness and practices and the consciousness and action needed for *successful* anticapitalist struggle?[3]

In the history of Marxist socialism, programs embodying a strategic orientation to bridge that gap have often been called 'transitional.' The *Communist Manifesto* is in this tradition, as are the *Theses on Tactics* and other declarations of the first four congresses of the Third (Communist) International. Its most comprehensive and eloquent expression was elaborated in *The Death Agony of Capitalism and the Tasks of the Fourth International*, the famous 'Transitional Program' adopted at the founding conference of Leon Trotsky's Fourth International in 1938 (Trotsky 1973a).

The hallmark of the transitional programmatic conception is its attempt to overcome the dichotomization of a 'minimum program' of struggle for reforms within capitalism and an abstract 'maximum program' that promises the eventual substitution of socialism for capitalism (a dichotomization formalized in the German Social Democracy's *Erfurt Programme* of 1895). A transitional program seeks to transcend this dichotomy by articulating a system of demands that anticipate the social and political content of a workers' state and the early stages of socialist construction. These demands (a sliding scale of wages and hours, workers' control of production, the expropriation of industry without compensation, workers' defence guards, and so on) are meant to intersect the immediate (largely defensive) struggles of the working class as these occur within capitalism, while at the same time projecting 'solutions' that, taken together, can disintegrate the social, political, and military power of the capitalist class. In the words of the Third International: 'In place of the minimum programme of the centrists and reformists, the Communist International offers a struggle for the concrete demands of the proletariat which, in their totality, challenge the power of the bourgeoisie, organize the proletariat and mark out the different stages of the struggle for its dictatorship' (Communist International 1980: 286 [1921]).

Fundamentally, the transitional program is predicated on the inevitability of capitalist crises and class struggles stemming from the inherent contradictions of capitalism. The program permits the vanguard of the working class to build a bridge, at first in practice, then in consciousness, between the immediate struggles of the working class and the programmatic goal of a workers' socialist government.

A basic theoretical presupposition of the transitional program is that socialists must take into account two sets of factors determining the development of working-class consciousness: on the one hand, that consciousness is profoundly conditioned by the fetishisms inherent in the capitalist relations of production and by ideologies rooted in the 'appearance of things' under capitalism; on the other hand, that it is shaped by the experience of struggle against the material depredations of the capitalist system, and that under conditions of systemic crisis the floodgates of consciousness can be opened to possibilities that are not 'normally' entertained by the great mass of working people.

Although sometimes conceived as akin to André Gorz's (1973) 'anticapitalist structural reforms,' transitional demands form part of an articulated program of *open-ended* anticapitalist struggle. Only when they are dissociated from the overall *system* of demands and thereby 'fetishized' (which invariably involves a qualitative attenuation of their thrust) can they be seen as 'reforms' serving a *closure* of struggle. Indeed, as a 'system' of demands, they lead 'unalterably to one final conclusion: the conquest of power by the proletariat' (Trotsky 1973a: 75).

The logic of the transitional programmatic conception is illustrated by even so 'modest' a transitional demand as the 'sliding scale of wages and hours.' The sliding scale of hours is not only the 'socialist solution' to the problem of unemployment under capitalism; it is a veritable prefiguration of 'the system of work in socialist society,' 'the total number of workers divided into the total number of hours' (ibid. 128). Utterly counterposed to the bourgeois-reformist conception of 'work-sharing,' it proposes that any shortening of the work-week in the interests of ameliorating the problem of unemployment should entail no diminution in the living standards of the working class. A concrete application of the demand is the call for '30 hours work for 40 hours pay' when workers are being laid off because of labour-saving technological innovation. The *social* logic of this demand is quite clear: technological innovation should accrue to the benefit of workers rather than capitalists. Similarly, the demand for a *full* sliding scale of wages (also known as 'indexation for inflation') seeks to guarantee the workers' share of national income by removing wage levels from the adjustments of the capitalist price structure. Overall, the thrust of the 'sliding scale of wages and hours' is to strike a blow against the reification of labour-power in the capitalist economy by systematically challenging its status as a commodity. Challenges of this sort to the Invisible Leviathan are absolutely necessary if the workers' movement is ever to advance its struggle to the level of expropriating capitalist industry and establishing a workers' government.

An adequate class-struggle socialist program must obviously address the many factors that may contribute to the fragmentation of working-class struggles. Transitional and democratic demands pertaining to the specific problems confronting women, minority, and immigrant workers must be integrated into the program if it is to build a 'bridge' wide enough and strong enough to accommodate the working class as a whole. Furthermore, the perspective of struggle around a transitional program must be linked to an *internationalist* strategy of organizing workers across national lines. Indeed, only through a conscious *internationalization* of the struggle can workers avoid tying their 'interests' to the competitive performance of their 'own' capitalists on the world market.

The transitional program and the strategic orientation it embodies for mobilizing the working class against capital is consistent with Marx's critique of capitalism in the sense that it challenges the *social logic* of value relations. But certain limitations of this programmatic-strategic conception should be noted. First, its efficacy is largely predicated on the existence of widespread sympathy for socialism as the pre-eminent goal of the labour movement, as well as on the existence of a layer of working-class militants who consciously seek the ousting of reformist labour leaders and the construction of a class-struggle leadership. Neither of these conditions obtain today in North America, and they are clearly less present in Europe now than at any other time in the twentieth century.

This leads directly to a second consideration. *Why* has the 'subjective will' to prosecute anticapitalist struggles been eroded so dramatically in recent years in the developed capitalist world? This is a very difficult question to answer, but it clearly involves more than capitalism's alleged (and very arguable) capacity to 'buy off' the working class. For discontent with the status quo has risen dramatically throughout the developed capitalist countries in the 1990s, and yet this has nowhere produced a widespread revival of socialist politics.

A factor of considerable importance in explaining this phenomenon has surely been the widespread and deepening 'crisis of confidence' in socialism as an attractive model of social, political, and economic organization that we have witnessed in recent years, a crisis now present even among those avant-garde elements of the working class who have traditionally been most committed to the socialist idea. This crisis consciousness can only be overcome to the extent that a new vision of socialism is successfully articulated and promulgated as an indispensable component of socialist practice. What this vision would entail, however, is inseparable from a critique of Stalinist 'real socialism.'

Value Theory and Socialist Construction

Until quite recently, the Soviet model of 'socialist construction' was an immensely powerful pole of attraction for major segments of the Western working class as well as for the impoverished masses of the colonial and semi-colonial world. The Soviets' successes in 'extensive economic growth' in the 1930s and again in the immediate postwar period (up to about 1965) commanded the admiration of the majority of those who longed to throw off the yoke of capitalism and imperialism, and to embark on the building of a socialist society free of want and extreme social inequality. Not surprisingly, many admirers of the Soviet achievement were inclined to regard the draconian, corrupt, repressive, and antidemocratic features of the Soviet system as 'necessary evils' – departures from socialist principle that were, in any case, hypocritically exaggerated by antisocialist forces. What seemed unarguable to those who 'wanted to believe' was that Soviet 'real socialism' had eliminated unemployment, modernized a vast and backward economy at breakneck speed, and provided by the 1950s a level of basic material security for its people that was, in some respects, superior to conditions prevailing in the developed capitalist countries. By the early 1960s Khrushchev's boast that the Soviet Union would soon reach the stage of full-fledged 'communism' appeared quite plausible to many who had already been awed by the rapid recovery of the Soviet economy in the aftermath of the terrible devastation of the Second World War.

As early as 1937, in *The Revolution Betrayed*, Leon Trotsky provided an incisive account of the impressive accomplishments of the Soviet planned economy while also pointing to the contradictions and limits of the Stalinist bureaucratic-command structure that administered it:

The progressive role of the Soviet bureaucracy coincides with the period devoted to introducing into the Soviet Union the most important elements of capitalist technique. The rough work of borrowing, imitating, transplanting and grafting was accomplished on the bases lain down by the revolution. There was, thus far, no question of any new word in the sphere of technique, science or art. It is possible to build gigantic factories according to a ready-made Western pattern by bureaucratic command – although, to be sure, at triple the normal cost. But the further you go, the more the economy runs into the problem of quality, which slips out of the hands of the bureaucracy like a shadow. The Soviet products are as though branded with the gray label of indifference. Under a nationalized economy, *quality* demands a democracy of producers and consumers, freedom of criticism and initiative – conditions incompatible with a totalitarian regime of fear, lies and flattery. (1970b: 275–6)

A faint echo of Trotsky's indictment of bureaucratic commandism in the Soviet 'degenerated workers state' was sounded some fifty years later by Mikhail Gorbachev as part of his call for 'restructuring' following the Brezhnev 'era of stagnation': 'In the last fifteen years the national income growth rates had declined by more than a half and by the beginning of the eighties had fallen to a level close to economic stagnation. A country that was once quickly closing on the world's advanced nations began to lose one position after another' (1987: 19).

Superficially, Gorbachev's reform policies of *glasnost* and *perestroika* might appear to have been close to Trotsky's programmatic admonition of 1932: 'Only the interaction of three elements, of state planning, of the market and of Soviet democracy can provide the country with correct leadership in the transitional epoch [to socialism]' (1973b: 275). But this was not really the case. It was soon apparent that Gorbachev's policies were inspired, not by Trotsky, the leader of the left opposition to Stalin, but more by Nikolai Bukharin, co-author with Stalin of the doctrine of 'building socialism in one country' and later the leader of the right opposition to Stalin's regime.

Bukharin was the prophet, within ostensibly Marxist thought, if not within the socialist tradition as a whole, of what is today referred to as 'market socialism' (Spartacist 1988). The attraction of this notion to reform-minded bureaucrats like Gorbachev is easy to understand. It is an approach that seeks to resolve the problems associated with 'transitional socialist economies' *without* introducing the political forms of an authentic workers' democracy and *without* seeking a socialist division of labour on an *international* scale. As the experiences of Yugoslavia, Hungary, and the Soviet Union amply confirm, it is also an approach that has been manifestly incapable of addressing the immense accumulated problems and contradictions of decades of Stalinist bureaucratic mismanagement, waste, and authoritarian rule.

The tendency of Stalinist bureaucracies, Gorbachev's included, to seek a solution to the crisis of the 'command-administrative' system through increasing reliance on market mechanisms reflected neither the 'practicality' nor the 'feasibility' of the 'market socialist' alternative. Rather, it reflected the belief of these bureaucratic oligarchies that 'market-oriented reform' was the *only* alternative to the status quo compatible with the perpetuation of their material priviliges and their monopoly of political power. We know now that the Gorbachevite turn to 'market socialism' in the USSR was simply the penultimate chapter in a process of 'counter-revolution' that began with Stalin's political expropriation of the working class in the 1920s and that culminated with the installation of Boris Yeltsin's openly pro-capitalist regime in 1991.[4]

It is not possible to enter here into a full-scale analysis of the lessons of 'socialist construction' in the former countries of 'actually existing socialism,' or of the factors leading to the terminal crisis of this system. But the still-strong influence of the 'market socialism' idea on socialist-minded workers and intellectuals, in East and West alike, suggests that the 'lesson' most widely drawn has been that the crisis of the Communist regimes was pre-eminently a crisis of 'planned economy' and that the indicated antidote was a reassertion of the role of market relations in coordinating economic activity and enforcing efficiency. True, most advocates of market socialism also invoke the necessity for democracy and human rights in a 'healthy' socialist society. But the prevailing tendency is to view democracy as an 'end in itself' rather than as a key ingredient in socialist economic development. Indeed, on this view, democracy for the producers and consumers is one of those 'institutional externalities' that may even impede economic efficiency and growth.

The optimal articulation of the three elements that Trotsky pointed to as indispensable to socialist economic development – central planning, the market, and workers' democracy – is undoubtedly problematic. But this articulation problem will remain endemically resistant to a satisfactory resolution so long as debate on the political economy of socialism is confined within the parameters of the discouraging dilemma, *either* bureaucratically centralized state planning *or* workers' self-management of enterprises within a 'socialist market economy.' Other possibilities deserve to be explored, and it is gratifying to see that the issue is now being seriously engaged by Marxists in a spate of recent publications (Spartacist 1988; Mandel 1986, 1992; Elson 1988; Bottomore 1990; Samary 1991; Laibman 1992; Flaherty 1992; URPE 1992). A touchstone for this discussion should remain Trotsky's own proposal for a democratically centralized planning system, which would continue to rely on (socialized) market mechanisms for as long as these may be required:

The problem of the *proportionality* of the elements of production and the branches of the economy constitutes the very heart of socialist economy ... The innumerable living participants in the economy, collective and individual, must serve notice of their needs and of their relative strength not only through the statistical determinations of plan commissions but by the direct pressure of supply and demand. The plan is checked and, to a considerable degree, realized through the market. The regulation of the market itself must depend upon the tendencies that are brought out through its mechanism. The blueprints produced by the departments must demonstrate their efficacy through commercial calculation ... The art of socialist planning does not drop from heaven nor is it presented full-blown into one's hands with the conquest of power. This art may be mastered only by struggle, step by step, not by a few but by millions, as a component part of the new economy and culture. (1973b: 265, 274, 260)

Elsewhere, Trotsky emphasized that planning is not a self-sufficient method of regulating the economic affairs of human beings, but is critically dependent on certain other principles of social and economic organization:

[A] successful socialist construction is unthinkable without including in the planned system the direct personal interests of the producer and consumer, their egoism – which in its turn may reveal itself fruitfully only if it has in its service the customary reliable and flexible instrument, money. The raising of the productivity of labour and bettering of the quality of its products is quite unattainable without an accurate measure freely penetrating into all the cells of industry – that is, without a stable unit of currency ... For the regulation and application of plans two levers are needed: the political lever, in the form of a real participation in leadership of the interested masses themselves, a thing which is unthinkable without Soviet [council] democracy; and a financial lever, in the form of a real testing out of *a priori* calculations with the help of a universal equivalent, a thing which is unthinkable without a stable money system. (1970b: 67–8)

This vision of socialist construction may seem to be something of a retreat from Marx's (implicit) program of transcending market and monetary relations in the creation of a society in which human beings *consciously* direct their affairs. But it should be borne in mind that Trotsky is speaking here of the *transition* to socialism, and that he regards 'socialist planning' as an 'art' that must be mastered by *millions*, 'as a component part of the new economy and culture.' What vistas will open up with the democratic involvement of millions of people in social and economic planning cannot be predicted from our present vantage point. All that can be said with certainty is that for some period following the 'conquest of power' by the working class and its allies, 'socialist planning' will continue to rely heavily on the assistance of market forces and monetary instruments.

But the question remains: Would the survival of money and the market signify the survival of the law of value? The answer is, yes, *up to a point.* The survival of market and money categories could only mean that society is continuing to allocate resources and distribute income in accordance with the measurement of labour-time. But in a centrally planned economy, under the democratic management of the associated producers and consumers, the measurment of wealth in terms of socially necessary labour-time would cease to be the *dominant* principle of economic regulation and resource allocation. Moreover, the abolition of private ownership in the means of production and of enterprise competition oriented toward profit maximization would undercut the two pillars of the *capitalist* law of value, rendering obsolete the quest for surplus-value as the motor force of economic activity. The survival of 'exchange-value' in such a post-capitalist society would not, in other words, entail the survival of surplus-value. Human activity could henceforth be geared toward the satisfaction of human needs and the all-round development of the human personality rather than toward the appropriation of wealth in the socially antagonistic form of private profit. But for this to happen, socialist 'exchange-value' would have to be the 'form of appearance' of a new set of social relations based pre-eminently upon cooperation, solidarity, and democracy, and not upon the invidious enterprise competition that currently fashionable models of market socialism unabashedly posit and even celebrate (Nove 1983, 1987; Le Grand and Estrin 1989).

This much is clear: the models of market socialism that have issued from the crisis of Stalinism could not fail to perpetuate and entrench all the characteristic evils associated with the value relation (from unemployment to the division of mental and manual labour) that Marxist socialism has always set its sights on eliminating. Marx's theory of value stands as a constant reminder of the *limits* to the historically progressive role of commodity exchange and as a challenge to reconstruct society on fundamentally different foundations. As such, it directs us to look beyond 'that which exists' to that which *ought to* and *could* exist once the constraints of the value-form are socio-historically transcended and human beings determine, in defiance of the 'eternal' law of value, to become masters of their own collective destiny.

11 'Modernity,' Postmodernism, and the Law of Value

Capitalism, Modernity, and Value

There have been many accounts of what is distinctive and 'new' in modernity relative to what came before it. But the accounts that have exercised the greatest influence on social theory have been: (1) the theory of 'industrial society,' originating in the thought of Saint-Simon and developed in diverse ways by Auguste Comte, Emile Durkheim, Ralf Dahrendorf, Raymond Aron, and a host of other theorists usually associated with the 'positivist' tradition of sociological theory; (2) the theory of capitalism associated with Max Weber, Georg Simmel, Werner Sombart, and Ferdinand Toennies, which emphasizes the *culturalist* discontinuities between precapitalist and capitalist social forms; and (3) the theory of capitalist society informed by Marx's theory of the generalization of the commodity form and the rise of the law of labour-value as the dominant principle of socio-economic organization. Each of these theoretical accounts – or, more precisely, *theoretical strategies* – recognizes a historical divide between pre-modern (traditional) and modern forms of social life. But, broadly speaking, the three strategies differ as to what should be highlighted in the epochal transition from the pre-modern to the modern. Theorists of industrial society emphasize the new relation to nature that humanity achieved with the momentous progress of science, technology, industry, division of labour, and so forth. The culturalist theorists of capitalist society emphasize the changed 'mental universe' brought about by modernization: the rationalization and disenchantment of the modern world (Weber), the new forms of sociation sponsored by money relations (Simmel), and the changed value orientations resulting from the displacement of community by market-mediated association (Toennies). Finally, Marxists emphasize the ascendance of new and historically unique social relations of production, which serve not only to promote a new human relation to nature (industrialism, centralization of production, and so on) but to sponsor in human beings a mode of thinking that gives a systematic impetus to the development of science and technology.

It may be somewhat schematic to do so, but there is heuristic value in pointing out that the theory of industrial society gives pride of place to Marx's 'material forces of production,' while the culturalist theory of capitalism tends to focus on Marx's 'ideal superstructure' (as well as those cultural products that fall outside a determinate social structure entirely). The *superiority* of Marx's theory of capitalism in relation to its two main competitors is precisely that it focuses on the social relations of production and reproduction that *mediate* the relationship between these two 'levels' – a relationship that remains tellingly indeterminate in all versions of non-Marxist social theory. The key to Marx's success in this respect consists precisely in his elaboration of a critique of the *naturalistic* conception of economic value – a conception that classical political economy shares with marginalism and that the theory of industrial society shares with the culturalist theory of capitalism. On the basis of this critique – otherwise known as the Marxian theory of value – Marx demonstrated the possibility and necessity of overcoming the *dualisms* that overrun all the main versions of modern bourgeois thought.

These considerations form the basis for assessing the 'first' crisis of modernity occasioned by the bifurcation of the inter-class bloc that spearheaded the bourgeois-democratic revolution – a crisis registered most fully by the culturalist theorists of capitalist society in company with such philosophers as Nietzsche and Heidegger, but also to some degree by the theorists of industrial society and the bourgeois optimists of neoclassical marginalism. This first crisis of modernist thought broke over what was to be a recurring theme of social-scientific and philosophical controversy in the twentieth century: the relationship between (objective, unconscious, law-bound) structures and (human, conscious, free) subjective agency.

The lineaments of this crisis can perhaps be most conveniently understood in relation to the philosophical legacy of Kant, whose ontological and epistemological dualism was, as he foresaw, well ahead of its time. The century spanning the appearance of Kant's philosophy and the neo-Kantian revival of the late nineteenth century (which influenced both Durkheim and Weber) saw a drift in bourgeois social thought from the certainty that capitalism simultaneously represents 'what is' and 'what ought to be' toward a stance that was far more sensitive to the irremediably irrational and indeterminate elements of the structure-agency relationship. In particular, the disaffection of the working class from its erstwhile bourgeois ally in the democratic struggle, the former's increased capacity for collective organization and action, and the emergence of a proletarian-socialist politics all found an intimately interrelated reaction in the evolution of bourgeois thought as a whole. The robust, vigorously anti-idealist scientism of the Enlightenment and of the heroic period of the bourgeois-democratic revolution gave way to a pervasive philosophical dualism that was more or less concealed by a mutual pact of non-interference between new currents of subjective idealism and an array of tepid neopositivisms. In the realm of economic theory, these developments were paralleled by the final dissolution of classical political economy and the rise of marginalism.

The common ideological motif of the early social and historical sciences of the bourgeois era – the conviction that capitalist social relations of production had a 'natural' foundation such that any challenge to them could only be construed as an irrational defiance of natural law – was to undergo a modification but not a substantive transformation with the development of a working-class/socialist reaction against it. However, it is important to appreciate the impetus to and character of this modification. On the one hand, classical political economy as a theory of *social structure* was decisively crippled by the crisis of its own 'supply-side' accounts of price formation (a crisis engendered by the inconsistencies of Ricardo's theory, the challenge of Marxism, and the inadequacies of Mill's cost-of-production theory of price). By effectively surrendering the terrain of a social-structural account of economic value to Marxism, classical political economy wrote its own death warrant. On the other hand, the ideological underpinnings of classical political economy's utopian belief in a harmony of interests within the capitalist class structure also came unhinged with the movement of the working class toward independent forms of political and industrial action (trade-union and socialist political organization). These two developments complemented and reinforced one another significantly: the resumption of class conflict called into question the efficacy of the market as the self-sufficient 'regulator' of social equilibrium, while the deficiencies of the social-structural theory of price seemed to find reflection in the inability of political economy to account for the 'irrational' (*collective* as well as anticapitalist) actions of the working class. In both instances, the rift between theory and reality – and between value and fact – could only further entrench a dualistic world-view already nurtured by a deepening division of mental and manual labour and by the proliferation of commodity production and exchange.

The upshot then is that the movement from classical political economy to marginalism involved a shift toward an increasingly *dualistic gnoseology*.

Classical political economy had sought to subsume the theory of action under its theory of the social structure, while laying claim to a monopoloy of competence in the interrogation of the social. Marginalist economics constitutively regarded the social order as intrinsically *divided*, its economic component constituted as the result of a multitude of (market-based) individual actions undertaken for the purpose of allocating scarce resources to alternative uses, its cultural component constituted as the result of an ensemble of practices not directly influenced by the rationality of the process of economic exchange. By accepting this duality of the social structure, marginalism *completed* the 'naturalization' of capitalist relations of production, as well as of 'economic value,' while delimiting the theoretical boundaries of economics and creating a niche for other social sciences to pursue the analysis of the sociocultural dimensions of the social structure. The indeterminate relationship between the socio-economic and sociocultural components of the social structure – expressed in the theoretical dichotomization of 'economy' and 'society' that marginalism sanctioned by 'abstracting economic relations from all social content' (Clarke 1982: 234) – served as starting-point for a whole series of antinomies and binomial oppositions that came to characterize the crisis in bourgeois 'modernist' thought.

Marginalism and classical sociology subscribed to a common dualism that sanctioned the division of social reality into 'economy' and 'society,' while carving out distinctive areas of specialization within an increasingly ideologized division of intellectual labour. But this shared dualism found a *uniform* expression neither *within* nor *between* the two disciplines. Thus, the tendency of economists to regard sociology as concerned with the province of the 'irrational' was strongly challenged by Max Weber (1978), who saw the historical process of rationalization as one occurring in such non-economic domains as religion and law as well as in the (market) economy. Indeed, for Weber, the emergence of the modern rational form of capitalism depended on a larger historical process of rationalization, the progress of which he traced in the evolution of religious theodicies.

Nevertheless, the 'rational value-orientation' of capitalist society was deemed to be its defining characteristic by marginalist economics and Weberian sociology alike, and the task of sociology, from both perspectives, was chiefly to 'restore some degree of historical variety to the naturalism of economics' (Clarke 1982: 236), while also distinguishing between the rational and non-rational elements impinging on social action and the relationship between the economic and the sociocultural. *Both* marginalism and Weberian social theory regarded the capitalist socio-economic order as a confluence of *natural law* and *human volition based on 'ideas,'* with no specifically 'social' intermediation between the two. Their 'differences,' such as they were, stemmed entirely from their different locations within a theoretical division of labour shaped by this common (dualistic) problematic.

The contrast between Weber's 'interpretive' sociology, with its focus on the subjective orientation to action and its attention to questions of culture, power, and conflict, and functionalist sociology, with its more Durkheimian focus on 'order' and the consensual and ritualistic bases of social reproduction, was to become an exemplar, *within* sociology itself, of an increasingly obvious disjunction between social theories stressing, respectively, a 'voluntarism' at the level of human action and an objectivist 'naturalism' at the level of the social structure. As Clarke emphasizes, *both* approaches involve highly questionable procedures of abstraction from the social relations of capitalist production – the voluntarist approach abstracting 'the individual' from these relations, while the naturalistic (neopositivist) approach abstracts nature itself. The two approaches may seem 'mutually exclusive' – but they are no less complementary for that fact. Indeed, within the framework of a common dualism, they maintain a symbiotic relationship, drawing strength from each other's deficiencies while tacitly acknowledging each other's 'achievements' as well. Their common refusal to consider the mediating role of Marx's 'social relations of production' – and hence also his law of value – closes the door to any escape from the dualistic problematic. The upshot, avers Clarke, is that 'modern sociology is condemned to exist within a world defined by a series of abstract dualisms which reflect the inadequacy of its foundations but which nevertheless structure sociological debate: structure-action; object-subject; positivism-humanism; holism-individualism; society-individual; explanation-understanding; order-conflict; authority-consent' (1982: 238–9). As it happens, this is an apt résumé not only of the crisis of 'modern sociology' but of modern bourgeois thought in general.

While recognition of the *social form* of capitalist production is a necessary and indispensable basis for the repudiation of the 'naturalization' of capitalist relations of production, together with the dualistic problematic that that conception entails, the history of Marxist thought demonstrates both that it is a hard-won recognition and that it is an insufficient basis for avoiding dualism. The crisis in bourgeois modernism has clearly been paralleled in recent years by a 'crisis of Marxism' that appears to have many filiations and points of contact with the schism between 'scientific' and 'life-philosophical' orientations that characterizes the malaise of bourgeois modernity. But the question is, Does this crisis result from Marxism's theoretical focus on the 'social relations of production' (including, of course, *value relations*), or does it arise instead from a rather harsh encounter between theoretical expectation and historical experience, between theory and practice? On the answer to this question hinges much in contemporary disputes between Marxists and a new levy of Marx-critics ('Analytical Marxists,' post-Marxists, postmodernists, poststructuralists, and so forth) who often affect opposition to capitalist modernity as well.

Like the bourgeois social theory of an earlier period, Marxism has been obliged to confront a major historical disappointment that has called into question many of its certitudes and engendered a very real crisis consciousness. The *bureaucratization of the workers' movement* (first in the trade unions and subsequently in the Social-Democratic and Communist parties) *and of the first workers' state* (the Soviet Union) has weighed no less heavily on the consciousness of Marxists, Western Marxists in particular, than did the persistence of class conflict on the intellectual heirs of the bourgeoisdemocratic revolution. It is therefore hardly surprising that a certain convergence has occurred between Western Marxism and bourgeois social theory with respect to a number of dualist tropes, and that this convergence has often blurred the dividing line between 'Marxist' and 'non-Marxist' approaches.

The limits to this 'convergence' should nevertheless be evident. For what must appear as *eternal* antinomies in bourgeois philosophy and social theory must appear as historically conditioned oppositions within Marxism. Moreover, such may be said even of Western Marxism's own tendency to divide into 'humanist' and 'scientific' camps.

On what basis, then, can it be maintained that the antinomies of the dualistic outlook are a 'necessary' feature of bourgeois thought but are fundamentally, even 'constitutively,' alien to Marxism? To answer this question we must consider the deeper roots of the dualist world-view. The fundamental source of the dualist outlook is the division of mental and manual labour as reinforced and ramified by the separation of exchange and use inherent in commodity relations. Bourgeois thought is defined negatively by its complete inability to conceive of a social order in which either of these phenomena are transcended. The dualistic 'collapse' of bourgeois thought therefore reunites it with the social conditions of its dominance: the division of the direct producers and their exploiters; the opposition between production for use and production for profit; the separation of head and hand, and the extension of this separation for the first time into the very heart of the labour process. The theoretical posture of justifying such conditions could only serve to revive and then 'unravel' the metaphysical system most responsible for problematizing the relationship between determinism and freedom, facts and values, reason and sense experience within modern thought – the Kantian system. In those disciplines most attuned to the subject-object relation, Kant's dualism was able to sanction a rivalry between two apparently 'opposite' approaches, which nevertheless complement one another and find a common ground in resisting all attempts at their mutual transcendence. At the theoretical level, Marxism stands as the most audacious of all such attempts – the materialist heir to the last significant idealist attempt at such a transcendence, the Hegelian system.

Yet it is above all at the level of *program* that Marxism resists the dualist outlook. Marx's programmatic vision of a classless, rationally planned, and democratically administered social order in which the contradiction between mental and manual labour would be progresssively overcome is a vision that finds translation at the level of theory in a repudiation of the notion that the dualities *specific to capitalism and class society* are ontologically rooted in the existence of 'two worlds' (subject-object, spirit-matter, noumena-phenomena, Müssen-Sollen, and so on). Hence, within the 'integrated' Marxist project, as within bourgeois thought, the relationship between theory and program is a dialectically interactive one, and program tends to generate theory.

But the reverse is, of course, also true; theory also generates (or influences) program, especially when the efficacy of that program seems most in doubt. The 'crisis of Marxism' is, in fact, pre-eminently an expression of the fact that Marxist intellectuals have developed grave doubts about the program that guided Marx in the elaboration of his theoretical perspectives. These doubts arise most generally from the *results* of the bureaucratization phenomenon mentioned earlier: the failure of the working class to realize its revolutionary potential under conditions of advanced capitalism, and its apparently related failure to maintain or assert control over the levers of state power in any of the countries where a transition to socialism has been ostensibly attempted. The question is thus posed: Does Marxist *theory* have the conceptual resources to explain these 'historical disappointments' in a way that remains consistent with its traditional *program*?

The harsh historical experience of 'labour bureaucracy' has not only been a 'test' of the viability and legitimacy of the Marxist program; it has also had serious implications for the *interpretation* of Marxism. The bureaucratic degeneration of both the classical Social Democracy and of the Soviet workers' state created highly favourable conditions for a 'monism' that decisively privileged objective structures over conscious human agency (much as classical political economy had done) and for the promulgation of a rigidly deterministic Marxism purged of 'voluntaristic,' 'ethical,' 'humanist,' or 'subjectivist' elements. The theoretical reflex against such bureaucratic 'official' versions of Marxism was, not surprisingly, to capsize this decidely undialectical monism in favour of a dualism involving a one-sided reassertion of the 'subject.' Thus was born the confrontation between the Two Marxisms – the inaugural moment of the 'crisis of Marxism.' Had the schizoid condition of modernity itself spelled the undoing of Marxism's own project of enlightenment, progress, and ... (post-capitalist) modernity?

Analytical Marxism, Poststructuralism, and Rationality

It is common nowadays for Marxism – that is, Marx's own Marxism – to be faulted for its conception of rationality. Indeed, the Achilles' heel of all forms of modernist thought is often said to be a too-confident and potentially sinister faith in Human Reason. Commenting on an early 'neo-Marxist' expression of this theme in Horkheimer and Adorno's *Dialectic of Enlightenment*, Leszek Kolakowski writes: 'The "dialectic" consisted in the fact that the [Enlightenment] movement which aimed to conquer nature and emancipate reason from the shackles of mythology had, by its own inner logic, turned into its opposite. It had created a positivist, pragmatist, utilitarian ideology and, by reducing the world to its purely quantitative aspects, had annihilated meaning, barbarized the arts and sciences, and increasingly subjected mankind to "commodity fetishism" ' (1978: 373). For Horkheimer and Adorno the single-minded pursuit of knowledge that would enable human domination of nature is an expression of 'subjective reason' and leads to the eclipse of that 'objective reason' which alone permits the valorization of such *ends* of human action as freedom and democracy. Subjective reason dissolves the unity of means and ends by denying that human *goals* can be determined on the basis of reason; and reason is thereby reduced to finding means to ends that may be motivated by simple 'economic self-interest' – or even those barbarous human tendencies that find a concentrated distillation in fascism.

The key problem with this argument from a Marxist standpoint is that it fails to give due weight to the role of capitalist social relations of production in the devolution of the bourgeois Enlightenment into subjective reason. The values of justice, equality, progress, brotherhood, freedom, democracy, liberty, and universality had a muscular presence in the Enlightenment – the French Enlightenment in particular – and were integral to the Reason that the bourgeois-democratic revolution championed against the superstition, religiosity, mythologies, status inequalities, absolutism, and overt injustices of the feudal order. But they were not values that could be consistently pursued by a New Society founded on capitalist social relations and increasingly committed to the rational adaptation of means to the inherently *non-universal* end of private capital accumulation. As the claims of these values were sublated by war, nationalism, colonial pillage, the oppressive realties of the industrial revolution, the resumption of class conflict, and the remorseless imperatives of the competitive pursuit of profit, the 'ethic' of the Enlightenment was passed on to, and necessarily transmuted by, the socialist heirs of the bourgeois-democratic revolution: the Jacobin-communists, the utopian socialists, the Red 48ers, the Social-Democrats, the Communards, and the Marxists. For Marx, the abandonment of Enlightenment values in favour of a narrowly defined 'subjective reason' was not at all the result of the Enlightenment's drive to 'dominate nature,' but was rather the consequence of the adaptation of 'reason' to the imperatives of capital. To reclaim the original unity of means and ends promised by Enlightenment reason required not just a critique of the technical-instrumental rationality that capital had exalted, but the negation of the capitalist social relations of production and the law of value promised by the immanent *anti-systemic* (that is, anticapitalist) rationality of the workers' movement toward socialism.

The concept of rationality posited by Marx is integral to his critical scientific project of disclosing the historical movement of capitalist society. But it has been challenged, implicitly and explicitly, from two different directions in recent years, at least partly in response to the perceived 'crisis of Marxism.' Poststructuralists, for their part, challenge Marxism's claim to 'objective knowledge' of capitalist society based on dialectical reason. On the other hand, 'Analytical Marxists,' particularly 'rational-choice theorists,' challenge Marx's findings on the grounds that they fail to conform to the principles of methodological individualism (Roemer 1988, Elster 1982) and subjective rationality. In this, of course, they reprise an old complaint of the marginalists concerning the rational foundations of Marx's law of value – a good place to begin.

Rationality and Irrationality in the Law of Labour-Value

The 'Analytical' or 'Rational-choice' school of neo-Marxism has been justifiably dubbed 'neoclassical Marxism' by its critics for having fully embraced the methodological principles of neoclassical economics in its efforts to (a) 'refute' Marx's theory of labour-value and his general analysis of capitalism's laws of motion, and (b) sustain the proposition that exploitation occurs under capitalism through mechanisms different from those specified by Marx.

The most influential theorist of 'rational-choice' Marxist economics is John Roemer, whose 'general theory of exploitation' is meant to be equally valid for all societies founded upon class inequality and differential access to productive resources. Roemer's criticisms of Marx's theory of value are unremarkable; they are the traditional ones of neoclassical economics, supplemented by certain neo-Ricardian observations. What is new in Roemer's work is his attempt to generate the phenomenon of exploitation as a theoretical result of neoclassical concepts.

Roemer asserts that his theoretical model explains 'some phenomena, in deriving them from logically prior data ... [The] data are: differential ownerships of the means of production, preferences and technology. Everything is driven by these data; class and exploitation are explained to be a consequence of initial property relations' (quoted in Lebowitz 1988). It would seem, as Lebowitz points out, that Roemer, 'like Marx,' starts from 'logically prior data' that 'are not the subject of his analysis (i.e. "unsubstantiated postulates")' (1988: 203). But whereas Marx's 'unsubstantiated postulates' are taken from 'history, from real life, the real concrete,' Roemer's are borrowed from the conceptual instrumentarium of neoclassical economics. Here we arrive at the real heart of the problem with Roemer's model: its inability to specify either the real conditions or the developmental tendencies of the capitalist mode of production. Capitalist *property* relations rather than capitalist social relations of production are both the starting-point and terminus of Roemer's analysis. But the specification of these property relations – the unequal distribution of property in the means of production – is insufficent to generate any conclusions beyond the banality that capitalism involves exploitation. Roemer's theory tells us little about the capitalist imperative to control the labour process, to reproduce the capital/wage-labour relation, and to subordinate the process of production to the goal of profit-making. And it tells us even less about the 'crisis tendencies' bred by the *contradictory* character of capitalist social relations of production.

The result of Roemer's approach is to problematize the relationship between a (neo-Marxian) theory of exploitation and the (ethical) imperative to achieve a society without exploitation. Nothing in Roemer's theory suggests an immanent tendency within capitalism to negate itself or to call forth the conclusion that capitalism not only 'ought' to be replaced by socialism but 'must' be so replaced. This lacuna in Roemer's 'Marxist economic philosophy' is the necessary result of his failure to break with the naïve naturalism, formalism, and one-sidedly subjective concept of rationality characteristic of marginalism. In responding to the rational-choice Marxists, then, we need to recapitulate some basic differences between Marx and the marginalists.

The marginalist concept of value, it bears repeating, is a naturalistic one. Value is conceived to be a *natural* phenomenon stemming from the unmediated relation of individual economic actors to 'things,' and therefore is considered an effectively 'eternal' aspect of human existence. The 'rationality' of this relation is by no means unconditional, for while it is promoted by the natural laws of the market-place, it is compromised by human irrationality stemming from 'non-economic' interests. We might say, following Fischer's (1982) terminology, that the marginalist concept of economic value is a typically 'two-tiered' theory involving *natural structures* (for example, the price structure) and *individual subjects* (who are 'free' to either abide by or defy the 'natural' imperatives of the market economy).

By contrast, the Marxist concept of value involves a 'three-tiered' theoretical approach. Between 'natural laws' and idea-oriented 'human agency' stand the social relations of production that mediate the natural and the ideal components of the social order. Value is conceived not as a natural phenomenon but as a determinate socio-historical form of the human imperative to articulate a division of labour, a relation between people.

The supreme importance of *subjective* rationality to modern social theory is well stated by Swedberg, Himmelstrand, and Brulin: 'The notion of rationality, if handled correctly, might provide a solution to the old problem in sociology of simultaneously accounting for the autonomy of the actor and the influence of the social surroundings on his or her actions. The concept of rationality safeguards the notion of the actor's autonomy through its stress on the importance of choice. If this choice plus its parameters could be properly accounted for in sociological terms, the ship so-to-speak would be in harbor' (1987: 183).

It is precisely in connection with the notion of the 'parameters' of rational action that the decisive difference between the two-tiered conception of economic value enunciated by marginalism and the three-tiered conception of Marxist value theory can be most clearly elucidated. Somewhat schematically it may be said that marginalism is predicated upon the notion that the capitalist economy is inherently rational in the sense that it operates in accordance with 'predictable natural laws' and encourages behaviour on the part of economic agents that conforms to them. Specifically, economic agents are encouraged to pursue the rational goal of maximizing their utilities by selecting means that are in harmony with the natural laws of the market-place. To the extent that such rationality can be imputed to the individual economic actor, the problem of the structure-agency relation, within 'the economy' at least, becomes soluble.

Marx's theory of value leads to very different conclusions about the 'rationality' of the capitalist mode of production. Economic rationality is defined not in terms of 'predictability,' but in far more 'substantive' terms: the degree to which the relations of production can systematically promote the productivity of labour and the progress of human culture. On this criterion of rationality, the capitalist mode of production must be regarded as a unity of contradictory elements – a unity that plays a substantively rational role in human development only up to the point at which the relations of production begin systematically to *restrain* the development of human capacities.

This insight leads directly to a contrast of the notions of individual (subjective) rationality and systemic (objective) rationality. The marginalist criterion of rationality is an *entirely* individualistic one: how well has the individual actor adapted the 'naturally available' means to a desired and 'naturally possible' end? By contrast, the three-tiered approach of Marxism permits *two* quite distinct criteria of rationality: the rationality of the social actor inserted within particular social relations of production, and the systemic rationality of the social structure (mode of production) itself. The contrast between the rationality of the individual capitalist and the rationality of agencies seeking to safeguard the interests of the *social capital as a whole* (political parties, the capitalist state, and so on) illustrates how the value-theoretical analysis of capitalism involves an appreciation of the ways in which 'rationality' and 'irrationality' operate at both the individual and collective (or systemic) levels.

Consider the following example. It is eminently 'rational' for individual capitalists to reduce their costs of production and enhance their competitive position by replacing living workers with machines. But such action may also end in a rise in the organic composition of the social capital as a whole, producing a decline in the average rate of profit – a substantively 'irrational' result unanticipated and undesired by the innovating capitalists. By introducing labour-saving technology, the individual capitalist may *believe* that she or he is selecting means that are rationally suited to the goal of a higher profit rate – and this may even be the case up to a point. But we know that a higher profit rate is not *only* a function of the 'natural' conditions of production, but pre-eminently of what is transpiring within the social structure of 'abstract labour' as a whole. Thus, the temporary advantage that a capitalist might gain by introducing labour-saving technology (an advantage reflected in a higher-than-average transitional rate of profit, signifying the capitalist's superior ability to meet the 'natural' challenges of production) is bound to disappear as competing capitals close the technological gap and with it the discrepancy between the OCC of the original innovator and the OCC of the social capital. Moreover, once this (temporary) advantage disappears, so too will the higher-than-average profit rate. A falling profit rate will ensue resulting from insufficient surplus-value production in relation to capital investment. Thus, what appears as a subjectively rational move on the part of an individual capitalist seeking to employ superior knowledge of natural laws (technology) in pursuit of higher profits may end in lower profits.

In the three-tiered theoretical conception of Marxist value theory, then, individual rationality must be adjudged in relation to systemic rationality as well as in relation to natural laws and contingencies. Marginalism, by contrast, considers that the rationality of individual actions can be judged in relation to a set of conditions in which it is assumed a priori that no contradiction can exist between 'the natural' and 'the social.'

This point has direct relevance to the way in which the Roemerian theory of exploitation, the 'game theory' of Jon Elster (1982) and Erik Olin Wright (1985), and the general methodological individualism of the rational-choice school of Analytical Marxism serve to sever the link between the substantive macro-rationality/irrationality of the social structure and the micro-rationality/irrationality of purposive agents inserted within that structure. First, the social results of human agency are seen to be a mere aggregation of individual actions, unaffected and unmediated by the collective expressions of the social relations of production (the distribution of social labour, the structure of abstract labour, class formation, the state, and so on). Second, the rationality of individual social actors is seen to be entirely a function of their subjectively perceived interests within the framework of the existing social structure. Finally, the possibility is never considered that the consciousness of individual actors may be affected through the reflexive monitoring of the *objective substantive irrationality* of capitalism as a system. Yet it is just this possibility that allows (even relatively privileged) members of the 'middle classes' to (rationally) take their stand with the working class in the struggle for an alternative social order, socialism.

Marxism rejects a one-sided concern with subjective rationality, understanding that the consciousness of individual agents is always the complex result of elements of rationality and irrationality operating at macro and micro levels, and through objective structures as well as subjective agents. Yet Marxism, too, has often viewed the structure-agency relation as relatively unproblematic to the extent that rationality can be imputed to 'the collective subject': that is, to the extent that a revolutionary class consciousness can be imputed to the working class. It has frequently been assumed by Marxists that the increasing 'systemic irrationality' of capitalism would bring in its wake an increasing 'rationality' on the part of the putative revolutionary subject. However, this is frequently not the case. While Marxism possesses theoretical resources that help to explain why working-class people have difficulty in achieving and retaining this rationality of revolutionary consciousness, the problem remains that the theory of ideology and the theory of capitalism's structural contradictions require articulation with one another.

It is precisely this articulation that the theory of value facilitates. On the one hand, Marx's value theory is the basis for disclosing the link between the real subsumption of labour by capital and the phenomenon of 'commodity fetishism.' On the other hand, the theory of value provides the basis for an understanding of the process of 'cognitive appropriation' and the dissemi-nation of a dualistic consciousness. The law of value, then, occupies the terrain of *both* structure and subject, providing conceptual resources to explain significant elements of both the 'objective' structural articulation of social labour *and* the social determination of particular modes of conscious-ness and cognition. Marx's 'value,' in brief, shows that 'objective structures' and 'subjective agency' belong to *the same world.*

Marx's concept of value is inseparable from his analytic focus on the social relations of production as the mediating link between 'natural laws' and 'human agency' under capitalism. The limits of this focus also suggest the limits of a value-theoretical perspective in the analysis of capitalism and of human agency within capitalist societies. It should go without saying that Marxist value theory neither provides, nor seeks to provide, a *full* account of either 'natural laws' or of human agency (influenced as it is by a plethora of factors irreducible to the prevailing relations of production). Accordingly, this theory should not be seen as a 'master-key' to the structure-agency relationship even as this manifests itself under capitalism. Precisely because no such master-key exists, neither structure nor subject should be accorded a *privileged* theoretical position. Nevertheless, Marx clearly and, I think, reasonably, intended that the theory of value should be seen as an objective theoretical *guide to action*, as a source of insight into the historical limits of the capitalist structure and into the conditions and possibilities of its tran-scendence.

The historical-materialist and value-theoretic focus on the social relations of production permits theoretical inquiry to go beyond the dualist preoccu-pations that have led so many non-Marxist theorists into an attenuation or even an outright rejection of the concept of objective truth (Anderson 1982). It is precisely this attenuation/rejection that provides a thematic unity to the two main strands within 'poststructuralist' thought: the 'sociological' post-structuralism of Michel Foucault, with its emphasis on the role of 'power relations' in constituting knowledge (Foucault 1972), and the 'textual' post-structuralism of Jacques Derrida, with its emphasis on the self-referential nature of the 'system of signs' and its insistence that 'there is nothing outside the text' (Derrida 1976: 158). Both of these schools of thought represent a development of 'structuralist' thought in a direction that involves the 'decentring' of structures without a reassertion of the role of the 'subject.' As Anderson pithily suggests, poststructualism thereby licenses a 'subjectivism without a subject' (1982: 54).

Both versions of poststructuralism have been subjected to incisive and devastating criticism in recent years (Anderson 1982, Dews 1987, Callinicos 1990, Palmer 1990, MacDonald 1990), and I shall not recapitulate those criticisms here. But it should be pointed out that the poststructuralist 'challenge' to the dialectical reason of Marxism stems mainly from a species of 'cynical reason' (Sloterdijk 1988), rather than from the sort of one-sided 'subjective reason' associated with marginalism and rational-choice Marxism. This 'cynical reason' is associated with the invocation of Nietzsche's 'will-to-power' theme, particularly in the case of Foucault, together with a reassertion of the universal applicability of Ferdinand de Saussure's model of structural linguistics to the interrogation of knowledge claims.

Both Foucauldian and Derridean poststructuralism seek to construct barriers against 'totalizing' tendencies in philosophy and social theory (of which Marxism is supposedly particularly guilty on some accounts). Yet, by positing 'power' as the master-category for the explication of the genealogy of modernity, and/or by privileging 'language' over practice in the constitution of the social, poststructuralists seem to fall victim to precisely those totalizing tendencies that they claim to deplore. Evidently, poststructuralist totalizations are to be preferred because they discourage notions of 'total social transformation' – but this simply assumes what needs to be demonstrated: that a total social transformation at the level of the social relations of production is neither needed nor desirable.

Significantly, the 'language model' that intruded so successfully into social theory on the wave of structuralism and poststructuralism is itself vulnerable to a historical-materialist critique to the extent that its provenance is a *dualist* one. Saussure's 'signifier' and 'signified' may be seen without too much difficulty as the binomial poles of a veritable archetype of the disjunction of an ontological unity, the 'sign.' In this regard, several attempts have been made by Marxist theorists to disclose a link between post-Saussurean semiotics and the social ontology of commodity relations (Timpanaro 1980, Lipietz 1985). Not surprisingly, even Derrida's poststructuralist strategy of 'deconstruction' – for all its self-conscious opposition to 'metaphysics' and its internalist critique of Saussurean semiotics – fails to really break from this dualistic tradition. As MacDonald incisively points out: 'The theory of deconstruction reveals how the lesser term of the dualism is repressed within the system; it brings the form of that repression to light. But no value belongs to that term. What deconstruction demonstrates is the necessity of both terms, and the inevitability of the privileging of the dominant term in all language and representation. It is clear from this that the hierarchy of philosophical dualisms stays undisturbed despite deconstruction's revelation of the internal interdependency of its terms' (1990: 237).

None of this should be construed as suggesting that the analysis of language, communication, or power/domination is 'alien' to historical materialism. The issue is not whether these shibboleths of poststructuralism should be explored, but whether they should be explored *in connection with* an analysis of the social relations of production and the determinate socio-historical forms of human labour, or whether they should be accorded a kind of ontological *privilege*, such that they become a rationale for *ignoring* the issue of the social relations of production. Again, it is quite apparent that the tendency of bourgeois thought is to accord a theoretical privilege to anything that sublates the issue of the social relations of production. To this extent, poststructuralism serves a highly useful purpose from the bourgeois standpoint as a major intellectual *diversion* from the theoretical and programmatic results of Marx's devastating critique of capitalist social relations.

Postmodernism: Condition or Fashion?

It is hardly accidental that most theorizations of the 'postmodern condition' are so heavily dependent on poststructuralist and Baudrillardian perspectives that sublate the analysis of the social relations of production while seeking to overcome the familiar duality of culture and industry by focusing precisely on that fearsome 'postmodern' complex: the culture industry. Postmodernists assured us throughout most of the 1980s that the 'new reality' was one in which the production of knowledge, fashions, simulacra, tastes, and even identities would count for far more than the production of Marx's 'value' and the crises this bred; and they added that it was only upon this essentially cultural terrain that conflicting visions of the future could be fought out. Yet the putative omnipotence of the established culture industry was such as to really deny the possibility of such contests resulting in 'the conscious construction of alternative social futures' (Harvey 1989: 34). For postmodern culture had supposedly fragmented the 'alienated subject' of Marx's social theory into a plethora of subjects incapable of pursuing the Enlightenment project 'with a tenacity and coherence sufficient to bring us some better future' (ibid.). This vision was nicely summarized by Terry Eagleton:

Post-modernism signals the death of ... 'metanarratives' whose secretly terroristic function was to ground and legitimate the illusion of a 'universal' human history. We are now in the process of wakening from the nightmare of modernity, with its manipulative reason and fetish of the totality, into the laid-back pluralism of the postmodern, that heterogeneous range of lifestyles and language games which has renounced the nostalgic urge to totalize and legitimate itself ... Science and philosophy must jettison their grandiose metaphysical claims and view themselves more modestly as just another set of narratives. (Quoted in Harvey 1989: 9)

The characteristic themes of postmodernist ideology are ultimately explicable in terms of a sea-change that has not produced a capitalism immune from the contradictions and crisis tendencies identified by Marx, but which is itself the product of a maturing of these contradictions in a climate of politico-ideological reaction (1980s Reaganism, Thatcherism, Mitterrand's 'austerity socialism,' and so forth). The extreme measures associated with the real 'successes' of neoconservatism in the 1980s (from union-busting and military Keynesianism to the erosion of the welfare state and the victory over Soviet power) has destroyed the illusion of the inexorable progress of 'modern societies' through gradual and incremental reforms; and the association of this vision with various 'metanarratives' of historical progress (including, quite mistakenly, Marx's program of *social revolution*) has disoriented many (formerly) left-wing intellectuals now identified with the postmodernist trend. Wallowing in impressionism, postmodernist intellectuals have mistaken their own disorientation and that of the labour movement with a permanent fragmentation of that ensemble of forces which retains the objective capacity to transform society, but which now lacks the will and vision to do so.

Postmodernism certainly exists as a fashionable intellectual and cultural current; but can we speak of a 'postmodern condition' that is significantly different from the 'condition of modernity'? It seems doubtful. Clearly, the rise of postmodernist thought coincided with a significant conjunctural transition in the history of twentieth-century capitalism; but the 'restructuring' that we are now witnessing changes nothing essential about the laws of motion of capitalism. Rather this restructuring has been necessitated by the increasing dislocations and crisis tendencies bred by the laws of labour-value and capital accumulation. It is a perverse logic that now insists that the rather desperate and destabilizing changes occasioned by the malaise of capitalism constitute proof of a postmodern renaissance of this moribund system; still more absurd is the competing postmodernist thesis of capitalism's transformation into 'post-capitalism' thanks to technologically driven social, economic, and cultural changes. What seems obvious to those not blinded by the glitter of the postmodernist cultural spectacle is that the most significant changes of recent years have their roots in a severe crisis of capitalist socio-economic relations (the 'economy'). Writing in the late 1980s, David Harvey observed that 'it is conventional these days ... to dismiss out of hand any suggestion that the "economy" (however that vague word is understood) might be determinant of cultural life even in (as Engels and later Althusser suggested) "the last instance". The odd thing about postmodern cultural production is how much sheer profit-seeking is determinant in the first instance' (1989: 336). Only three years later, the watchword of the American presidential elections was to become 'It's the economy stupid!', and hypocritical postmodern indifference to the course of economic events lost much of its ill-deserved fashionability. The severe and persistent recession that gripped most of the advanced capitalist world in the early 1990s confirmed that the brave new world of capitalist (or 'post-capitalist') 'post- modernity' was looking more and more like the deeply troubled capitalism of early twentieth-century 'modernity.' New times, certainly. A new 'stage' of capitalism's world-historical crisis – perhaps. A postmodern 'transcendence' of capitalism – hardly.

Bureaucracy, the Law of Value, and the Crisis of Capitalist Modernity

At the ideological and political levels, contemporary capitalism is weathering the current crisis remarkably well. Intellectuals remain preoccupied with ideas that pose no fundamental challenge to the existing order, while the labour movement is paralysed by its leadership's refusal to question the rules of the capitalist game. We are currently experiencing the worst conjunctural crisis of the world capitalist economy since the Great Depression of the 1930s; but instead of working people waging a vigorous defence of their living standards and rallying to a socialist project of scrapping capitalism, we are witnessing the persistent appeal of 'cyncical reason' and of irrationalist finger-pointing. With remarkable success, the capitalists and their agents have been able to convince most that the current crisis is an inevitable product of 'globalization,' 'restructuring,' 'living beyond our means,' 'the deficit,' 'restricted trade,' 'the welfare state,' 'bad government policies of the past,' 'too many immigrants,' 'women in the workforce,' and so on – anything, that is to say, but the irrationalities and contradictions of capitalist production. This state of affairs, transient as it may be, continues to generate a hospitable climate for postmodernist ideology, precisely because the latter, like all conservative ideologies, rests on 'the idea that *prejudice* is so deeply built into our traditions of thought that no amount of rational criticism can hope to dislodge it' (Christopher Norris, quoted in Callinicos 1990: 94). But the present disorientation of intellectuals, leftists, trade unionists, and would-be progressives has a more immediate point of origin than any alleged popular preference for prejudice over reason. There is a very good reason why many people are loath to identify the source of our current difficulties in capitalism; for to do so is to immediately invite the argument that there is no good alternative, and that we must therefore muddle through as best we can, all the while respecting the parameters, the logic, and the integrity of the capitalist order.

It is a compelling argument, made all the stronger by the failure of many Marxists and socialists to understand the real significance of the sorry experience of Stalinism in the former Soviet bloc as well as the ignominious record of Western labour reformism in recent years. The problem of 'labour bureaucracy' has indeed brought the mainstream of the international labour and socialist movements up against a seemingly insurmountable brick wall. In this context, the association of Marx's 'economics' with the fatalism and objectivism that characterized the *failed* projects of reformist socialism and Stalinism can only encourage a reappraisal of the former that subverts an understanding of the *unified* theoretical and political project that was Marx's chief legacy. For if, as I have argued previously, Marx's own criterion for truth is finally a practical one, the collapse of Stalinist 'real socialism' in the Soviet bloc cannot fail to influence perceptions of the veracity of Marx's theory of value, his critique of capitalism, and his program of human emancipation. The crisis of bureaucratic rule in the Stalinist states has clearly found partial but unmistakable expression as a crisis of 'actually existing planned economy.' The lesson being drawn here – concerning the alleged indispensability of 'free market' mechanisms to the optimization of economic efficiency – would seem to decisively vitiate Marx's programmatic goal: the realization of a society in which the relations of 'people to people' are no longer dominated by 'objective bonds' and in which 'universally developed individuals, whose social relations, as their own communal relations, are ... subordinated to their own communal control' can fulfil the promise of a non-alienated 'individuality' marked by 'universality and the comprehensiveness of ... relations and capacities' (Marx 1973: 162). In short, if the Soviet experience of 'building socialism' is any indication, Marx's project of socialist disalienation appears to be in serious trouble as a guide to changing reality – and with it the value theory upon which it is at least partially predicated.

This general conclusion, however, assumes that the hegemonic forms of 'Marxist practice' in recent decades *have been* informed by Marx's theory of value, his critique of capitalist production, and his theory of alienation. But on this score there is considerable room for doubt. Indeed, there is really no reason to believe that Marx would have endorsed the view that his theory of value enjoins the working class to conciliate the bourgeoisie with a program of reforms *within* the framework of capitalism, or the view that progress toward a rationally planned socialist economy can be made *without* the democratic involvement of the associated producers and consumers, and *without* the benefit of an international socialist division of labour. On the contrary, Marx's value theory points socialist practice precisely in the direction of a revolutionary confrontation with a capitalist order that *relies on* the operations of the law of value to divide, disorient, and blackmail the working class into playing by capital's 'rules of the game.' And just as decisively, Marx's value-theoretic critique of capitalist alienation suggests that the material and social bases for authentic socialism can only be laid through a commitment to internationalist (universalist) principles and an *extension* of individual human capacities – something that is impossible so long as society remains in the grip of a bureaucratic dictatorship.

This last consideration returns us to a key problem alluded to earlier: the capacity of Marxism to account theoretically for the persistence of the bureaucratic phenomenon in the labour and socialist movements, and to specify adequately the conditions under which it can be subdued. To do so Marxists are obliged to confront critically that 'modernist metanarrative' that has somehow escaped the 'counter-terrorist' excoriation of conservative postmodernism: Max Weber's account of the bureaucratic rationalization of the modern world. In doing so, they will be assisted by a considerable volume of Marxist and non-Marxist organizational theory and empirico-historical evidence that effectively refutes the Weberian thesis that 'no alternative' exists to 'rational-legal bureaucracy' within 'complex' organizations (see Clegg 1990 for a good survey, and Meszaros 1989 for a pitiless Marxist dissection of Weber's thesis). Weber's related sophistry that 'socialism' will remove the last remaining obstacle ('the market'!) to a complete 'bureaucratization of the world' must also be stripped of the ill-deserved credibility it has enjoyed owing to the damage done by Stalinism. The rise of Stalinist bureaucratism in the first country to attempt the 'construction of socialism' proves not the Weberian thesis of the inevitability of socialist bureaucracy ('the Russian Communists were obliged to adopt bureaucratic methods to promote efficiency') but rather the Marxist thesis that bureaucracy is fundamentally rooted in social antagonisms and that it is inimical to the development of a healthy and efficient socialism. It should, after all, be recalled that the consolidation of the Stalinist bureaucratic oligarchy occurred in the context of the market-oriented New Economic Policy of the early to mid-1920s and not as a result of the institutionalization of central planning in the late

1920s (the *specific form* of which was determined above all by the anterior fact of bureaucratic dictatorship).

The most fundamental failing of Weber's theory of bureaucracy has been identified by Ernest Mandel:

Max Weber assumes that bureaucratic rule is inherently rational. And that is not the case. Bureaucratic rule implies a combination of partial rationality and global irrationality, which exactly reflects the parallel combination in market economy and generalized commodity production – that is, capitalism itself – with whose historical rise the bureaucratic systems are closely bound up. It expresses the necessity of a more rationally functioning state to protect the interests of property-owners, one that will assure legal security, non-arbitrary use of monetary systems, safeguards against economic policies that hinder the flow of commodities, and so on. *But these increments in rationality, for each person, firm or state taken separately, lead to a historically increasing irrationality of the system (the world) in it totality.* And of that Weber is not aware. (1992: 182)

For Mandel, as for the classical tradition of revolutionary Marxism, the contradictions of advanced capitalism necessitate the scrapping of both the 'free market' and bureaucracy as the dominant (complementary) modes of social organization in favour of a system of socialist 'self-administration' – a system whose material and social prerequisites (a radical reduction in the work-week, a highly productive economy, a well-educated population) are being brought into being by capitalism itself.

Despite the recent asseverations of Vincent (1991) and Sayer (1991) that Marxists should pay greater heed to Weber, the Weberian 'metanarrative' of a modern world trapped by the inexorable logic of bureaucratic rationality cuts against an understanding of the historical limits of capitalism, bureaucracy, and the law of value. But such a recognition hardly absolves Marxists of the responsibility to outline the broad contours of an alternative social order or the need to adumbrate the organizational, programmatic, and strategic measures required to counter the very real and disabling problem of labour bureaucracy in the anticapitalist struggle. Partly this will be a labour of recovery – for much of value concerning these matters was said by an earlier generation of Marxists (Luxemburg, Lenin, Trotsky, Gramsci, Rakovsky, and others), only to be marginalized or forgotten amidst a storm of social-democratic and Stalinist obloquy and distortion. But Marxists must also shed their traditional reticence to 'construct in thought' an appealing vision of an alternative socialist society, not least because such a vision is more than ever necessary to motivating an authentically socialist human agency. Only on this condition can the 'cynical reason' of postmodernism be overcome and confidence in human progress recaptured, for only then can we begin to anticipate an end to the abhorent rule of capital – and the Invisible Leviathan.

Notes

Chapter 1

1 According to the Organization for Economic Cooperation and Development (Economic Outlook, June 1992), the average annual rate of growth of labour productivity in manufacturing *slowed* in most developed capitalist countries in the 1970s and 1980s relative to the 1950s and 1960s; but productivity nevertheless increased in *absolute* terms in all these economies, as well as in the 'Newly Industrializing Countries' and other parts of the 'developing world.' For data on the long-term falling trend of the average rate of profit throughout the capitalist world since the Second World War, see T.P. Hill, *Profits and Rates of Return* (Paris, 1979), and chapter 8 below. Official data from the United States, and the European Community, reviewed by Chris Harman in *International Socialism* 58 (1993), suggest that, since 1970, the average rate of profit has been fluctuating in a much lower 'range' than was the case in the immediate postwar period. The conclusion is unmistakable: absolute declines in the rate of return on capital are fully compatible with on-going absolute gains in labour productivity – a result anticipated and theoretically explained by Marxist economic theory far more adequately than by any contending school of economic thought.

2 This 'underutilization' of human productive potentialities is manifested in many ways, among them: low levels of agricultural productivity in many parts of the Third World, levels that could be greatly increased if Third World agricultural producers were provided with better-quality and more up-to-date tools and implements; the high levels of structural unemployment and underemployment that have long afflicted 'the South' and that are now rapidly becoming the norm in 'the North' as well; and increases in the wasteful reallocation of social labour from 'productive' to 'reproductive' activities that serve only the perpetuation of the capitalist institutional order. 'Official' – and therefore highly conservative –

estimates of unemployment and underemployment in the global economy were approaching eight hundred million people in 1993 (i.e., 17 per cent of world population).

3 According to OECD historical statistics reviewed by Glyn (1992), the OECD countries registered average annual growth rates in GDP of 4.9 per cent from 1960–73, 2.7 per cent from 1973–9, and 2.7 per cent from 1979–90 before plummeting under the impact of the global depression of the early 1990s. Since the OECD countries are central to the performance of the world capitalist economy as a whole, any growth slowdown there must negatively affect the 'developing' countries as well. For an analysis of the link between problems of underdevelopment and the environment, see the World Commission on Environment and Development (1987).

Chapter 2

1 This is rather more than a 'fashion' for some Marxists. Some of the value theorists whom I will characterize as 'neo-orthodox in chapter 5 argue that value, the law of value, and even commodity production are categories that can have no meaning in precapitalist social formations – a position apparently foreshadowed by I.I. Rubin's (1973) critique of Engels's approach to the 'historical transformation problem,' i.e., the problem of the transformation of the labour-values of simple commodity production into the 'prices of production' of capitalist commodity production. John Weeks's position in this regard is particularly extreme: 'To treat the exchange of products in precapitalist societies as evidence of commodity production is to presuppose the underlying social relations of the most developed form of exchange, particularly the monetization of the means of production' (1981: 36). Weeks insists that value relations must always and everywhere be associated with the 'law of socially necessary labour time' and the 'law of the tendency of the rate of profit to equalize.' If this is so, however, the historical *origin* of capitalist commodity production becomes a complete mystery, as Mandel (1977: 15) has noted.

Few value theorists, even neo-orthodox theorists, share Weeks's extreme view. Rubin would certainly disagree: 'We can say: labour-value (or commodity) is a historical ''pruis'' in relation to production price (or capital). It existed in rudimentary form before capitalism, and only the development of the commodity economy prepared the basis for the emergence of the capitalist economy. But labour-value in its developed form exists only in capitalism' (1973: 256). This point is further extended by Ben Fine: 'Each commodity-producing society has a set of relations of production which determine both the conditions under which value is formed (what sort of value is produced) and the conditions which lead to a divergence of market price from value' (1986: 149). See also Marx 1977: 1059–60.

Chapter 6

1 The latest contributors to the confusion surrounding this issue are Kitching (1988) and Macy (1988), whose arguments I interrogate in depth in Smith 1994. See Meszaros 1970, Mandel 1971, and Schweitzer 1982 for comprehensive summaries of earlier rounds of debate concerning the relation of the young to the mature Marx.

Chapter 7

1 In principle, it would seem desirable to treat variable capital in the same way as constant capital – i.e., by distinguishing between its stock and flow expressions. But any such procedure immediately underlines some significant differences between constant capital and variable capital, for it is apparent that capitalists *do not invest* in labour-power in the same way they do in means of production. Not only is the rate of turnover enormously different between constant and variable capital; it is so great that it is not unrealistic to assume that the variable-capital 'stock' is, in value terms, non-existent. The justification for this assumption is well stated by Mage: 'Most large businesses in practice segregate the "variable" portion of their circulating capital in a special payroll account, whose maximum size is slightly above the average payroll. But since production workers are generally paid *after* the close of the payroll period, the "stock of variable capital" is always equalled or even exceeded by the liability "wages payable", so that its *net* value is actually zero or even negative! Marx was quite well aware of this, when in Volume I [of *Capital*] he wrote "the laborer is not paid until after he has expended his labor-power ... [H]e has produced, before it flows back to him in the shape of wages, the fund out of which he himself is paid, the variable capital" ' (Mage 1963: 37–8). In the formula s/C, changes in the value of labour-power are reflected in the numerator, i.e., in the aggregate surplus-value, which serves as an index of the total value of the living labour consumed in production. This index is determined at any given time by the rate of surplus-value, s/v.

Chapter 8

1 I hasten to add that the relationship between theories of crisis and programmatic perspectives is always a mediated one; hence, underconsumptionist theorists are by no means 'destined' to pursue a reformist or Keynesian orientation, even though their theory might favour this.
2 There is no 'fatalism' associated with Marx's theory because crises, of various degrees of acuity, can always be 'counted on' to restore the conditions of profit-

able accumulation. But they cannot be counted on to restore a 'progressive historical role' to capitalism if that role has already been exhausted.

3 Mage's method of specifying the value categories has been mentioned in passing by a number of sympathetic commentators as well as by at least one critic (Ernest Mandel, 1975: 176). But none of these commentators has engaged with his approach in any sustained way. See Wright 1978, Hodgson 1974, and Gonick 1983. Mage's approach has therefore remained a 'novelty,' while the more conventional specifications of the value categories have retained an almost unchallenged grip on Marxist economic theory.

4 Baran and Sweezy 1966: 72. See also Foster 1986.

5 Shaikh 1987: 121. 'Adj. profit rate' is the profit rate adjusted for variations in capacity utilization.

6 Weisskopf 1979: 341–78 and Wolff 1986: 87–109. See also Reati 1986: 56–86, and Bowles, Gordon, and Weisskopf 1986: 132–67.

7 See Marx (1981b: 407). The expression 'variable capital sui generis' is mine, not Marx's.

8 The distinction between productive and unproductive labour has little to do with whether the product of labour is a 'material object' or a 'useful effect.' What it concerns centrally is whether or not the labour in question is directly productive of surplus-value (via direct participation in the production of commodities). See Smith 1993 for an extended discussion of the problem of unproductive labour.

9 See Sweezy 1942, Gillman 1957, Shaikh 1987, Moseley 1987, and Mandel 1975. It should be noted that some commentators distinguish between unproductive labour in the sphere of circulation and unproductive labour employed by the state. For example, Mandel treats the wages of state employees as elements of 'social surplus value,' but appears to view the labour of circulation workers as 'exchanged with capital' (although he does not specify whether this is variable or constant capital).

10 'Capital exists as capital only in so far as it passes through the phases of circulation, the various moments of its transformation, in order to be able to begin the production process anew, and these phases are themselves phases of its realization – but at the same time ... of its devaluation. As long as capital remains frozen in the form of the finished product, it cannot be active as capital ... This loss of capital means in other words nothing else but that time passes it by unseized, time during which it could have been appropriating alien labour, surplus-labour time, through exchange with living labour' (Marx 1973: 546).

11 There is an interesting analogy to be drawn between such circulationist strategies and the 'labour-saving' strategies pursued by industrial capitalists. Both are eminently 'rational' from the standpoint of the individual capitalist enterprise seeking to enlarge its share of social surplus-value; but both pose a threat to the average rate of profit of the social capital as a whole, by increasing non-labour costs relative to living labour expended. For an interesting discussion of this issue, see Lebowitz 1972. Lebowitz diverges from the present analysis by treat-

ing 'merchants' variable capital' as *actual* variable capital and by applying the idea of 'organic composition' to circulation capital.

12 Marx's own critique of such 'capital fetishism' is to be found in 'Results of the Immediate Process of Production,' in Marx 1977.

13 Mage's failure to recognize this point constitutes the biggest weakness of his empirical study of the U.S. economy. He treats *all* tax revenues as constant capital.

14 In empirical studies of the Marxian ratios, it is necessary, in my view, to define variable capital as the *after-tax* wage-bill of productive workers. The productive worker's *real* income is the income used to reproduce her capacity to work and to support her family, not the 'income' that she allegedly 'contributes' to the state. Certain transfer payments form components of 'variable capital' – but such additional income is small in comparison with the taxes deducted from 'gross wages.'

15 This value-theoretical appreciation of the state as part of the 'machinery' of social reproduction has implications for the elaboration of a theory of the capitalist state – in particular for specifying the *limits* within which the state can operate. By itself, however, this formula is an insufficient basis for theoretically adjudicating between contending Marxist theories of the state, although it could be seen as favouring the 'capital-logic' or 'forms-analytic' *strategy* of 'deriving' the state's forms and functions from the laws of motion and contradictions of capitalism. The collection of 'capital-theoretic' studies of the state in Holloway and Picciotto (1978) suggest a whole range of specific starting-points for the 'derivation' of the capitalist state. This is both a strength and weakness of this volume, since the contributors share the common fault of 'fixating' on particular manifestations of the capital and value relations and then deriving the functions of the state from a consideration of the political, extra-economic, or economic imperatives generated by *particular* contradictions considered in isolation from the *totality* of contradictions characterizing capitalism. If we accept the premiss that the forms and functions of the capitalist state are derivable from a consideration of the contradictions that this state seeks to attenuate as a 'special apparatus' within capitalist reproduction, then it is surely necessary to recognize that the capitalist state emerges *historically* in response to an *ensemble of contradictions*, the basic elements of which are always present within a given capitalist society, but whose 'ordering' in terms of state 'priorities' is only *conjuncturally* determinable. On the basis of this 'internal critique' of the capital-theoretical approach to the state, it seems to me possible to meet most of the objections to it registered by Gough (1979), Jessop (1982), and other 'political' – or 'class' – theoretical state theorists.

16 Mage's study is most profitably compared with that of Gillman, while my own study invites comparison with Sharpe's (1982). See also Webber and Rigby (1986: 33–55), who establish a rising trend in the value composition of capital (C/v) and the rate of surplus-value, alongside a surprisingly consistent fall in the

rate of profit from 1950 to 1981; but they do so by abstracting the manufacturing sector from the rest of the economy, a procedure that I regard as theoretically inadmissible. Marx's average rate of profit is calculable only with reference to the *social capital* as a whole.

17 The OCC defined as $C/v + s_4$ has a trend line that rises from 3.48 in 1947 to 5.97 in 1980 ($r^2 = 0.93$, p.<.0001). By contrast, the trend line for $C/v + s_5$ rises only from 2.022 in 1947 to 2.203 in 1980 ($r^2 = 0.38$).

18 The trend line for the ratio s_4/v rises from 0.546 in 1947 to 0.810 in 1980 ($r^2 = 0.56$). For the ratio s_5/v it rose from 1.632 in 1947 to 3.894 in 1980 ($r^2 = 0.97$).

19 The trend line for s_5/C *rises* from 0.3190 in 1947 to 0.3678 in 1980 ($r^2 = 0.55$). But the trend line for s_4/C falls from 0.100 in 1947 to 0.074 in 1980 ($r^2 = 0.46$). When s_4/C was treated as the dependent variable and $C/v + s_4$ as the independent variable, an r^2 of 0.69 was obtained, indicating that much of the downward trend in the rate of profit is accounted for by the upward trend in the OCC.

20 For data on productivity and the real wages of production workers, see Shaikh 1987: 118–22; and Smith 1984: 281–3.

Chapter 10

1 Ellen Meiksins Wood, in her important book *The Retreat from Class*, identifies Poulantzas as the 'forerunner' of a (non-class-struggle) 'new "true" socialism' that has been embraced by many erstwhile Marxists, among them Gorz (1982) and Laclau and Mouffe (1985). As Wood demonstrates well, Poulantzas's erroneous theoretical conceptions of class were very much in the service of a Maoist and then a Eurocommunist politics oriented toward subordinating the independent workers' movement to a class-collaborationist 'popular front' alliance. The influence of such Stalinist conceptions continues to inform the theory and politics of many who now identify themselves with 'post-Marxist' socialism. For further critical perspectives on this trend, see Panitch (1986) and Geras (1990).

2 Not the least of these 'cultural' circumstances concerns the issue of whether the value of labour-power is normatively equated with an individual or a family wage. Marx suggests that the value of labour-power must take into account the wage labourer's obligation to support non-wage-earning family members (a spouse, dependent children, etc.). But this is not always the case, especially under conditions of increased labour-force participation by women (which may or may not be the result of a decline in the real wages of male workers and which may or may not promote such a decline). Related to this issue is the still-unresolved debate surrounding the contribution of unpaid domestic labour to the reproduction of the commodity labour-power and therewith ('indirectly') to the production of surplus-value in the 'public' economy. Some of the major contributions to these discussions include Gerstein 1973; Seccombe 1974; Fox 1980;

and Humphries 1977. See also Ursel 1992 for a historical analysis of how state intervention has affected the interrelationship between productive and 'reproductive' spheres in Canada.

3 In providing some elements of an answer to this question I will focus on narrowly defined 'programmatic' issues and leave the strategic and tactical issues of working-class organization and forms of struggle to the side.

4 In saying this I am, of course, following Trotsky's judgment that the Soviet Union was a 'degenerated workers' state' from 1924 on. Central to Trotsky's analysis is the idea that the Stalinist bureaucracy was by no means a finished 'ruling class' but rather a 'parasitic oligarchy' that would either be removed by a working-class political revolution or pave the way for a return to capitalism. On this view, the Soviet 'transitional' society was not indicative of 'the general laws of modern society from capitalism to socialism . . . but a special, exceptional and temporary refraction of those laws under the conditions of a backward revolutionary country in a capitalist environment' (Trotsky 1970a: 7). Accordingly, the lessons of the Soviet experience pertain mainly to 'the application of *socialist* methods to the solution of *pre-socialist* problems' (1970b: 57) under conditions of extreme *bureaucratic deformation* of these methods.

References

Abercrombie, Nicholas, and John Urry. 1983. *Capital, Labour and the Middle Classes*. London: Allen and Unwin

Adorno, Theodor, and Max Horkheimer. 1972. *Dialectic of Enlightenment*. New York: Herder and Herder

Amin, Samir. 1985. 'Modes of Production, History and Unequal Development.' *Science & Society* 49:2

Anderson, Perry. 1979. *Lineages of the Absolutist State*. London: Verso
– 1982. *In the Tracks of Historical Materialism*. London: Verso

Arrighi, Giovanni. 1991. 'World Income Inequalities and the Future of Socialism.' *New Left Review* 189

Baran, Paul, and Paul Sweezy. 1966. *Monopoly Capital*. New York: Monthly Review Press

Baudrillard, Jean. 1981. *For a Critique of the Political Economy of the Sign*. St Louis: Telos Press

Benton, Ted. 1985. 'Realism and Social Science.' In Roy Edgley and Peter Osborne (eds), *Radical Philosophy Reader*. London: Verso

Bhaskar, Roy. 1979. *The Possibility of Naturalism*. Brighton: Harvester

Blackburn, Robin. 1972. 'Introduction.' In Robin Blackburn (ed.), *Ideology in Social Science*. Fontana/Collins

Boehm-Bawerk, Eugen von. 1975. *Karl Marx and the Close of His System*. Ed. Paul Sweezy. London: Merlin Press

Bortkiewicz, Ladislaus von. 1975. 'On the Correction of Marx's Fundamental Theoretical Construction in the Third Volume of *Capital*.' In Paul Sweezy (ed.), *Karl Marx and the Close of His System*. London: Merlin Press

Bottomore, Tom. 1990. *The Socialist Economy: Theory and Practice*. New York and London: Guilford Press

Bowles, Samuel, David M. Gordon, and Thomas Weisskopf. 1986. 'Power and Profits: The Social Structure of Accumulation and the Profitability of the Postwar U.S. Economy.' *Review of Radical Political Economics* 18:1, 2

Braverman, Harry. 1974. *Labor and Monopoly Capital: The Degradation of Work in the Twentieth Century.* New York: Monthly Review Press

Brenner, Robert. 1977. 'The Origins of Capitalist Development: A Critique of Neo-Smithian Marxism.' *New Left Review* 104

Bukharin, Nikolai. 1972. *Economic Theory of the Leisure Class.* New York: Monthly Review Press

Callinicos, Alex. 1990. *Against Postmodernism: A Marxist Critique.* New York: St Martin's Press

Carchedi, Guglielmo. 1977. *On the Economic Identification of Social Classes.* London and Boston: Routledge and Kegan Paul

– 1986a. 'The Logic of Prices as Values.' In Ben Fine (ed.), *The Value Dimension: Marx versus Ricardo and Sraffa.* London and New York: Routledge and Kegan Paul

– 1986b. 'Two Models of Class Analysis.' *Capital and Class* 29

– 1987. 'Class Politics, Class Consciousness, and the New Middle Class.' *The Insurgent Sociologist* 14:3

– 1991. *Frontiers of Political Economy.* London and New York: Verso

Clarke, Simon. 1982. *Marx, Marginalism and Modern Sociology: From Adam Smith to Max Weber.* London and Basingstoke: Macmillan

Clawson, Dan. 1980. *Bureaucracy and the Labor Process.* New York: Monthly Review Press

Clegg, Stewart. 1990. *Modern Organizations: Organization Studies in a Postmodern World.* London: Sage Publications

Cohen, G.A. 1978. *Karl Marx's Theory of History: A Defence.* Princeton University Press

– 1981. 'The Labour Theory of Value and the Concept of Exploitation.' In Ian Steedman et al., *The Value Controversy.* London: Verso

– 1983. 'Forces and Relations of Production.' In Betty Matthews (ed.), *Marx: A Hundred Years On.* London: Lawrence and Wishart

Colletti, Lucio. 1972. *From Rousseau to Lenin.* London: Verso

Communist International. 1921, 1980. 'On Tactics.' In *Theses, Resolutions and Manifestos of the First Four Congresses of the Third International.* London: Ink Links

Corrigan, P., H. Ramsay, and D. Sayer. 1979. *For Mao.* London: Macmillan

Derrida, Jacques. 1976. *Of Grammatology.* Trans. Gayatri C. Spivak. Baltimore: Johns Hopkins University Press

– 1982. *Margins of Philosophy.* Chicago: University of Chicago Press

Deutscher, Isaac. 1973. *Marxism in Our Time.* San Francisco: Ramparts Press

De Vroey, Michel. 1981. 'Value, Production and Exchange.' In Ian Steedman et al., *The Value Controversy.* London: Verso

Dews, Peter. 1987. *Logics of Disintegration.* London: Verso

– 1937. *Political Economy and Capitalism.* London: Routledge and Kegan Paul

- 1973. *Theories of Value and Distribution Since Adam Smith.* Cambridge: Cambridge University Press
Dumenil, G., M. Glick, and J. Rangel. 1987. 'The Rate of Profit in the United States.' *Cambridge Journal of Economics* 11:4
Eldred, Michael. 1984. 'A Reply to Gleicher.' *Capital and Class* 23
Elson, Diane. 1979. 'The Value Theory of Labour.' In Diane Elson (ed.), *Value* (see below).
- 1988. 'Market Socialism or Socialization of the Market?' *New Left Review* 172
- (ed.). 1979. *Value: The Representation of Labour in Capitalism.* London: CSE Books
Elster, Jon. 1982. 'Marxism, Functionalism and Game Theory.' *Theory and Society* 11 (July)
Emmanuel, Arghiri. 1972. *Unequal Exchange.* New York: Monthly Review Press
- 1974. 'Myths of Development versus Myths of Underdevelopment.' *New Left Review* 85
Engels, Friedrich. 1970. *The Origin of the Family, Private Property and the State.* In *Selected Works of Marx and Engels*, vol. 3. Moscow: Progress
- 1895, 1981. 'Supplement and Addendum to Volume Three of *Capital.*' In Karl Marx, *Capital Volume Three.* New York: Vintage
Farjoun, Emmanuel. 1984. 'The Production of Commodities by Means of What?' In Ernest Mandel and Alan Freeman (eds), *Ricardo, Marx, Sraffa.* London: Verso
Feyerabend, Paul. 1988. *Against Method.* London: Verso
Fine, Ben. 1982. *Theories of the Capitalist Economy.* New York: Holmes and Meier
- 1986. 'Introduction.' In Ben Fine (ed.), *The Value Dimension.* London: Routledge and Kegan Paul
Fine, Ben, and Laurence Harris. 1979. *Rereading Capital.* New York: Columbia University Press
Fischer, Norman. 1982. 'The Ontology of Abstract Labor.' *Review of Radical Political Economics* 14:2
Flaherty, Diane. 1992. 'Self-Management and Socialism: Lessons from Yugoslavia.' *Science & Society* 56:1
Foley, Duncan. 1986. *Understanding Capital: Marx's Economic Theory.* Cambridge, Mass.: Harvard University Press
Foster, John Bellamy. 1986. *The Theory of Monopoly Capitalism.* New York: Monthly Review Press
Foucault, Michel. 1972. *The Archeology of Knowledge.* London: Tavistock
- 1980. *Power/Knowledge.* New York: Pantheon
Fox, Bonnie (ed.) 1980. *Hidden in the Household: Women's Domestic Labour under Capitalism.* Toronto: Women's Press
George, Susan. 1988. *A Fate Worse than Debt.* Harmondsworth: Penguin
Geras, Norman. 1983. *Marx and Human Nature: Refutation of a Legend.* London: Verso

– 1990. 'Seven Types of Obloquy.' In Ralph Miliband and Leo Panitch (eds), *Socialist Register 1990*. London: Merlin Press

Gerstein, Ira. 1973. 'Domestic Work and Capitalism.' *Radical America* 7:4, 5

– 1986. 'Production, Circulation and Value.' In Ben Fine (ed.), *The Value Dimension*. Reprinted from *Economy and Society* 5:3 (1976)

Giddens, Anthony. 1981. *A Contemporary Critique of Historical Materialism*. Berkeley and Los Angeles: University of California Press

– 1990. *The Consequences of Modernity*. Cambridge: Polity Press

Gillman, Joseph. 1957. *The Falling Rate of Profit*. London: Dobson

Gleicher, David. 1985. 'A Rejoinder to Eldred.' *Capital and Class* 24

Gleick, James. 1987. *Chaos: Making a New Science*. New York: Viking

Glyn, Andrew. 1992. 'The Costs of Stability: The Advanced Capitalist Countries in the 1980s.' *New Left Review* 195

Gonick, Cy. 1983. 'Boom and Bust: State Policy and the Economics of Restructuring.' *Studies in Political Economy* 11

Gorbachev, Mikhail. 1987. *Perestroika: New Thinking for Our Country and the World*. New York: Harper and Row

Gorz, André. 1973. 'Reform and Revolution,' In *Socialism and Revolution*. New York: Anchor

– 1982. *Farewell to the Working Class: An Essay on Post-Industrial Socialism*. Boston

Gottlieb, Roger. 1984. 'Feudalism and Historical Materialism: A Critique and a Synthesis.' *Science & Society* 48:1

Gough, Ian. 1979. *The Political Economy of the Welfare State*. London and Basingstoke: Macmillan Press

Habermas, Jurgen. 1971. *Knowledge and Human Interests*. Boston: Beacon Press

– 1987. *The Philosophical Discourse of Modernity*. Cambridge: Polity Press

Harman, Chris. 1993. 'Where Is Capitalism Going?' *International Socialism* 58

Harvey, David. 1989. *The Condition of Postmodernity*. Oxford: Basil Blackwell

Hilferding, Rudolf. 1975. *Boehm-Bawerk's Critique of Marx*. In Paul Sweezy (ed.), *Karl Marx*. London: Merlin Press

Hilton, R.H. (ed.). 1976. *The Transition from Feudalism to Capitalism*. London: New Left Books

Himmelweit, Susan, and Simon Mohun. 1981. 'Real Abstractions and Anomalous Assumptions.' In Ian Steedman et al., *The Value Controversy*. London: Verso

Hodgson, Geoff. 1974. 'The Theory of the Falling Rate of Profit.' *New Left Review* 84

– 1975. *Trotsky and Fatalistic Marxism*. Nottingham: Spokesman

– 1980. 'A Theory of Exploitation without the Labour Theory of Value.' *Science & Society* 44:3

Holloway, John, and Sol Picciotto (eds). 1978. *State and Capital: A Marxist Debate*. Austin: University of Texas Press

Humphries, Jane. 1977. 'Class Struggle and the Persistence of the Working Class Family.' *Cambridge Journal of Economics* 1

Itoh, Makoto. 1980. *Value and Crisis: Essays on Marxian Economics in Japan.* New York: Monthly Review Press

Jameson, Fredric. 1990. 'Postmodernism and the Market.' In Ralph Miliband and Leo Panitch (eds), *Socialist Register 1990.* London: Merlin Press

Jessop, Bob. 1982. *The Capitalist State.* Oxford: Martin Robertson

Kay, Geoffrey. 1979. 'Why Labour Is the Starting Point of Capital.' In Diane Elson (ed.), *Value: The Representation of Labour in Capitalism.* London: CSE Books

Keat, Russell, and John Urry. 1982. *Social Theory as Science.* London: Routledge and Kegan Paul

Kitching, Gavin. 1988. *Karl Marx and the Philosophy of Praxis.* London and New York: Routledge

Kolakowski, Leszek. 1978. *Main Currents of Marxism.* Oxford and New York: Oxford University Press

Krader, Lawrence. 1975. *The Asiatic Mode of Production.* Assen: Van Gorcum

Kuhn, Thomas S. 1970. *The Structure of Scientific Revolutions.* 2nd edition. Chicago: University of Chicago Press

Laclau, Ernesto, and Chantal Mouffe. 1985. *Hegemony and Socialist Strategy.* London: Verso

Laibman, David. 1982. 'Technical Change, the Real Wage and the Rate of Exploitation: The Falling Rate of Profit Reconsidered.' *Review of Radical Political Economics* 14:2

– 1984. 'Modes of Production and Theories of Transition.' *Science & Society* 48:3

– 1992. 'Market and Plan: Socialist Structures in History and Theory.' *Science & Society* 56:1

Latouche, Sergio. 1976. 'Quelques repères pour analyser la signification historique de la théorie du Professeur Piero Sraffa.' *Cahiers d'Economie Politique* 3

Lebowitz, Michael. 1988. 'Is "Analytical Marxism" Marxism?' *Science & Society* 52:2

Lebowitz, Michael. 1972. 'The Increasing Cost of Circulation and the Marxian Competitive Model.' *Science & Society* 36:3

– 1973–4. 'The Current Crisis of Economic Theory.' *Science & Society* 37:4

– 1976. 'Marx's Falling Rate of Profit: A Dialectical View.' *Canadian Journal of Economics*, May

– 1991. 'The Significance of Marx's Missing Book on Wage-Labor.' *Rethinking Marxism* 4:2

Le Grand, Julian, and Saul Estrin (eds). 1989. *Market Socialism.* Oxford: Clarendon Press

Lenin, V.I. 1970a. *Imperialism: The Highest Stage of Capitalism.* Peking: Foreign Languages Press

– 1970b. *The State and Revolution.* Moscow: Progress

Leontieff, Wassily. 1982. 'The Distribution of Work and Income.' *Scientific American*, September

Lindsey, J.K. 1980.. 'The Conceptualization of Social Class.' *Studies in Political Economy* 3

Lipietz, Alain. 1985. *The Enchanted World.* London: Verso

Locke, John. 1968. 'The Second Treatise of Government.' In Michael Curtis (ed.), *The Great Political Theories.* New York: Avon

Lovejoy, Arthur. 1966. 'Natural Dualism.' In Morris Weitz (ed.), *20th Century Philosophy: The Analytic Tradition.* New York: The Free Press

Lukács, Georg. 1971. *History and Class Consciousness: Studies in Marxist Dialectics.* London: Merlin Press

Lyotard, Jean-François. 1984. *The Postmodern Condition: A Report on Knowledge.* Manchester: Manchester University Press

Macdonald, Eleanor. 1990. 'Derrida and the Politics of Interpretation.' In Ralph Miliband and Leo Panitch (eds), *Socialist Register 1990.* London: Merlin Press

McKelvey, Charles. 1991. *Beyond Ethnocentrism: A Reconstruction of Marx's Concept of Science.* Westport, Conn.: Greenwood Press

Macy, Michael W. 1988. 'Value Theory and the ''Golden Eggs'': Appropriating the Magic of Accumulation.' *Sociological Theory* 6 (Fall)

Magdoff, Harry. 1969. *The Age of Imperialism.* New York: Monthly Review Press

– 1992. 'Globalization – To What End?' In Ralph Miliband and Leo Panitch (eds), *Socialist Register 1992.* London: Merlin Press

Mage, Shane. 1963. *The Law of the Falling Tendency of the Rate of Profit: Its Place in the Marxian Theoretical System and Relevance to the U.S. Economy.* Ph.D. thesis, Columbia University

Mandel, Ernest. 1967. 'Economics of the Transition Period.' In Ernest Mandel (ed.), *Fifty Years of World Revolution.* New York: Merit

– 1968. *Marxist Economic Theory.* New York: Monthly Review Press

– 1971. *The Formation of the Economic Thought of Karl Marx.* New York: Monthly Review Press

– 1975. *Late Capitalism.* London: New Left Books

– 1977. 'Introduction.' In Karl Marx, *Capital Volume One.* New York: Vintage

– 1981. 'Introduction.' In Karl Marx, *Capital Volume Three.* New York: Vintage

– 1986. 'In Defense of Socialist Planning.' *New Left Review* 159

– 1992. *Power and Money: A Marxist Theory of Bureaucracy.* London and New York: Verso

Mandel, Ernest, and Alan Freeman (eds). 1984. *Ricardo, Marx, Sraffa: The Langston Memorial Volume.* London: Verso

Marx, Karl. 1873, 1977. 'Afterword to the Second German Edition.' In Marx, *Capital Volume One.*

– 1881, 1983. 'First Draft of a Reply to Vera Zasulich.' In T. Shanin (ed.), *Late*

Marx and the Russian Road. New York: Monthly Review Press
- 1953. 'Die Wertform'. In *Kleine Okonomische Schriften.* Berlin: Dietz Verlag
- 1964. *The Economic and Philosophical Manuscripts of 1844.* New York: International Publishers
- 1965. *Capital I.* Moscow: Progress
- 1965. Pre-Capitalist Economic Formations. New York: International Publishers
- 1968. 'Letter to Kugelmann, July 11, 1868.' In Karl Marx and Friedrich Engels, *Selected Correspondence.* Moscow: Progress
- 1970, 1859. 'Preface' to *A Contribution to the Critique of Political Economy.* Moscow: Progress
- 1973. *Grundrisse.* Trans. Martin Nicolaus. Harmondsworth: Penguin
- 1977. *Capital Volume One.* Trans. Ben Fowkes. New York: Vintage
- 1977. 'Results of the Immediate Process of Production.' Appendix to *Capital Volume One.* New York: Vintage
Marx, Karl. 1978a. *Theories of Surplus Value.* 3 vols. Moscow: Progress Publishers
Marx, Karl. 1978b. *Capital III.* Moscow: Progress
Marx, Karl. 1981a. *Capital Volume Two.* Trans. David Fernbach. New York: Vintage
Marx, Karl. 1981b. *Capital Volume Three.* Trans. David Fernbach. New York: Vintage
Marx, Karl. 1989. *Readings from Karl Marx.* Ed. Derek Sayer. London: Routledge
Marx, Karl, and Friedrich Engels. 1846, 1947. *The German Ideology.* New York: International Publishers
- 1965. *Selected Correspondence.* Moscow: Progress Publishers
- 1970. *Selected Works.* 3 vols. Moscow: Progress Publishers
Meek, Ronald. 1956. *Studies in the Labor Theory of Value.* 2nd edition. New York: Monthly Review Press. Reprinting with new introduction of 1956 edition. N.d. for 2nd ed.
- 1973. 'Marginalism and Marxism.' In Black, Coats, and Goodwin (eds), *The Marginal Revolution in Economics.* Durham
Meszaros, Istvan. 1970. *Marx's Theory of Alienation.* London: Merlin Press
- 1989. *The Power of Ideology.* New York: New York University Press
Moreau, François. 1991. 'The Condition of the Working Class under Capitalism Today: The Case of Mexico.' *Socialist Alternatives* 1:1
Morishma, Michio. 1973. *Marx's Economics.* Cambridge: Cambridge University Press
- 1974. 'Marx in the Light of Modern Economic Theory.' *Econometrica*
Moseley, Fred. 1986. 'Estimates of the Rate of Surplus-Value in the Postwar United States Economy.' *Review of Radical Political Economics* 18:1, 2
- 1987. 'Marx's Crisis Theory and the Postwar U.S. Economy.' In R. Cherry et al. (eds), *The Imperiled Economy*, vol. 1. New York: URPE

Murray, Patrick. 1988. *Marx's Theory of Scientific Knowledge.* Atlantic Highlands, NJ: Humanities Press

Nove, Alec. 1983. *The Economics of Feasible Socialism.* London: George Allen and Unwin

– 1987. 'Markets and Socialism.' *New Left Review* 161

Okishio, Nobuo. 1961. 'Technical Change and the Rate of Profit.' *Kobe University Economic Review* 7

Ollman, Bertell. 1976. *Alienation: Marx's Conception of Man in Capitalist Society.* Cambridge: Cambridge University Press

Palmer, Bryan. 1990. *Descent into Discourse.* Philadelphia: Temple University Press

Panitch, Leo. 1986. *Working-Class Politics in Crisis: Essays on Labour and the State.* London: Verso

Parijs, Phillippe van. 1980. 'The Falling Rate of Profit Theory of Crisis: A Rational Reconstruction by Way of Obituary.' *Review of Radical Political Economics,* Spring

Pilling, Geoffrey. 1974. 'Imperialism, Trade and "Unequal Exchange": The Work of Arghiri Emmanuel.' *Economy and Society* 2

– 1986. 'The Law of Value in Ricardo and Marx.' In Ben Fine (ed.), *The Value Dimension* (see above). Originally appeared in *Economy and Society* 1 (1972)

Poulantzas, Nicos. 1978. *Classes in Contemporary Capitalism.* London: Verso

Reati, Angelo. 1986. 'The Rate of Profit and the Organic Composition of Capital in West German Industry from 1960 to 1981.' *Review of Radical Political Economics* 18: 1, 2

Ricardo, David. 1951. *Principles of Political Economy and Taxation.* In P. Sraffa (ed.), *Works, Volume I.* Cambridge: Cambridge University Press

Robinson, Joan. 1942. *An Essay on Marxian Economics.* London: Macmillan

– 1968. *Economic Philosophy.* Harmondsworth: Penguin

Roemer, John E. 1988. *Free to Lose: An Introduction to Marxist Economic Philosophy.* Cambridge: Harvard University Press

Rosdolsky, Roman. 1977. *The Making of Marx's 'Capital'.* London: Pluto Press

Rubin, I.I. 1973. *Essays on Marx's Theory of Value.* Montreal: Black Rose Books

Samary, Catherine. 1991. 'To Live Better and More Freely: Of Ends and Means.' *Socialist Alternatives* 1:1

Samuelson, Paul (and Anthony Scott). 1968. *Economics: An Introductory Analysis.* 2nd Canadian edition. Toronto: McGraw-Hill

Sayer, Derek. 1987. *The Violence of Abstraction: The Analytic Foundations of Historical Materialism.* Oxford and New York: Basil Blackwell

– 1991. *Capitalism and Modernity: An Excursus on Marx and Weber.* London and New York: Routledge

Sayer, Derek, and Philip Corrigan. 1983. 'Late Marx: Continuity, Contradiction and Learning.' In Teodor Shanin (ed.), *Late Marx and the Russian Road.* New York: Monthly Review Press

Schumpeter, Joseph. 1962. *Capitalism, Socialism and Democracy.* New York: Harper and Row

Schwartz, J. (ed.). 1977. *The Subtle Anatomy of Capitalism.* Goodyear Publishing

Schweitzer, David. 1982. 'Alienation, De-alienation and Change: A Critical Overview of Current Perspectives in Philosophy and the Social Sciences.' In S.G. Shoham (ed.), *Alienation and Anomie Revisited.* Messina: Ramot Educational Systems

Seccombe, Wally. 1974. 'The Housewife and Her Labour under Capitalism.' *New Left Review* 83

Seton, F. 1957. 'The "Transformation Problem." ' *Review of Economic Studies* 24

Shaikh, Anwar. 1977. 'Marx's Theory of Value and the "Transformation Problem." ' In J. Schwartz (ed.), *The Subtle Anatomy of Capitalism.* Goodyear Publishing

– 1978. 'Political Economy and Capitalism: Notes on Dobb's Theory of Crisis.' *Cambridge Journal of Economics*, June

– 1979–80. 'Foreign Trade and the Law of Value.' 2 parts. *Science & Society* 43:3 and 44:1

– 1981. 'The Poverty of Algebra.' In Ian Steedman et al., *The Value Controversy.* London: Verso

– 1987. 'The Falling Rate of Profit and the Economic Crisis in the U.S.' In R. Cherry et al. (eds), *The Imperiled Economy*, vol. 1. New York: URPE

Shanin, Teodor (ed.). 1983. *Late Marx and the Russian Road: Marx and the 'Peripheries of Capitalism.'* New York: Monthly Review Press

Sharpe, Andrew. 1982. 'The Evolution of the Rate of Surplus Value, Organic Composition of Capital, and Rate of Profit in Canada, 1926–80.' Paper presented to the Political Economy Session of the Canadian Political Science Association annual meeting, Ottawa, 9 June 1982

Sloterdijk, Peter. 1988. *Critique of Cynical Reason.* London: Verso

Smith, Adam. 1970. *The Wealth of Nations.* Harmondsworth: Penguin

Smith, Murray E.G. 1984. 'The Falling Rate of Profit.' Master's thesis, University of Manitoba

– 1989. The Value Controversy and Social Theory: An Inquiry into Marx's "Labour Theory of Value." ' Ph.D. thesis, University of British Columbia

– 1991a. 'Respecifying Marx's Value Categories: A Theoretical and Empirical Reconsideration of the "Law of the Falling Rate of Profit." ' *Studies in Political Economy* 35

– 1991b. 'Understanding Marx's Theory of Value: An Assessment of a Controversy.' *Canadian Review of Sociology and Anthropology* 28:3

– 1992. 'The Value Abstraction and the Dialectic of Social Development.' *Science & Society* 56:3

– 1993. 'Productivity, Valorization and Crisis: Socially Necessary Unproductive Labor in Contemporary Capitalism.' *Science & Society* 57:3

– 1994. 'Alienation, Exploitation and Abstract Labour.' *Review of Radical Political Economics* 26:1

Sohn-Rethel, Alfred. 1978. *Intellectual and Manual Labour: A Critique of Epistemology.* London and Basingstoke: Macmillan

Spartacist. 1988. *'Market Socialism' in Eastern Europe.* New York: Spartacist

Sraffa, Piero. 1960. *Production of Commodities by Means of Commodities.* Cambridge University Press

Stalin, Joseph. 1972a. 'Dialectical and Historical Materialism.' In Bruce Franklin (ed.), *The Essential Stalin.* New York: Anchor Books

– 1972b. 'Economic Problems of Socialism in the U.S.S.R.' In Franklin (ed.), *The Essential Stalin*

Steedman, Ian. 1981. *Marx After Sraffa.* London: Verso

Steedman, Ian, et al. 1979. *The Value Controversy.* London: Verso

Swedberg, R., U. Himmelstrand, and G. Brulin. 1987. 'The Paradigm of Economic Sociology: Premises and Promises.' *Theory and Society* 16:2

Sweezy, Paul. 1968 [1942]. *The Theory of Capitalist Development.* New York: Monthly Review Press

– 1975. 'Editor's Introduction.' In Paul Sweezy (ed.), *Karl Marx and the Close of His System* (by E. Boehm-Bawerk), and *Boehm-Bawerk's Critique of Marx* (by R. Hilferding). London: Merlin Press

– 1981. *Four Lectures on Marxism.* New York and London: Monthly Review Press

Therborn, Goran. 1980. *Science, Class and Society.* London: Verso

Thompson, Paul. 1989. *The Nature of Work.* 2nd edition. Basingstoke and London: Macmillan

Timpanaro, Sebastiano. 1980. *On Materialism.* London: Verso

Trotsky, Leon. 1969. *The Permanent Revolution & Results and Prospects.* New York: Merit Publishers

– 1970b, 1937. *The Revolution Betrayed.* New York: Pathfinder

– 1970a. *In Defense of Marxism.* New York: Pathfinder

– 1971. *The Third International after Lenin.* New York: Pathfinder

– 1973a. *The Transitional Program for Socialist Revolution.* New York: Pathfinder

– 1973b. *Writings of Leon Trotsky 1932.* New York: Pathfinder

URPE (Union for Radical Political Economics). 1992. 'The Future of Socialism.' Special issue of *Review of Radical Political Economics* 24:3, 4

Ursel, Jane. 1992. *Private Lives and Public Policy: 100 Years of State Intervention in the Family.* Toronto: Women's Press

Vincent, Jean-Marie. 1991. *Abstract Labour: A Critique.* New York: St Martin's Press

Vitkin, Mikhail. 1981. 'The Asiatic Mode of Production.' *Philosophy and Social Criticism* 8:1

Wallerstein, Immanuel. 1983. *Historical Capitalism.* London: Verso Books

Walras, Leon. 1954. *Elements of Pure Economics*. London

Webber, M.J., and D.L. Rigby. 1986. 'The Rate of Profit in Canadian Manufacturing, 1950–81.' *Review of Radical Political Economics* 18:1, 2

Weber, Max. 1978. *Economy and Society: An Outline of Interpretive Sociology.* 2 vol. Los Angeles: University of California Press

– 1976. *The Protestant Ethic and the Spirit of Capitalism*. London: Allen and Unwin

Weeks, John. 1981. *Capital and Exploitation*. Princeton: Princeton University Press

Weisskopf, Thomas. 1979. 'Marxian Crisis Theory and the Rate of Profit in the Post-War U.S. Economy.' *Cambridge Journal of Economics* 69

Winternitz, J. 1948. 'Values and Prices: A Solution of the So-Called Transformation Problem.' *Economic Journal* 58

Wolff, Edward. 1986. 'The Productivity Slowdown and the Fall in the U.S. Rate of Profit, 1947–76.' *Review of Radical Political Economics* 18:1, 2

Wood, Ellen Meiksins. 1986. *The Retreat from Class: A New 'True' Socialism.* London: Verso

World Commission on Environment and Development. 1987. *Our Common Future*. Oxford: Oxford University Press

Wright, Erik Olin. 1985. *Classes*. London: Verso

– 1978. *Class, Crisis and the State*. London: Verso

Yaffe, David. 1975. 'Value and Price in Marx's *Capital*.' *Revolutionary Communist* 1

Index

THE STATE AND ECONOMIC LIFE

Editors: **Mel Watkins**, University of Toronto; **Leo Panitch**, York University

This series, begun in 1978, includes original studies in the general area of Canadian political economy and economic history, with particular emphasis on the part played by the government in shaping the economy. Collections of shorter studies, as well as theoretical or internationally comparative works, may also be included.

1 The State and Enterprise: Canadian manufacturers and the federal government 1917–1931
TOM TRAVES

2 Unequal Beginnings: Agriculture and economic development in Quebec and Ontario until 1870
JOHN MCCALLUM

3 'An Impartial Umpire': Industrial relations and the Canadian state 1990–1911
PAUL CRAVEN

4 Scholars and Dollars: Politics, economics, and the universities of Ontario 1945–1980
PAUL AXELROD

5 'Remember Kirkland Lake': The history and effects of the Kirkland Lake gold miners' strike, 1941–42
LAUREL SEFTON MACDOWELL

6 No Fault of Their Own: Unemployment and the Canadian welfare state 1914–1941
JAMES STRUTHERS

7 The Politics of Industrial Restructuring: Canadian textiles
RIANNE MAHON

8 A Conjunction of Interests: Business, politics, and tariffs 1825–1879
BEN FORSTER

9 The Politics of Canada's Airlines from Diefenbaker to Mulroney
GARTH STEVENSON

10 A Staple State: Canadian industrial resources in cold war
MELISSA CLARK-JONES

11 Women's Work, Markets, and Economic Development in Nineteenth-Century Ontario
MARJORIE GRIFFIN COHEN